To my parents
Dorothy Tannen
and
Eli Tannen
who introduced me to oral and literate tradition
respectively

Spoken and Written Language:

Exploring Orality and Literacy

DEBORAH TANNEN, *Editor*
Georgetown University

VOLUME IX in the Series

ADVANCES IN DISCOURSE PROCESSES

Roy O. Freedle, *editor*

ABLEX Publishing Corporation
Norwood, New Jersey 07648

Printed in the United States of America

Library of Congress Cataloging in Publication Data
Main entry under title:

Spoken and written language.

   (Advances in discourse processes; v. 9)
   Includes index.
   1. Discourse analysis—Addresses, essays, lectures.
I. Tannen, Deborah. II. Series.
P302.S6   401'.41   81-12865
ISBN 0-89391-094-5   AACR2
ISBN 0-89391-099-6 (pbk.)

ABLEX Publishing Corporation
355 Chestnut Street
Norwood, New Jersey 07648

Contents

Preface to Series

Roy Freedle

Series Editor

This series of volumes provides a forum for the cross-fertilization of ideas from a diverse number of disciplines, all of which share a common interest in discourse—be it prose comprehension and recall, dialogue analysis, text grammar construction, computer simulation of natural language, cross-cultural comparisons of communicative competence, or other related topics. The problems posed by multisentence contexts and the methods required to investigate them, while not always unique to discourse, are still sufficiently distinct as to benefit from the organized mode of scientific interaction made possible by this series.

Scholars working in the discourse area from the perspective of sociolinguistics, psycholinguistics, ethnomethodology and the sociology of language, educational psychology (e.g., teacher-student interaction), the philosophy of language, computational linguistics, and related subareas are invited to submit manuscripts of monograph or book length to the series editor. Edited collections of original papers resulting from conferences will also be considered.

Preface to Volume IX

As discourse analysis has turned linguistic attention to texts, it is crucial to understand the relationship between various kinds of texts. The spoken vs. written modes constitute one of the basic distinguishing characteristics of texts and is a natural stepping-off point for such an inquiry. Furthermore, all the issues of applied linguistics–how language affects and is used in everday interaction, education, and various special settings—will be enlightened by an understanding of 1) the relationship of spoken to written language, and 2) how language attitudes and conventions associated with orality and literacy influence discourse.

The present volume addresses these issues of discourse analysis and embodies two crucial features that have characterized much recent work in this area. It is broadly interdisciplinary, including research in anthropology, psychology, and literature as well as linguistics, which is at the core. And it is deeply humanistic, looking at language always in context and as a human endeavor.

This volume is the first of two which have developed out of what was originally intended to be a single large collection devoted to spoken and written language seen from the broad perspective of orality and literacy. The second collection, *Coherence in Spoken and Written Discourse*, will also contain an annotated bibliography.

Many of the papers in the present collection owe much to the insight of anthropological and literary work on orality and literacy. However, they go beyond this dichotomy to investigate the characteristics and effects of changing traditions, and to suggest that distinctions between orality and literacy on the one hand, and spoken vs. written language on the other, do not suffice to characterize real discourse. For one thing, there are various oral and literate traditions, and there are different ways of realizing these in both spoken and written language.

The authors of these collected papers demonstrate that complexities found in discourse in context reflect not only its spoken or written mode but its interactive goals and structures: genre, register, and speech event all play significant roles. A number of the chapters consider the relationship of literary to conversational language and find them closer, and distinctions between them foggier, than had previously been thought. Finally, we have a view of individuals and societies caught in changing traditions of orality and literacy intertwined with each other and with chirography, print, and technology.

DT

Acknowledgements

As always, there are more people to thank than I can name. My thinking about spoken and written language, like all my thinking about discourse, reflects continuing dialogue with Wallace Chafe, John and Jenny Cook-Gumperz, and Robin Tolmach Lakoff. As this book developed, discussions with students and colleagues were invaluable, especially with Allen Browne, Dennis Jarrett, Ron Scollon, Roger Shuy, and Cynthia Wallat. I am also grateful to Dennis Jarrett for help with initial editing.

On March 19-21, 1981, I had the privilege to organize and chair the 32nd Annual Georgetown University Round Table on Languages and Linguistics, 'Analyzing Discourse: Text and Talk'. (In a way, the collection of papers from that conference, published by Georgetown University Press, is a companion volume to this). On Thursday, March 18, I also chaired an all-day pre-conference session on spoken and written language, at which many of the contributors to the present collection and its forthcoming partner (*Coherence in Spoken and Written Discourse*), as well as Professor Walter J. Ong, S. J., presented their work. I am grateful to them all for coming and participating.

Finally, I want to thank Roy Freedle, series editor, for advise and support, and the staff of Ablex for being a pleasure to work with.

Introduction

By way of introduction it seems useful to provide 1) a brief summary of past research on oral and literate tradition, 2) a summary of how I found this research useful to my own, and 3) a brief preview and overview of how the chapters in this collection build on this research. 1) and 2) are accomplished in Chapter 1, 'The Oral/Literate Continuum in Discourse.' This introduction will address 3).

After summarizing research in linguistics, anthropology, psychology, and literature on orality and literacy, I suggest in Chapter 1 that strategies that have been associated with orality grow out of emphasis on interpersonal involvement between speaker/writer and audience, and that strategies that have been associated with literacy grow out of focus on content. I then demonstrate how these dimensions illuminate findings of my research on 1) Greek and American narratives told about the same film 2) formulaic language 3) storytelling in conversation among Americans of different ethnic and geographic backgrounds and 4) spoken and written versions of a personal narrative.

The chapters in the first section examine differences between spoken and written language from a number of perspectives. In Chapter 2, Hildyard and Olson ('On the Comprehension and Memory of Oral vs. Written Discourse') find, based on experiments with children in third and fifth grades, that LISTENERS attend more to what is MEANT and READERS attend more to what is WRITTEN, that is, the actual words presented in the text. In Chapter 3, Chafe ('Integration and Involvement in Speaking, Writing, and Oral Literature') reports differences in syntactic and other linguistic structures between spoken dinnertable conversation and written academic prose produced by the same individuals. He finds that his written samples are more INTEGRATED whereas the spoken are more FRAGMENTED, and that his written samples are more DETACHED whereas the spoken are more INVOLVED.

Chafe's final section notes that these features need not be associated with writing and speaking, for he demonstrates that ritual Seneca (an American Indian language) has much in common with written English.

Chapters 4 and 5 are based on non-English discourse. Clancy ('Written and Spoken Style in Japanese Narratives') finds significant differences in written and spoken narratives produced in Japanese about the same film. She suggests that the differences grow out of cognitive and social demands of speaking and writing in the respective contexts. Li and Thompson ('The Gulf Between Spoken and Written Language: A Case Study in Chinese') show that modern written Chinese differs from modern spoken Mandarin, and that this gulf is, in part, created and maintained by the influence of the logographic writing system.

The chapters in the second section further explore the relationship between spoken and written language and suggest ways that what has been associated with one mode can be seen in discourse of the other. Some of the papers in this section tackle such related questions as the nature of the literary in discourse.

In Chapter 6, Heath ('Protean Shapes in Literacy Events: Ever-Shifting Oral and Literate Traditions') demonstrates, based on ethnographic observation of interaction involving written materials in a working-class all-Black community of the Carolinas, that 'the nature of oral and written language and the interplay between them is ever-shifting, and these changes both respond to and create shifts in the individual and societal meanings of literacy'.

Such 'ever-shifting' traditions are further explored and demonstrated in Chapters 7 through 10 as well as 13. Green, Polanyi, and Bright show that features of discourse that have been thought 'literary' are found in spoken discourse; Rader and Lakoff show that what has been thought 'oral' is found in writing.

In Chapter 7, Green ('Colloquial and Literary Uses of Inversions') finds that subject-verb inversions, previously thought to be confined to literary written discourse, are used in both spoken and written language, and that types of inversions can be discriminated on the basis of colloquial versus literary register. In Chapter 8, Polanyi ('Literary Complexity in Everyday Storytelling') closely analyzes narratives spontaneously produced in natural conversation and demonstrates that they contain 'the same complexities in manipulating point of view, identity of reference, and multiplicity of meaning that have hitherto been treated as special qualities of literary language'. Bright ('Poetic Structure in Oral Narrative'), Chapter 9, renders a close analysis and translation of a Karok (American Indian) myth in order to investigate the relationship between prose and poetry and 'the position of literary art with respect to the difference between speech and writing'.

In Chapter 10, Rader ('Context in Written Language: The Case of Imaginative Fiction') expands the text of a very short story written by a novice writer to show that literary fiction, though written, is not decontextualized—a quality that has been regarded as quintessentially 'written'—but rather is maximally contextualized, demanding maximal rather than minimal filling-in by readers. She suggests, moreover, that such reader participation is basic to the literary reading experience.

The last section explores the human as well as linguistic effects of changing oral and literate traditions. These papers suggest that we are confronting more complex distinctions than simply orality vs. literacy, and the implications and ramifications of such changing traditions are also complex, for individuals and societies.

In Chapter 11, Goody ('Alternative Paths to Knowledge in Oral and Literate Cultures') discusses how the introduction of literacy entails a devaluation of knowledge not associated with books. He illustrates this with examples from his observations among the African society of the LoDagaa and suggests implications for problems of modern technological Western societies.

In Chapter 12, Becker ('The Poetics and Noetics of a Javanese Poem') introduces readers to a macapat poem, a highly stylized form of discourse 'still sung and composed today, still in an archaic language'. This chapter gives a glimpse of a discourse style heavily influenced by literary Sanskrit, and also gives a view of the anguish of the poet, 'the elite of a chirographic culture under the sustained attack of a culture well into print'. The emotional power of the poem for us derives in part from the fact that we too are caught in a transitional era.

This view of ours as a transitional era is at the core of the final chapter, by Lakoff ('Some of my Favorite Writers are Literate: The Mingling of Oral and Literate Strategies in Written Communication'). Whereas Goody contends that the onslaught of literacy can be felt in our attitudes toward knowledge, Lakoff suggests that we are entering a new era of a new nonliteracy—a technological one—in which the oral is again being valued over the literate. She demonstrates this by showing that writing has come to reflect 'forms imitative of the oral mode'.

The division of chapters into sections is always somewhat arbitrary. Although aspects of the papers reflect the divisions outlined here, summaries necessarily oversimplify, and other aspects of the same papers could have yielded other organizations. All the chapters overlap in their focus on the relationship between spoken and written language and its uses in human interaction.

Deborah Tannen

1 The Oral/Literate Continuum in Discourse*

Deborah Tannen
Georgetown University

I
ORAL VS. LITERATE TRADITION

A number of scholars in varying fields pioneered research in the sixties examining the effects of writing on cognitive and social processes (Goody and Watt 1963; Havelock, 1963; Ong, 1967). The seventies brought continued work by the same scholars (Goody, 1977; Havelock, 1971; Ong, 1977) as well as others (Cole & Scribner, 1974, Cook-Gumperz & Gumperz 1981; Kay, 1977; Olson, 1977; Scribner & Cole, 1980).

Lord (1960), following Parry, had demonstrated that oral epics were not memorized but reconstructed at each telling through the imposition of formulaic phrases on the skeleton of a familiar plot. Havelock (1963) surmised that the difference between oral reconstruction and rote memory associated with oral vs. literate tradition, respectively, is not just a habit of expression but represents a difference in approach to knowledge and thought. In literate society, knowledge is seen as facts and insights preserved in written records. As Ong (1967) also points out, in oral culture, formulaic expressions (sayings, cliches, proverbs, and so on) are the repository of received wisdom.

Formulaic expressions function as wholes, as a convenient way to signal knowledge that is already shared. In oral tradition, it is not assumed that the ex-

*This is an expanded, revised, and partly rewritten version of a paper entitled "Implications of the oral/literate continuum for cross-cultural communication" which was delivered at the Georgetown University Round Table on Languages and Linguistics 1980, Current Issues in Bilingualism, and published in the volume by the same name, edited by James Alatis. Washington, D.C.: Georgetown University Press.

pressions contain meaning in themselves, in a way that can be analyzed. Rather, words are a convenient tool to signal already shared social meaning. Thus, in an oral tradition, as has been pointed out elsewhere (Tannen & Oztek 1977), it does not matter whether one says 'I could care less' or 'I couldn't care less'. The expression is, in either case, a handy way to make reference to a familiar idea. As Olson (1977) puts it, 'the meaning is in the context'. In contrast, in literate tradition, 'the meaning is in the text'.

Ong observes that in oral tradition, thought is 'exquisitely elaborated' through a stitching together of formulaic language which he calls 'rhapsodic'. In literate tradition, thought is analytic, sequential, linear. Olson notes that truth, in oral tradition, resides in common-sense reference to experience, whereas in literate tradition it resides in logical or coherent argument. It is the oral sense of truth that comes naturally. Hence, says Olson, most people cannot distinguish between a conclusion that is logical and one with which they agree.

Ong explains furthermore that 'knowing' in oral tradition is achieved through a sense of identification with the speaker or the characters in the spoken discourse. This follows Havelock's assertion that understanding in oral tradition is subjective. It explains the fact—puzzling and disturbing to modern scholars—that Plato would have banned poets from participation in education in the Republic. Because of their ability to move audiences emotionally, poets were a dangerous threat to the transition to literacy, by which people were to learn to suspend their emotions and approach knowledge through analytic, logical processes.

Olson points out that children learn language through use of formulas; Wong Fillmore (1979) has demonstrated this for second language acquisition. That is, children do not learn the meanings of individual words and rules for putting them together, like Tinker toys and sticks. Rather, they learn strings of words associated with fixed intonation and other paralinguistic features, to be uttered in certain social settings. By trying the expressions out in various settings, they arrive at correct associations—or at least they approximate correct associations more and more closely.

I have noticed that when children do learn that words have literal meanings, they go through a stage of overapplication of this principle. This accounts for their inclination, at a certain age, to interrupt their parents during adult conversation with complaints like 'That's not what he said', and offer corrections that do not change the sense at all, to the parents' great annoyance. This stage of language development furnishes Hank Ketcham with numerous Dennis the Menace jokes which derive humor from the boy's literal interpretation of words that were meant formulaically.

In a broad sense, then, strategies associated with oral tradition place emphasis on shared knowledge and the interpersonal relationship between communicator and audience. In this, they 'elaborate' what Bateson (1972) calls the metacommunicative function of language: the use of words to convey something about the relationship between communicator and audience. Literate tradition emphasizes what Bateson calls the communicative function of language: the use of words to convey information or content. This gives rise to the idealization that language can be 'autonomous' (Kay, 1977)—that is, that words can carry meaning all by themselves, and that it is their prime function to do so.

Scollon and Scollon (to appear) caution against generalizing the 'bard and formula' notion of orality propounded by scholars whose work I have discussed here. The Scollons note that oral traditions can differ strikingly, and they demonstrate this with Athabaskan examples. They suggest instead a distinction between focused and nonfocused situations. The former is one in which 'there are strong limitations on negotiation between participants'; the latter is one in which 'the highest value is on mutual sense making among the participants.'

This analysis reinforces the hypothesis that it is not 'orality' per se that is at issue but rather the relative focus on communicator/audience interaction on the one hand, as opposed to the relative focus on content on the other, or, as John Gumperz would put it, to what degree interpersonal involvement or message content carry the signalling load.

All the scholars whose work I have cited point out that literate tradition does not replace oral. Rather, when literacy is introduced, the two are superimposed upon and intertwined with each other. Similarly, no individual is either 'oral' or 'literate.' Rather, people use devices associated with both traditions in various settings. Goody & Watt (1963) suggest that oral tradition is associated with the family and ingroup, while literate tradition is learned and passed on in the decontextualized setting of the school. Certainly this is typically true (although surely the school has its own context and is considered decontextualized only by reference to the different contexts of home and family). But strategies associated with one or the other tradition can be realized in any setting and in any mode, as my own research and other chapters in the present volume demonstrate.

Cook-Gumperz and Gumperz (1981) point out that strategies associated with literate tradition have been conventionalized in Western countries for oral use in public settings. In fact, it is clear that many middle class families employ strategies associated with literate tradition in the home. This can be seen in their prodding children to 'get to the point' and 'stick to the point'. An outgrowth of such attitudes, too, can be seen when parents and teachers tell children that their talk ought to be 'logical', that, for example, 'two negatives makes a positive', as if sentences can and ought to be analyzable from constituent parts, like mathematical equations. In fact, in interaction, it does not matter how many negative particles a sentence contains, except insofar as more may be better, as in vernacular Black English, which requires negative concord (Labov, 1969).

II

I would like to sketch briefly how I have found the notion of oral vs. literate tradition—or, more precisely, an oral/literate continuum reflecting relative focus on involvement vs. content—useful in my own rsearch on discourse. It is important to stress that it is the awareness of strategies that have been associated with oral and literate tradition that has been enlightening. I have come to believe, and the present collection of papers demonstrates, that these strategies are not limited to orality vs. literacy, and certainly not to spoken vs. written language, but rather can be seen to interplay in spoken and written discourse in various settings.

GREEK AND AMERICAN NARRATIVES

I first applied the oral/literate paradigm when I was analyzing narratives told by Greek and American women about a film (Tannen, 1980b).[1] The film, commissioned in connection with a project directed by Wallace Chafe at the University of California, Berkeley, takes about six minutes and has sound but no dialogue. It shows a series of simple events: a man is picking pears; a boy comes along on a bike and takes a basket of pears; he falls off his bike and is helped by three other boys; they start to leave but find and return his hat, and he then gives them three pears; they eat the pears as they walk past the pearpicker, who has just discovered that he is missing a basket. The movie was shown to twenty American women who were asked to tell what they had seen. I took the film to Greece and elicited narratives from twenty Greek women in a similar format.

In comparing the narratives told by American women in English and Greek women in Greek, I found that the Greeks told 'better stories', constructing them around a theme and omitting details that didn't contribute to that theme (hence their narratives were considerably shorter). In contrast, the Americans tended to include many details—seemingly, as many as they could recall—and list them, as though performing a memory task. The Americans were also concerned with getting temporal sequence right.

Second, the Greek speakers often made judgments about the characters' behavior (for example, the boy should not have stolen the pears or should have thanked his helpers sooner), or about the film's message (for example, that it showed a slice of agricultural life, or that little children help each other). In contrast, the Americans used their judgment to comment on the filmmaker's technique (for example, that the costumes were unconvincing or the soundtrack out of proportion). To do this, they often used jargon associated with cinema ('soundtrack', 'camera angle', 'the camera pans').

In summary, then, the Greeks seemed concerned with presenting themselves as acute judges of human behavior and good storytellers, while the Americans were concerned with presenting themselves as acute recallers (or good experimental subjects). Put another way, the Americans seemed to be operating on a set of expectations ('frame' or 'script') for being the subject of an experiment, while

---

[1]Narratives about this film are also the basis of analysis in Clancy (this volume), Tannen (to appear), Michaels and Collins (to appear), and a collection of papers in Chafe (1980).

the Greeks seemed to refer to expectations ('frame' or 'script') for everyday conversation. (See Tannen, 1979a, for an extended analysis of this notion of 'frame').

Given these patterns, there remained a question in my mind about what these differences meant. Here the oral/literate paradigm proved illuminating. By referring to expectations about being the subjects of an experiment, the Americans were drawing on their willingness to approach a school task for its own demands. Furthermore, they were focusing on the content of the film (its details and temporal sequence), treating it as a decontextualized object. Finally, when they called in their critical faculties, they turned them on the film as a film, again drawing upon a tradition of critical objectivity. In contrast, the Greeks tended to draw upon interactive experience which was more focused on interpersonal involvement: telling the story in way that would interest the interviewer, and regarding the characters in the film not as actors wearing costumes but as people exhibiting certain behavior. Equally adept at marshalling critical faculties, the Greeks applied them in a different way: to interpret the film's human message (no small task in a short film with minimal plot). Thus, cultural differences resulted in elaboration, or focus, or signalling load, being placed on different aspects of the interaction—on the one hand, message content, and on the other, interpersonal involvement. In both cases, speakers were responding in culturally conventionalized ways. (The foregoing analysis is presented and discussed in detail in Tannen, 1980b).

FORMULAIC LANGUAGE

As I thought about these dimensions, I realized that they cast light upon work I had done earlier on modern Greek. One early study (Tannen & Oztek, 1977) examines formulaic expressions.

Most Americans feel that they ought not to use formulaic language. They feel that fixedness implies insincerity; hence the word 'cliche', with its negative connotation. This attitude persists despite the fact that no one can talk without extensive use of formulaic speech. Fillmore (1979) suggests that 'a large portion of a person's ability to get along in a language consists in the mastery of formulaic utterances'. Nonetheless, many Americans, when uttering formulas, make apologies ('I know this is a cliche, but. . .' 'Everyone must say this, but. . .') or otherwise mark their expressions with verbal or nonverbal equivalents of quotation marks.

In contrast, many speakers of Greek and Turkish seem to be happiest if they can find a fixed way of saying what they mean. For one thing, this lends to their utterance the weight and legitimacy of received wisdom: if everyone says it, it must be true. Second, it assures them that they are making a socially appropriate conversational contribution.

Situational formulas of the type found in Turkish and Greek are rigid collocations that are always said in particular social settings. Their omission carries meaning; it is perceived as a social gaffe or an intended slight, just as in American culture hanging up the telephone without saying 'goodbye' constitutes a positive act that might be reported: 'S/he hung up on me.' Rigid situational formulas are a prototype of formulaic language, or one end of a continuum of fixedness in language use, the other end of which might be a totally new thought expressed in a totally original syntactic pattern. There is a range of relative fixedness and relative novelty along the continuum, including use of familiar combinations of words, familiar syntactic patterns, and so on. As Jarrett (1978) demonstrates for blues lyrics, all utterances are 'inevitably traditional', although the degree of fixedness may range from use of clearly recognizable formulas to totally new lines which are formulaic in their adherence to recognizable patterns of rhythm, metaphor, register, syntax, and so on. Similarly, in everyday interaction, individuals differ with respect to the relative frequency of their use of more or less formulaic language, and cultures differ with regard to value placed on relative fixedness vs. relative novelty in expression. These differences with respect to value placed on formulaicness vs. novelty of expression corresponds to Olson's (1977) and Ong's (1967) observations about oral vs. literate tradition. Formulaicness is valued when wisdom is seen as knowledge passed down through the generations. Novelty is valued when wisdom is seen as new information. (A similar argument about relative value placed on two kinds of knowing is the thesis of the chapter by Goody in this volume).

WHAT TO SAY: COMMONPLACES, PERSONALIZING, PHILOSOPHIZING

The use of formulaic or well-worn expressions is closely associated with what is said; form and content are intertwined. Just as Greeks find it more appropriate to use familiar expressions, so they are more disposed to express sentiments that are familiar and often reiterated.

These differing propensities showed up in the pear narratives as well. For one thing, in telling about the film, the Greeks in the study were not only more likely to try to find a theme or general meaning for the film, but in so doing they often chose culturally familiar themes such as the beauty of agricultural life. Their readiness to make use of culturally familiar explanations showed up in many ways. For example, in explaining why the boy fell off his bicycle, almost half (nine) of the Greeks made reference to the appearance of a girl, cuing a familiar boy-meets-girl 'script' (see Tannen 1979a for discussion of scripts, frames, schemata). The Americans did not do this. They only mentioned the girl if they were making reference to her in their explanation of causality of the fall.

Another related dimension is the tendency to talk in terms of personal experience and to instantiate rather than talk in abstract or general terms. For example, several of the Greeks followed up their summaries of what happened in the film with their own ideas of what it all meant, in a way that sounds to Americans like 'philosophizing'. One Greek speaker made much of the 'conflicts' in the film, and another focused on the many 'falls', relating this to her pessimistic outlook in general and the difficulty she was experiencing in her own life at the time (Tannen, 1980b).

The difference in tendency to personalize showed up in another cross-cultural study dealing with Greeks and Americans (Tannen, 1976), as well as in a follow-up study that included Greek-Americans (Tannen, 1981a). In order to investigate interpretive patterns of indirectness in conversation, I presented Greeks, Americans, and later Greek-Americans with a sample conversation:

> Wife: John's having a party. Want to go?
>
> Husband: Okay.
>
> Wife: (Later) Are you sure you want to go to the party?
>
> Husband: Okay, let's not go. I'm tired anyway.

In answering questions on a questionnaire, and then explaining why they chose the answers they did, many Greek respondents (and Greek-Americans as well) made reference to their own experience: 'That's the way my husband would do it', or 'That's how it happens in my house'. Others explained their answers by instantiating the conversation: 'The wife is probably home all day while her husband works, so she'd probably want to go to the party'. In contrast, most Americans answered in terms of the dialogue itself: 'The husband said OK, and Ok means yes'. Thus, the Greek respondents were more likely to instantiate, to personalize, to talk in terms of broader context. The Americans, on the other hand, were more apt to approach the task by focusing on the conversation as an artifact, to talk objectively and theoretically—or at least in ways that appear so.

Another interesting finding of this study was the 'brevity effect'. Those Americans who made reference to the brevity of the response OK explained that OK means yes; because it was brief, it was casual and hence sincere. In contrast, all Greeks who referred to the brevity of the husband's OK, explained that OK means no; because it was brief, it was unenthusiastic. Therefore there seemed to be an 'enthusiasm constraint' operating for many Greek respondents. Put another way, the Greeks expected more elaboration in expression of desire to go (at least in a conversation between husband and wife about a party)—that is, elaboration of the interpersonal or emotive channel.

STORYTELLING IN CONVERSATION

Another extended study which was informed by an awareness of strategy differences suggested by oral/literate continuum research concerned conversational microanalysis, or what I have called conversational style (Tannen, 1979b, 1981b,

1981c, in press), a notion closely related to what Gumperz (1977) calls conversational inference. The data for my study were two and a half hours of naturally occurring conversation at Thanksgiving dinner among Americans of different ethnic and geographic backgrounds. Initially intending to describe the linguistic features which made up each participant's style, I found clusters of features in the speech of participants such that those from New York of Jewish background could be said to share 'a style', and those not from New York and not Jewish clearly did not share this style. The features of the speech of the New York Jews which I am idealizing as an identifiable style could be understood as employing strategies associated with oral tradition—that is, placing the signalling load on interpersonal involvement in a conventionalized way. In contrast, the approach to conversation and its interpretation which was demonstrated and discussed (during playback) by the non-New York participants exhibited approaches to language which have been associated with literate tradition, that is, placing more of the signalling load on message content.

One section of the above study (Tannen, 1979b) closely examines narratives told by participants in the Thanksgiving dinner. Because narrative analysis is a research area with a long history in the linguistic literature, and because participants' narrative styles demonstrate features and devices found more generally in their conversational styles, the following discussion will recapitulate some aspects of my findings on storytelling in conversation.

A framework for the analysis of narratives in conversation is provided by Labov (1972), based on stories told by black teenagers. Labov notes that in telling a story, a speaker's main job is to make clear to the audience what the point of the story is—to answer in advance the 'withering question', 'So What?' Speakers communicate the point of a story—i.e. their attitude toward what is being said—by means of 'evaluation', either external or internal. External evaluation is the obvious kind: the teller steps outside the story to poke the reader verbally and say, 'Hey, here's the point'. This can be done by such comments as 'And this was the incredible thing', or by explaining, for example, 'When he said that, I felt awful'. Internal evaluation is not so obvious. It resides in all levels of verbalization such as expressive phonology, speeding up or slowing down, repetition, lexical choice, and so on. Direct quotation is a common form of internal evaluation. By putting words in the mouth of the characters, the teller communicates what happened from inside the story. Nonetheless, by deciding what words to put in the character's mouth, the teller is building the story toward the desired point.

Labov suggests that middle class white speakers tend to use more external evaluation, while inner city blacks use more internal evaluation. He notes as well that internal evaluation makes a better story. I believe this explains the often perceived phenomenon of 'good storytellers' among working-class people, rural people, or members of certain cultures, including Jews and Greeks. This phenomenon results from use of strategies that build on interpersonal involvement to create the sense of identification, or involvement, with characters and tellers of stories which has been linked to oral tradition (though obviously need not be). The alternative way of knowing, through intellectual or objective understanding, has been linked to literate tradition (but, as the present analysis demonstrates, can operate in speaking just as well). In this schema, internal evaluation contributes to the sense of identification, while external evaluation makes explicit what the point is—a feature of literate-based strategies.

As Kay (1977) points out, use of language typically associated with literacy in an industrial society is 'autonomous'. Whatever is needed for comprehension is included in the words of the text (external evaluation). In contrast, nonautonomous language depends on 'simultaneous transmission over other channels, such as the paralinguistic, postural and gestural'—the basic tools of internal evaluation. Of course, this split is an idealization; what we are dealing with is a continuum: more or less reliance on features of spoken-like vs. written-like language. Lexical choice, by writers as much as by speakers, constitutes internal evaluation. However, a word may be spoken with a certain intonation, tone, gesture, and facial expression that would add to the evaluation, whereas the written word must stand alone.

In the analysis of stories told over dinner, it became clear that the New Yorkers of Jewish background employed more internal evaluation and avoided explicitly stating the points of their stories. Their strategy seemed to be—and this was supported by participants' comments upon hearing the tape—to capitalize upon shared background by not telling the point straight out, simultaneously building upon and reinforcing a sense of 'being on the same wave length'. The fact that the lack of external evaluation seemed inappropriate to the native Californians can be seen in their on-the-spot reactions as well as their comments during playback. For example, one New Yorker told the following story:[2] (K is Kurt; D is David; and I am the speaker designated T).

---

[2]Transcription conventions are a combination of my own and many gleaned from the following sources: the Chafe narrative project, University of California at Berkeley; Schenkein (1978); and the Gumperz project, University of California at Berkeley, based on conventions developed by John Trim. All names are pseudonymous except mine. (A discussion of the advantages, disadvantages, and complexities of being both analyst and participant can be found in Tannen, 1979b).

  . .noticeable pause or break in rhythm (less than .5 second)

  . . .half-second pause, as measured by stop watch; an extra dot is added for each additional half-second pause, hence . . . . full second pause, and so on

  ` secondary stress

  ´ primary stress

  italics mark emphatic stress

  CAPS mark very emphatic stress

  ⌐high pitch, continuing until punctuation

  ⌐very high pitch, continuing until punctuation

  ' high pitch on word

  , phrase final intonation: 'more to come'

  . sentence final falling intonation

(1) K: Í have a little sèven-year-old student . . . a little
       gírl who wears those. . . . . . .⌐_____   Shé . . is *too* →
          p |
(2) T: └─She wears those? [chuckle]──┘

   K: múch. Can yóu imagine? She's séven years old,
          acc

       and she síts in her chair and she goes . . . [squeals
                          acc───────]
       and squirms in his seat.]

(3) T: Oh:: Go::d. . . . She's only SEVen?

(4) K: And I say well . . hów about let's do sò-and-so. And
                                              acc

       she says . . .⌐Ok̆ay. . . .⌐Jùst like thát.
               ───────]   [squealing]

(5) T: ⌐Oh: : : : :
       p

(6) D: |What does it méan.
       p,acc

(7) K: It's just so . . .⌐she's acting like such a little gírl
                       p
       already.

There are two listener/respondents taking an active part in this story. Our reactions are opposite. I show agreement and understanding not by lexicaling them but by responding in like style. In (3) I say, 'Oh:: Go::d,' using exaggerated tone and lengthened vowels, and I repeat part of Kurt's story in a 'disbelieving' tone of voice: 'She's only SEVen?' My tone says, 'That really is amazing.' In (4) Kurt continues his story, and in (5) I again show appreciation by use of a paralinguistically exaggerated response, 'Oh::::::.' In contrast, David asks (6) 'What does it mean?'

Here is clear evidence, in the text itself, that one listener 'got the point' of the story while the other didn't—or at least that David did not approve of the way

---

→ arrow indicates talk continues without break in rhythm; see next line
? yes/no question rising intonation
: indicates lengthened vowel sound
p under line indicates spoken softly
acc under line indicates spoken quickly, continuing until punctuation unless otherwise indicated
ʔ is the traditional linguistic symbol for glottal stop, as in the expression of warning, ʔuh ʔoh
[brackets] indicate comments on nonverbal characteristics
  penned brackets on two lines indicate overlapping speech.

  Two people talking at once.
penned brackets with reversed flaps indicate
  latch.

    Second speaker begins without pause following first speaker's utterance.

the story was told, as will be shown below. The most significant part of this evidence lies in my responding in like style.

Kurt's telling of this 'story' is marked by exaggerated paralinguistic and prosodic features. He uses marked shifts from high to low pitch; speeding up and slowing down; postural and gestural cues. In (1) and (4), he mimics the movements as well as the voice of the girl he is talking about; he places his hands on his knees and squirms in a stereotypically female manner. My response is similar in a number of ways. I pick up on Kurt's words and repeat them back to him, (3) 'She's only SEVen?' with paralinguistically exaggerated phonology. The result is a rhythmically and paralinguistically synchronous and matched speaker/listener interchange.

In contrast, David's question (6) 'What does it mean?' is uttered in flat intonation. Not only does the content of his question make it clear that he does not get the point of the story. In addition, the rhythm and tone of his question are in contrast to Kurt's and my utterances. In playback, David commented that perhaps he did not so much miss Kurt's point as feel annoyed that Kurt had not made it. That is, he felt that the point of the story should be stated in external evaluation. He complained that even in answer to his question (6), Kurt did not tell the point of the story. Kurt's 'explanation' (7) is 'She's acting like such a little girl already'. David commented that 'such a little girl' means to him 'just like a person' or 'grown up', as in 'such a little young lady' as opposed to 'like an infant'. What Kurt meant and should have said was that she was acting like a 'coquette.' David continued that it made him uncomfortable when Kurt squealed and squirmed to imitate the girl's manner. This acting-out of the story seemed to him a breach of good taste.

It is particularly interesting that Kurt, in answering David's direct question, still did not 'explain' the point of the story. I submit that it seemed to him self-evident, as it seemed to me.

Thus, Kurt communicated the point of his story through internal evaluation, by presenting the character in a way that seemed to him self-evidently demonstrative of the point. He made much use of paralinguistic and kinesic features—the essence of oral tradition, building upon shared sociocultural knowledge and redundancy of channels. David expected something more like Kay's 'autonomous' use of language, in which the message is carried by and made explicit in words.

Another aspect of cross-cultural differences in storytelling has to do not only with how the point is communicated but what the point can be. Thus it becomes clear that for the New Yorkers of Jewish background, stories were most commonly told to illustrate the speaker's feelings about something. In some sense, Kurt's story is about his feelings about little girls using girly mannerisms. The non-New Yorkers, in contrast, told stories about events in which their feelings were not only not dramatized but often not expressed. This led to another set of mismatches: the New Yorkers had trouble getting the point of the non-New Yorkers' stories, since they were looking for meaning in the speaker's attitude toward the events.

At one point the conversation turned to a discussion of heredity vs. environment, as exemplified by adopted children. Kurt told the following story, again about a student:

(1) K: In fact onè of my stùdents told me for the first time,

I taught her for over a yéar. . . . That she was

adópted. And then I thought . . ?uh? . . . *that*
        acc ——————————]   acc
            p

explains . . *so* many things.

(2) T: What.⌐That she was →

(3) K: └Cause she's só:: dífferent ⌐from her móther

    T: └smarter than she

    K: should have been? or stùpider →

    T: ⌐ than she should've been. [chuckle]

(5) K: └ It wasn't smárt or stùpid, àctually, it was just she

was *so* different. . . . . Just '*diff*erent.

    T: hm

The point of the story emerges in the first sentence in which Kurt illustrates his emotional reaction to hearing that his student was adopted in the grunt, 'uh', uttered between two glottal stops, accompanied by a facial expression of surprise. This sense of surprise in effect carries the message that the student was different from her parents, and this had been puzzling to Kurt before he learned that she was adopted. I have suggested (Tannen, 1979b) that the questions asked by me in this interchange do not show lack of understanding or lack of approval of the way the story is being told. Rather, they function as 'cooperative prompts', eliciting information which Kurt would have told anyway. They serve to encourage him to tell what he was planning to tell—a show of enthusiasm on the listener's part. Evidence for this lies in the fact that the story continues over the overlap of the question; the question does not stop the storyteller or interfere with the rhythm of his story; rather the questions and story continue in an interwoven fabric of continuous and rhythmically smooth speech.

In contrast, when David tells a story about a child who is adopted, Kurt reacts with a question that interrupts the flow of David's speech and shows Kurt's impatience.

(1) D: My u::m . . . my aúnt's two kids are adopted, and
        they were both adopted from different . . . . famili?
        different móthers.

(2) K: Yeah. And?

(3) D: $\llcorner$ And they're just 'different from each
other and different from anyone in my fámily. . . . .

                        K hm

They're not like each óther at áll.

All listeners to the tape of this conversation agree that Kurt's 'Yeah. And?' sounds impatient. David himself, during playback, said that it sounded like Kurt was impatient, and David hypothesized that it was his slower pace that was causing the impatience. Indeed, David speaks more slowly than Kurt, and his hesitation over 'families' vs. 'mothers' creates a stalling in the telling. I hypothesize, however, that another part of Kurt's impatience results from the fact that David has not given any hint of how he feels about what he is telling. The flat intonation is in striking contrast to Kurt's storytelling style, although in terms of actual information communicated in the content, David gives no less information than Kurt did, and both are saying that the adopted children are 'just different' from their adopted families. But in David's story there is no element of his own emotional involvement, as there is in Kurt's. This pattern is not limited to these stories but appears in numerous stories told by members of the two groups.

By focusing on personal emotions, and by using internal evaluation through exaggerated paralinguistic and nonverbal cues, the New Yorkers in this study were using strategies more inherently oral. By sticking to events and relying on lexicalization, the natives of Los Angeles were using strategies more influenced by literacy. The effect in communication between members of the two groups was slight mutual impatience and annoyance, and incomplete comprehension. Of course, these phenomena were not gross but comparatively subtle and became clear only after microanalysis. All participants left the gathering feeling they had had a good time, and friendships among them endured. However, the nature of their rapport is certainly influenced by such habitual differences, and consequences of such stylistic differences are potentially significant in interaction not favorably biased by ties of friendship and congenial setting.

An important aspect of these examples is that the speakers whose strategies are somehow more "oral" are nonetheless highly literate people. Most examples of speakers who use "oral" strategies have been American blacks (Cook-Gumperz & Gumperz, 1981; Aronowitz, to appear; Kochman, 1975; Michaels and Collins, to appear), and this phenomenon has been linked to the fact that black children frequently perform poorly on literacy tests in school. However, the group I have found using oral strategies, Americans of East European Jewish background, have exhibited no weakness in literate tasks. Furthermore, Labov's (1972) observations about middle class white speakers' narrative strategies do not hold for these middle class white speakers. This serves to demonstrate that matters are more complex than had been thought. It will not do to label some people as oral and others as literate. Individuals and groups can make use of strategies that build on interpersonal involvement and make maximal use of paralinguistic and prosodic channels that are lost in writing; or strategies that focus on content and make maximal use of lexicalization, as these serve their context-bound needs and as these have been conventionalized in their speech habits.

SPOKEN VS. WRITTEN LANGUAGE

A recent study (Tannen, 1982, 1980a) confronts head on the question of orality and literacy and spoken vs. written language. It undertakes a close analysis of two narratives, one written and one spoken, by the same person about the same events. The study results in findings similar to those of Rader (this volume). My analysis is of a story spontaneously told by a woman in conversation with friends about a man in her office. When she was later asked to write down what she had told, she wrote not expository prose (as did most others who were given similar instructions) but a short story. Close analysis of her two versions of the narrative indicates that, in writing the short story, she combined features that might be expected in writing with others that might be expected in speaking. Specifically, her written version exhibited increased features of syntactic complexity which Chafe (this volume) calls 'integration' and which he found in expository prose. But in addition, she used more rather than fewer features which Chafe calls 'involvement' and which he found in casual conversation: details, imageability, direct quotation, repetition of sounds, words, and phrases. Thus, creative writing is a genre which is necessarily written but which makes use of features associated with oral language because it depends for its effect on interpersonal involvement or the sense of identification between the writer or the characters and the reader.

CONCLUSION

Kay (1977) suggests that the notion of autonomous vs. nonautonomous speech accounts for Bernstein's (1964) controversial hypothesis of elaborated vs. restricted codes. Kay writes (1977:22) that

> autonomous speech packs all the information into the strictly linguistic channel and places minimal reliance on the ability of the hearer to supply items of content necessary either to flesh out the body of the message or to place it in the correct interpretive context.

I suggest that the addition of background information is a kind of elaboration. Therefore, autonomous or literate-based language is not necessarily always elaborated, nor is oral-based or nonautonomous speech always restricted. Rather, there is a difference in which levels of signalling or which aspects of the communicative channel are elaborated. The use of exaggerated paralinguistic features such as pace, pitch shifts, amplitude shifts, expressive phonology, expressive tone quality, and so on constitutes elaboration of the paralinguistic channel. Similarly, the study of conversational strategies shows that Greeks expected more 'enthusiasm' in expression of preferences and that Jewish American participants in the Thanksgiving dinner expected more active listener participation in the form of expressive reactions, prompting questions, and mutual revelation of personal experience (Tannen, 1979b). This is elaboration of another sort. In the autonomous or literate-based mode, the content and verbal channel are elaborated, while the oral-based strategy elaborates paralinguistic channels and emotional or interpersonal dynamics.

These are some of the research areas in which I have found useful the notion of an oral/literate continuum, or, more precisely, a continuum of relative focus on interpersonal involvement vs. message content.[3] The chapters that follow further elaborate these themes.

REFERENCES

ARONOWITZ, ROBERT Reading tests as texts. Coherence in spoken and written discourse, ed. by Deborah Tannen. Norwood, NJ: Ablex, to appear.

BATESON, GREGORY. 1972. Steps to an ecology of mind. New York: Ballantine.

BERNSTEIN, BASIL. 1964. Elaborated and restricted codes: Their social origins and some consequences. American Anthropologist 66.6.

CAZDEN, COURTNEY AND E. LEGGETT. 1978. Culturally responsive education: A discussion of Lau Remedies II. Los Angeles: National Dissemination and Assessment Center, California State University.

CHAFE, WALLACE (ED.). 1980. The pear stories: Cultural, cognitive, and linguistic aspects of narrative production. Norwood, NJ: Ablex.

COLE, MICHAEL AND SYLVIA SCRIBNER. 1974. Culture and thought: A psychological introduction. New York: Wiley.

COOK-GUMPERZ, JENNY AND JOHN J. GUMPERZ. 1981. From oral to written: The transition to literacy. Variation in writing, ed. by Marcia Farr Whiteman, Hillsdale, NJ: Erlbaum.

FERGUSON, CHARLES A. 1959. Diglossia. Word. 15.325-40.

FILLMORE, CHARLES J. 1979. On fluency. Individual differences in language ability and language behavior, ed. by Charles J. Fillmore, Dan Kempler, and William S.-Y. Wang. New York: Academic Press.

FILLMORE, LILY WONG. 1979. Individual differences in second language acquisition. Individual differences in language ability and language behavior, ed. by C. J. Fillmore, D. Kempler, and W. S.-Y. Wang. New York: Academic Press.

GOODY, JACK R. 1977. The domestication of the savage mind. Cambridge: Cambridge University Press.

GOODY, JACK R. AND IAN WATT. 1963. The consequences of literacy. Comparative Studies in Society and History, 5.

---

[3]The distinction between oral and literate traditions resembles a number of other theoretical schemata, including Hall's (1977) high/low context continuum, field dependence vs field independence (Cazden & Leggett, 1978), R. Lakoff's (1979) communicative styles camaraderie vs. distance, and Diglossia (Ferguson, 1959).

GUMPERZ, JOHN J. 1977. Sociocultural knowledge in conversational inference. Georgetown University Round Table on Langauges and Linguistics 1977, ed. by Mariel Saville-Troike, 191–211. Washington, D.C.: Georgetown University Press.

HALL, EDWARD. 1977. Beyond culture. Garden City, N.Y.: Doubleday.

HAVELOCK, ERIC. 1963. Preface to Plato. Cambridge: Harvard University Press.

———. 1971. Prologue to Greek literacy. Cincinnati: University of Cincinnati Press.

JARRETT, DENNIS. 1978. The singer and the bluesman: Formulations of personality in the lyrics of the blues. Southern Folklore Quarterly, 42:1.

KAY, PAUL. 1977. Language evolution and speech style. Sociocultural dimensions of language change, ed. by B. Blount and M. Sanches. New York: Academic Press.

KOCHMAN, THOMAS. 1975. Orality and literacy as factors of Black and white communicative behavior. International Journal of the Sociology of Language 3. 95–118.

LABOV, WILLIAM. 1972. Language in the inner city. Philadelphia: University of Pennsylvania Press.

———. 1969. The logic of nonstandard English. University Round Table on Languages and Linguistics 1969, ed. by J. Alatis Georgetown Washington, D.C.: Georgetown University Press.

LORD, ALBERT. 1960. The singer of tales. Cambridge: Harvard University Press.

MICHEALS, SARA AND COLLINS, JIM. To appear. Oral discourse styles: classroom interaction and the aquisition of literacy. Coherence in spoken and written discourse, ed. by Deborah Tannen. Norwood, NJ: Ablex.

OLSON, DAVID R. 1977. From utterance to text: The bias of language in speech and writing. Harvard Educational Review 47.3.

ONG, WALTER J. 1977. Interfaces of the word. Ithaca N.Y.: Cornell University Press.

———. 1967. The presence of the word. New Haven: Yale University Press.

SCHENKEIN, JIM. 1978. Studies in the organization of conversational interaction. New York: Academic Press.

SCOLLON, RON, AND SUZANNE B.-K. SCOLLON. To appear. Cooking it up and boiling it down: Abstracts in Athabaskan children's story retellings. Coherence in spoken and written discourse, ed. by D. Tannen, Norwood, N.J.: Ablex.

SCRIBNER, SYLVIA AND MICHAEL COLE. 1981. The psychology of literacy. Cambridge: Harvard University Press.

TANNEN, DEBORAH. 1976. An indirect/direct view of misunderstandings. M. A. Thesis, University of California, Berkeley.

———. 1979a. What's in a frame? Surface evidence for underlying expectations. New directions in discourse processing, ed. by R. O. Freedle, 137–181. Norwood, N.J.: Ablex.

———. 1979b. Processes and consequences of conversational style. Ph.D. dissertation, University of California, Berkeley.

———. 1980a. Spoken and written language and the oral/literate continuum. Proceedings of the sixth annual meeting of the Berkeley Linguistics Society. University of California, Berkeley.

———. 1980b. A comparative analysis of oral narrative strategies: Athenian Greek and American English. The pear stories, ed. by Wallace Chafe. Norwood, N.J.: Ablex.

———. 1981a. Indirectness in discourse: Ethnicity as conversational style. Discourse Processes 4:3.

———. 1981b. The machine-gun question: An example of convesational style. Journal of Pragmatics 5:5.

———. 1981c. New York Jewish conversational style. International Journal of the Sociology of Language 30:133–149.

———. In press. Conversational style. Psycholinguistic models of production, ed. by H. Dechert and M. Raupach. Hillsdale, N.J.: Erlbaum.

———. 1982. Oral and literate strategies in spoken and written narratives. Language, 58:1.

TANNEN, DEBORAH AND PIYALE C. OZTEK. 1981. Formulaic expressions in Turkish and Greek. Proceedings of the Third Annual Meeting of the Berkeley Linguistics Society. University of California, Berkeley, 1977. Rptd in Conversational routine, ed. by F. Coulmas. The Hague: Mouton.

EXAMINING DIFFERENCES IN SPOKEN AND WRITTEN LANGUAGE

2 On the Comprehension and Memory of Oral vs. Written Discourse*

Angela Hildyard and David R. Olson
Ontario Institute for Studies in Education

INTRODUCTION

In general, our memory for what we have heard or read is not perfect. Various parts of a story or conversation are forgotten. Other parts are remembered even though they were not explicitly mentioned. This phenomenon is not new (Bartlett, 1932/1977) but it has recently been the focus of much research (Bower, 1976; Stein & Glenn, 1978; Warren, Nicholas & Trabasso, 1978) which shows that we tend to remember important structural information and forget irrelevant detail. One concern of this paper is to determine whether written as opposed to orally presented text disposes comprehenders to treat that text differently. This is a matter of some general theoretical significance in that written language and literacy offer a possible explanation for the linguistic and cognitive effects associated with modernity (Goody, 1977; Havelock, 1973).

To date, only a few researchers have included reading versus listening as a variable in experimental design. Sachs (1967, 1974) and Begg (1971) have both been concerned with the difference in the ability of adult readers and listeners to differentiate a previously presented sentence from a paraphrase. They have found that readers remember more of the surface structure features of the sentence (Sachs) and for a longer period of time (Begg) than listeners. On the other hand Horowitz and Berkowitz (1967) and Horowitz (1968) have compared the free recall protocols of adults who heard or read stories of varying complexity. They found that the recall protocols of the listeners were more accurate and contained

*This research was funded by The Ontario Ministry of Education and the Social Sciences and Humanities Research Council of Canada. We wish to thank Robin Campbell for his helpful comments on the manuscript.

19

more of the important text units than the protocols of the readers. Smiley, Oakley, Worthen, Campione, and Brown (1977) have looked at the recall patterns of Grade 7 students (13-years-old) and found that, like the adults, the Grade 7 listeners recalled more story units (propositions) than the Grade 7 readers. Berger and Perfetti (1977) report similar findings with Grade 5 children: the listeners included a significantly greater number of propositions in their free recall and obtained significantly higher scores on factual comprehension than did the readers.

These findings may not be strictly incompatible; readers and listeners may tend to extract different kinds of information from oral and written statements. Listeners may tend to recall more of the gist of the story and readers may recall more of the surface structure or verbatim features of the story.

Theoretical reasons may be offered as to why this may reasonably be the case. Although there are a large number of ways that speech differs from writing (Olson, 1977; Rubin, 1978; Vachek 1976; Havelock, 1963; McLuhan, 1962) the important one for an analysis of comprehension and memory of connected discourse, in this case, simple narratives, is the way that meaning is preserved in oral and written language. In oral language, the point, intention or significance of the language, the 'speaker's meaning' is preserved in the mind of the listener; as the actual words, syntax, and intonation are ephemeral, they are rapidly exchanged for those interpreted meanings which can be preserved. In written language, the words and syntax, the 'sentence meaning', is preserved by the artifact of writing, and mental recall becomes the precise reproduction of that artifact.[1,2]

Those differences between what is preserved in oral and written language which are most relevant to the present study are a class of implicit inferences which Grice (1975) labels Conversational Implicatures. Schank (1975) and Hildyard and Olson (1978) refer to this class of inferences as Enabling Inferences,

---

[1]Theoretical distinctions created for one purpose do not necessarily translate into those serving a different purpose. Nonetheless, it may be useful to indicate some homologies. Sentence meaning as we use the term is roughtly equivalent to the literal meaning of that sentence and equivalent to the logical or propositional structure underlying and expressed by that sentence. That propositional content of the sentence is similar but not equivalent to the sense of the sentence. Rather, it is equivalent to the sense plus the reference. Suppose two childen argue thus:

A: My dad is bigger than your dad

B: My dad is bigger than your dad.

These two sentences have the same sense, but express different underlying propositions: a greater than b; b greater than a, and therefore represent different sentence meanings.

[2]Havelock (1963, 1976) points out that with the emphasis on literacy both in classical Greece and in post-reformation England there was a great concern to make sentences say exactly, neither more nor less than what they meant. Poetry and proverbial sayings, which mean both more and less than what they say, were rejected as means of expressing truth both by Plato and 2000 years later by members of the Royal Society of London who, according to their historian Spratt (1667/1966), were devoted both to the advancement of science and to the improvement of the English language as a medium of prose.

namely, those informal inferences which the reader or listener must draw in order to make the discourse comprehensible. As Glenn (1978) states, subjects make inferences until they can understand and/or recall the passage' (p. 245).

To illustrate, if told

There was a terrible squeal of brakes. They saw the girl lying in the road.

it is necessary to infer that a vehicle struck the girl. That inference serves to tie together the distinct premises. Furthermore, the speaker (or writer) can count on the listener or reader to import this conceptual link. According to the cooperative principle (Grice, 1975) which holds between the speaker and listener, if it were not the case that the girl was struck by a vehicle which produced the loud squeal of brakes, then the speaker would have said so. Hence, it is safe and appropriate for the listener to make the inference. Of course a reader will also make the inference in order to understand the story, but if, as we suggest, s/he is led to try to reconstruct the written message, what in fact the story had said, s/he will differentiate the statements themselves from the inferences derived and try particularly to remember the former.

Not all inferences are critical to the comprehension of the discourse as a whole. There are a set of Pragmatic inferences which serve to elaborate, in a noncritical way, upon the given information. Thus, if told The cookies are in a container, we may reasonably but not logically infer that The cookies are in a cookie jar. Such pragmatic inferences tend to instantiate the sentence through the generation of information which could plausibly be found in the listener/reader's knowledge structure (Anderson & Ortony, 1975).

The interpretation of a conversation or a discourse must involve, therefore, far more than a literal interpretation of the explicitly presented sentences. Comprehension must also include the extraction of the speaker's intention, the generation of inferences essential to the coherence of the discourse or conversation, and the generation of inferences peripheral to the central theme. The critical question is whether readers and listeners process these various aspects of meaning in the same way. As suggested above, reading a text may be expected to produce a bias towards the detection and memory of the sentence meaning, for what was said, while listening may be expected to have a bias towards the detection and memory of the speaker's meaning, for what was intended or meant.

THE EXPERIMENT

Applying this general conception to the experimental study of the comprehension and memory of stories, we may predict that listeners, in their attempt to construct a coherent interpretation of the message, will attend primarily to those statements which are central to the theme of the message, incorporating Enabling Inferences into their interpretations when necessary, paying attention primarily to what WAS MEANT. Readers, on the other hand, have a permanent record of the sentence per se and pay attention to all the specified details, both relevant and irrelevant, which are explicitly represented in the text; to what, in fact, WAS SAID. Hence we may expect readers to be far more aware of which statements were actually contained in the message as opposed to those which are compatible with the information but were not explicitly stated. Moreover, any superiority of the readers over the listeners in differentiating inferences from explicitly presented sentences should be especially apparent for Enabling Inferences, since these are the inferences the listener will have included in the representation of the ongoing discourse in order to make it coherent and, therefore, more memorable (Glenn, 1978).

These expected differences between reading and listening were incorporated into hypotheses as follows. First, it was hypothesized that, in understanding a narrative story, listeners would attempt to build a representation which honors primarily central or structural information. Irrelevant or incidental details will be less well remembered. Readers, however, are more likely to pay attention to all specified details, including incidental ones, and hence will be better able to verify statements concerning them. Secondly, it was hypothesized that readers would be more aware than listeners of what statements were actually presented in the narrative. The listeners should be particularly inaccurate in their judgments of those propositions central to the story structure but which were in fact implicit.

If becoming literate involves learning that language can be specialized for specific functions, then we might expect to obtain differences not only between reading and listening conditions but also between good and poor readers. Several recently reported studies, concerned with good and poor readers' comprehension of narratives, provide partial confirmation of this prediction. For example, Smiley et al (1977), in their study of good and poor readers in Grade 7 (13 years of age), found that the good readers recalled more of a story and proportionally more of the structurally important story units than did the poor readers. Berger and Perfetti (1977) also found that good readers in Grade 5 (11 years of age) recalled more story units than did poor readers. These latter researchers, however, did not differentiate between structurally important and structurally irrelevant propositions. With respect to the ability to differentiate inferences from explicitly presented statements, Waller (1976) reports that good Grade 5 readers are more aware of what is explicit in a series of statements than are poor readers. However, Waller was concerned with recognition memory for sentences presented in the context of 3 line stories rather than longer meaningful narratives. To provide further information about the effect of reading level on the comprehension and memory of narratives in listening, as opposed to reading, the subjects in the present study were classified as good, average, or poor readers.

Finally, since the hypotheses predicted that subjects woud treat structurally important information differently from incidental or irrelevant information, it is necessary to provide some means of identifying what is important in a narrative.

Several authors (e.g. Bower, 1976; Glenn, 1978; Meyer, 1975; Stein & Glenn, 1978; Thorndyke, 1977) have suggested that stories can be considered in terms of a series of constitutents including the setting, the characters, a plan of action, the action, and the final outcome. While there is disagreement between story grammarians as to the exact nature of the inter-relationship of the various constituents, it is generally agreed that these structurally important units serve to introduce new information.

For purposes of the present study, structural information was defined as that information necessary for the introduction of new events and necessary for the coherence of the main story theme. Thus, structural information could be implicit (an Enabling Inference) or explicitly stated in the story. Incidental story information was defined as information which served to elaborate upon an event or episode in a non-critical way such that its deletion would not interfere with the comprehension of the story as a whole. This incidental information could similarly be implicit (a Pragmatic Inference) or explicit.

Method

Materials

Four different narrative stories 12 to 14 lines long were written. The stories described common childhood events. All the stories had been used in previous studies (e.g. Hildyard & Olson, 1978) and were known to be within the reading competence of the average third grade child.

The stories were accompanied by four different classes of statements:

Structural Explicit. These were statements which were explicitly presented in the story and which were concerned with propositions central to the structure or theme of the story.

Structural Implicit. These statements also concerned facts central to the main story structure, but were never presented explicitly and were, therefore, inferred. Structural Implicit statements are equivalent to the Enabling Inferences (Conversational Implicatures) described earlier.

Incidental Explicit. These were statements about details non-relevant to the structure or theme of the story as a whole. The statements concerned non-relevant explicitly mentioned facts.

Incidental Implicit. This last statement type included statements about non-relevant details which could be inferred from the story. Incidental Implicit statements are equivalent to the Pragmatic Inferences described earlier.

A story together with a set of statements is shown in Table I.

Each story was accompanied by 12 statements, such that across the four stories 12 exemplars of each item type were prepared. It was not possible to present

TABLE I

Example of Story and Statement Types

Susan and Jonathan

Susan and Jonathan lived in a house in the middle of the city. At the end of their backyard there was a large maple tree. Susan and Jonathan often played under the maple tree in their sandbox. One morning they found something in the sand. It was tiny and white. Susan went into the house to find a container to put it in. She went up to her bedroom and came back carrying a black and white box. It's too big, said Jonathan.

So Susan found a handkerchief and some kleenex. They put the handkerchief on the bottom of the box and laid the tissues on top of the handkerchief. Jonathan carefully laid the strange thing on the tissues.

Next morning their teacher was interested in what they had found and gave the whole class a lesson on how birds' eggs hatch.

1. Structural Implicit:
   Susan and Jonathan found a bird egg.
2. Structural Explicit:
   What they found was small and white.
3. Incidental Implicit:
   The sand box was at the end of the backyard.
4. Incidental Explicit:
   They lived in the city.

---

equal numbers of each statement type with each story, since to do so resulted in the stories being stilted and awkward. The statements were presented in a forced choice format and the subject was required to select the most appropriate alternative. The two alternative statements were written so that only attention to the story itself would permit the selection of the correct alternative. That is, given the general story theme either alternative would be feasible, but, in the context of the specific story details, one alternative was clearly more appropriate. To illustrate, the two alternative statements for the Structural Implicit statement shown in Table 1 were as follows:

1A.   Susan and Johnathan found a bird egg.

1B.   Susan and Jonathan found a stone.

The order of the most appropriate alternative (A or B) was randomized across the total set of statements. The order of presentation of the set of statement types for each story was arranged such that an answer to an early statement would have minimal effect on an answer to a later statement.

Two pilot studies were conducted with adults to ensure the validity of the Structural/Incidental and Implicit/Explicit dimensions and to ensure that only attention to the narrative itself would enable the subject to select the most appropriate alternative. On the basis of this pilot data, several items were rewritten and others discarded. The remaining 48 statements were the ones ultimately employed in this study.

Two distractor tasks were also prepared, one for the readers and one for the listeners. These distractor tasks were presented between a story and its accompanying statements. Different tasks were used for the two groups in an attempt to ensure that the interference effects would be equivalent across the two modes of presentation (cf. Brooks, 1968). The task for the readers involved checking along a line of letters to count and record the number of occurrences of a specific letter (a, e, or o). Five of these counting tasks were presented after each story. The listeners were required to listen to a string of words, count, and subsequently record the number of occurrences of words starting with a specific letter (m, s, t). Five word strings were presented after each story.

All materials were collated into booklets. The booklets for the readers contained the four stories, four sets of statements, plus four sets of distractor tasks, in the order, story, distractor task, statements (appropriate to the preceding story), and so on. The four stories were presented in a random order fixed across subjects. The statement sheets were set out as follows. The two alternative statement pairs were written one above the other and were numbered 1A, 1B, through 12A, 12B. At the right hand side of the response sheet were two columns: one for the child to check the most appropriate statement, and the second for the child to write Yes (the statement was presented in the story) or No (the statement was not presented in the story).

The booklets for the listeners contained a set of four blank sheets for the child to record the answers to the distractor tasks, plus four sheets for responses to the statements. The left hand side of this response sheet contained the numbers 1A, 1B, through 12B, but not the statements themselves. The right hand side contained two columns: one for the child to check the most appropriate statement, and the second for the child to write Yes (the statement was presented in the story) or No (it was not presented in the story).

Subjects

36 children from Grade 3 and 36 children from Grade 5 participated in the study. They were selected from two Grade 3 and two Grade 5 classrooms. The selection, which was made by the class teachers, was according to reading level: six good, six average, and six poor readers from each class were included.

Half the children at each grade level listened to the narratives, and half read them. Equal numbers of good, average, and poor readers were assigned to the reading/listening groups.

Procedure

The children were tested in groups of 18; that is, subjects in each grade and each experimental condition were seen separately. Different instructions were given to the readers and listeners. The readers were told that they would be required to read some stories and then answer some questions. They were informed that the questions were of a special kind requiring the selection of the most appropriate answer from two alternatives. The children were instructed to read both alternatives carefully and to put a checkmark against the most appropriate one, i.e., the one which fit in best with the story. They were then told to try to decide whether the statement they picked as the better, or more appropriate, one had actually been presented in the story. Specifically, the children were asked to Pick the best answer and then decide Did the story actually say this? Several examples were given to ensure that all the children understood that they were to make two responses and to ensure that they were aware of the difference between a statement which is explicitly presented and a statement which is compatible with the explicit propositions but which is inferred.

The children worked through the stories and distractor tasks in the predetermined order. They were requested to read each story just once and were encouraged to seek assistance if they had trouble reading any of the words. The children worked at their own rate. The task took between 30 and 45 minutes to complete, depending upon the child's reading level.

The children in the listening groups were told that they would hear some stories and some questions. They were informed that their task was to select the most appropriate answer from two alternatives. They were instructed to place a checkmark against alternative A or B, whichever was the more appropriate, and then to decide whether that alternative had actually been presented in the story. They recorded Yes or No as the readers had done. Several examples were presented, to ensure that all the children understood the task. The experimenter then read out the first story, followed first by the distractor task and then by the set of statements. The order of presentation of the stories was the same as for the readers. The entire procedure took approximately 30 minutes.

Note that the readers were required to read all the experimental materials (stories, distractor tasks, and statements). The listeners heard the stories, distractor tasks, and statements.

Approximately one week after the initial testing, the children were given a grade appropriate Gates-MacGinitie reading comprehension test. The children were tested in their classes. All the children in a class participated.

Results

In order to validate the teachers' assignment of children to the three reading levels in each of the two grades, Gates-MacGinitie grade level equivalent scores were calculated for each group in the experiment. Mean reading scores (and standard deviations) for the Grade 3 and Grade 5 children in each of the experimental groups are shown in Table II.

Analyses of variance computed on these data showed that, for both grade levels, the good readers were significantly better than the average readers, who were significantly better than the poor readers ($F > 35.3$; all Newman-Keuls,

TABLE II
Mean (and standard deviation) Reading Scores
for the Good, Average and Poor Grade 3 and Grade 5 Readers
in the Reading and Listening Groups

	Good	*Average*	*Poor*
Grade 3			
Reading Group	5.27(.83)	3.68(.36)	2.07(.64)
Listening Group	5.33(.57)	3.32(.41)	2.03(.38)
Grade 5			
Reading Group	7.75(1.09)	5.27(.29)	4.17(.55)
Listening Group	7.88(1.29)	5.40(.47)	3.9 (.65)

$p < 0.001$). Also, for each grade the reading scores for the listeners were equivalent to those of the readers (both $F < 1.00$). Obviously the teachers' assignment of children to the three reading levels was extremely accurate. Reading level was therefore included as a factor in each of the subsequent analyses.

The first analysis concerned the child's selection of the most appropriate statement. The six-way ANOVA (Grade × Reading/Listening × Reading level × Structural/Incidental × Implicit/Explicit × Subjects), computed on the total correct forced-choice selection for each statement type (max = 12), revealed the following significant main effects and interactions[1]: Reading level ($F(2,60) = 10.22$, $p < 0.001$); Structural/Incidental ($F(1,60) = 56.7$, $p < 0.001$); Implicit/Explicit ($F(1,60) = 19.65$, $p < 0.001$); Reading/Listening × Structural/Incidental ($F(1,60) = 14.97$, $p < 0.001$); Reading/Listening × Implicit/Explicit ($F(1,60) = 11.89$, $p < 0.001$); Grade level × Reading/Listening × Implicit/Explicit ($F(1,60) = 9.73$, $p < 0.01$).

The main effect of reading level was such that the good readers performed significantly better than the average and poor readers (Newman-Keuls: $p < 0.01$). Note that this superiority of the good readers held across both grade levels, for both the Reading and the Listening conditions and for all statement types.

All other main effects and interactions are contained within just two interactions, which will be considered in detail. Figure 1 shows the interaction of Reading/Listening with Structural/Incidental. A test for simple main effects (Kirk, 1968) indicated that both the readers ($p < 0.05$) and the listeners ($p < 0.001$) made fewer errors in selecting the correct Structural statements than in selecting the correct Incidental statements. The readers (86% correct) and listeners (88% correct) performed at approximately the same level on the Structural items. Performance on the Incidental items was not equivalent, however, and the readers (81% correct) obtained significantly higher scores ($p < 0.01$) than the listeners (72% correct). Here, then, is support for the first hypothesis: both readers and listeners score highly on items which are relevant to the structure of the story, but listeners are poorer than readers on items concerning irrelevant details.

---

[1]A quasi F statistic was not calculated because unequal numbers of each statement type were queried after each story.

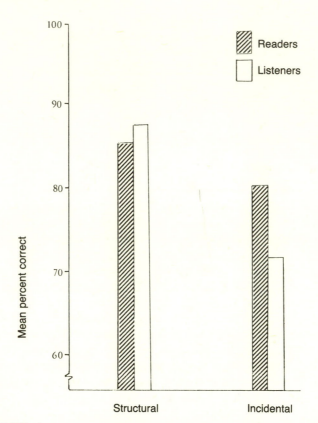

FIGURE 1. Percent correct Selection of the most Appropriate Structural and Incidental statements by Readers and Listeners.

The means for the significant three-way interaction of Grade level by
Reading/Listening by Implicit/Explicit are shown in Table III. A test for simple
interaction effects indicated a significant interaction only in the Grade 3 data
($p < 0.001$; Grade 5: $F < 1.0$). A test of simple main effects showed that the
Grade 3 readers recalled significantly more explicit (89%) than implicit (75%)
facts ($p < 0.001$), and the performance of these Grade 3 readers on Explicit facts
was significantly higher than the performance of the Grade 3 listeners (89% vs.
77%; $p < 0.01$). In other words, the Grade 3 readers excelled in their selection of
correct alternatives for the explicitly presented facts. Note, however, that overall
performance in all cells was relatively high; hence the lack of interaction in the
Grade 5 data may simply be the result of a ceiling effect.

The next analysis examined children's judgments as to whether or not the
statement had actually been presented in the story as opposed to being inferred by
the subject. The mean number of correct responses are shown in Table IV. Inspection of individual subjects' data indicated that many of the Grade 3 children and

TABLE III
Mean Percent Selection of the More Appropriate
Implicit and Explicit Statements
by Grade 3 and Grade 5

	Readers	Listeners
Grade 3		
Implicit Statements	75	78
Explicit Statements	89	77
Grade 5		
Implicit Statements	83	81
Explicit Statements	86	83

several of the Grade 5 children were operating with a response bias. In an attempt to remove the effects of this response bias, a five-way ANOVA (Grade × Reading level × Reading/Listening × Structural/Incidental × Subjects) was computed, with the child's d' score as the dependent variable. The significant main effects were as follows: Grade (F(1,60) = 8.61, p < 0.01); Reading/Listening (F(1,60) = 5.45, p < 0.025); Reading level (F(2,60) = 6.36, p < 0.01). None of the interactions was significant.

The Grade 5 children (mean d' = 1.27) were more accurate in differentiating inferences from explicit statements than were the Grade 3 children (mean d' = 0.87). The good readers (mean d' = 1.4) were similarly more accurate than the average (mean d' = 1.04) and the poor (mean d' = .70) readers (Newman-Keuls: p < 0.01). Finally, those children who read (mean d' = 1.23) were able to differentiate inferences from statements which were actually in the text with a higher degree of accuracy than those who listened (mean d' = .92). Thus, when the effects of response bias are removed, these data are exactly as predicted: children who read are able to pay closer attention to the explicit statements, and are therefore better able to differentiate these explicit statements from inferences. This ability, moreover, is related to literate competence.

TABLE IV
Grade 3 and Grade 5 Readers' and Listeners' Success in
Rejecting Implicit Inferred Statements and in Accepting
Explicit Statements as Having Been in the Text

	Readers'		Listeners'	
	Implicit	Explicit	Implicit	Explicit
Grade 3				
Structural	42	85	31	86
Incidental	44	86	40	76
Grade 5				
Structural	60	80	39	91
Incidental	61	85	54	82

Discussion

The Grade 3 and Grade 5 subjects in this study were all able to extract the story meaning, as evidenced by their extremely high performance in selecting those statements best fitting into the general story structure. However, as Figure 1 showed, those children who listened to the narrative stories were found to be better able to remember statements which were concerned with the central events of the story than statements about irrelevant or peripheral events. The Grade 3 and Grade 5 children who read the narrative stories better remembered these irrelevant details. In other words, children appear to listen more to what was MEANT, but to read more for what was SAID. Alternatively, listening results in particular memory for the thematic or central aspects of the story, whereas reading distributes memory across all aspects of the story represented in the written text.

The pattern obtained for the recall of structural/incidental statements was complementary to that obtained for explicit/implicit statements. For listeners in both Grade 3 and Grade 5, the selection of the correct alternatives was as accurate for Implicit statements as for Explicit statements, regardless of their structural importance. For readers of both grade levels, however, the selection of correct alternatives was more accurate for Explicit items than for Implicit ones, with this advantage of Explicit over Implicit reaching significance for the Grade 3 children. In general, then, the readers were better at recalling the facts explicitly mentioned in the text. Note, moreover, that this effect occurred even though the children were requested not to re-read the stories. In other words, these data are not due simply to the fact that readers are able to re-read the written message. Rather, these data provide support for the hypothesis that one listens for what was meant, the story gist, but reads what was, in fact, written.

The superiority of the high reading level subjects over the average and low reading level subjects, in selecting the correct statement regardless of whether the story was heard or read, complements the earlier findings of Smiley et al (1977) and Berger and Perfetti (1977). For whatever reason, children who read well also listen well. Perhaps they have appropriately specialized reading and listening skills; alternatively, some procedures for language comprehension are suitable for both oral and written language. And perhaps good readers have learned to treat even orally presented stories as if they were written texts and interpret and remember them accordingly.

That the listeners listened for gist, that is, both explicit and implicit structural information, while the readers paid closer attention to all details, again both structural and incidental, is interesting in the light of a recent paper by Monaco and Harris (1978). Monaco and Harris have argued that, contrary to story grammar theory, the hierarchical depth of a unit of information alone does not determine its probability of recall. They suggest that, 'Any description of story comprehension must take into account the role of the comprehender; his/her efforts, especially in terms of attention, also determine how much or how little information will be remembered' (p. 396). However, as Monaco and Harris' subjects read the narratives, we would expect only small differences between sentences of high hierarchical level (Structural) and those of low hierarchical level (Incidental). Had Monaco and Harris required their subjects to listen to the narratives, they may well have found that hierarchical depth WAS related to recognition and recall.

In judging whether or not the statements had actually been presented in the story, both the readers and the listeners were biased towards a "Yes" response, with the result that performance on statements which were Explicit and called for a Yes response was markedly better (mean of 84% correct) than performance on the Implicit statements which called for a No response (mean of 46% correct). To remove this response bias, d' scores were calculated; as predicted, readers and listeners differed in their ability to differentiate statements which were inferred from those that were explicit in the text. The children who read were better able to differentiate what had been said from what had been inferred. The children who listened, on the other hand, were less aware of what was presented explicitly and what was inferred. Presumably, listeners had incorporated the additional information contained in the inferences into the general story representation in their attempts to make the story memorable and coherent. Contrary to the predictions, however, the listeners did not experience greater difficulty in detecting the structural inferences than incidental ones. Rather, listeners had as much difficulty in differentiating what was said from what was inferred for those inferences central to the story theme as for those which served merely to elaborate upon that theme.

The Grade 5 children were superior to the Grade 3 children in detecting these inferences. This suggests that the ability to differentiate between explicit statements and inferred but appropriate statements is developmental in nature. That the good readers were better able than the poor or average readers to differentiate what was said from that was meant (and inferred) suggests that this competency is also tied to the acquisition of literacy. It is not simply that the good readers are better able to interpret stories and produce more inferences in this process, but rather that they have begun to develop a greater awareness of what was said and what they added in the course of interpretation. That is, they have a better idea of sentence meaning. And as the isolation of sentence meaning is heightened by reading as opposed to listening, we may suggest that the good readers' superiority in differentiating what was said from what was meant in the listening task may be one example of the feedback of a skill specialized by reading to a skill involved in listening.

Summary

In summary, it appears that readers and listeners do adopt somewhat different strategies in comprehending narrative discourse. The listeners pay primary attention to the theme of the story, building a coherent representation of what was meant. The readers, on the other hand, are able to pay closer attention to the meaning of the sentences per se, recalling more incidental but mentioned details and being more accurate in their judgments of what was in fact stated in the text. Furthermore, the acquisition of literate skills appears to involve a greater awareness of the sentence meaning, an awareness that shows up not only in comprehending written texts but those presented orally as well. It is, we may say, a reflection of the bias of written language towards literal meaning, to the meaning preserved in the text.

REFERENCES

ANDERSON, RICHARD C. & ORTONY, ANDREW. On putting apples into bottles: A problem of polysemy. *Cognitive Psychology,* 1975, *7,* 167–180.

BARLETT, FREDERICK C. Remembering. New York: Cambridge University Press, 1977 (first published 1932).

BEGG, IAN. Recognition memory for sentence meaning and wording. *Journal of Verbal Learning and Verbal Behavior,* 1971, *10,* 176–181.

BERGER, N. S. & PERFETTI, CHARLES A. Reading skill and memory for spoken and written discourse. *Journal of Reading Behavior,* 1977, *9,* 7–16.

BOWER, GORDON H. Experiments on story understanding and recall. *Quarterly Journal of Experimental Psychology,* 1976, *28,* 511–534.

BROOKS, LEE R. Spatial and verbal components of the act of recall. *Canadian Journal of Psychology,* 1968, *22,* 349–368.

BROWN, PENELOPE & LEVINSON, STEPHEN Universals in language usage: Politeness phenomena. In E. N. Goody (Ed.), *Questions and politeness: Strategies in social interaction.* Cambridge: Cambridge University Press, 1978.

GLENN, CHRISTINE G. The role of episodic structure and of story length in children's recall of simple stories. *Journal of Verbal Learning and Verbal Behavior,* 1978, *17,* 229–247.

GOODY, ESTHER N. Towards a theory of questions. In Esther N. Goody (Ed.), *Questions and politeness: Strategies in social interaction.* Cambridge: Cambridge University Press, 1978.

GOODY, JACK R. *The Domestication of the Savage Mind.* Cambridge: Cambridge University Press, 1977.

GORDON, DAVID & LAKOFF, GEORGE. Conversational postulates. In Peter Cole & Jerry L. Morgan (Eds.), *Syntax and semantics, Vol. 3: Speech acts.* New York: Academic Press, 1975.

GRICE, H. P. Logic and conversation. In Peter Cole & Jerry L. Morgan (Eds.), *Syntax and semantics, Vol. 3: Speech acts.* New York: Academic Press, 1975.

HAVELOCK, ERIC. *Preface to Plato.* Cambridge, Mass.: Harvard University Press, 1963.

——. *Origins of western literacy.* Toronto: Ontario Institute for Studies in Education, 1976.

HILDYARD, ANGELA & OLSON, DAVID R. Memory and inference in the comprehension of oral and written discourse. *Discourse Processes,* 1978, *1,* 91–117.

HOROWITZ, MILTON W. Organizational processes underlying differences between listening and reading as a function of complexity of material. *Journal of Communication,* 1968, *18,* 37–46.

HOROWITZ, MILTON W. & BERKOWITZ, ALAN. Listening and reading, speaking and writing: An experimental investigation of differential acquisition and reproduction of memory. *Perceptual and Motor Skills,* 1967, *24,* 207–215.

KIRK, RODGER E. Experimental Design: Procedures for the behavioral sciences. Belmont, California: Brooks/Cole Publishing Company, 1968.

McLUHAN, MARSHALL. *The Gutenberg galaxy.* Toronto: University of Toronto, 1962.

MEYER, BONNIE J. F. The organization of prose and its effect on memory. *Bulletin of the Psychonomic Society*, 1978, *11*, 393–396.

OLSON, DAVID R. From utterance to text: The bias of language in speech and writing. *Harvard Educational Review*, 1977, *47*, 257–281.

RUBIN, ANDEE. A theoretical taxonomy of the differences between oral and written language. In Rand J. Spiro, Betrona C. Bruce and William F. Brewer (Eds.), *Theoretical issues in reading comprehension*. Hillsdale, N.J.: L. Erlbaum, 1980, pp.411–438.

SACHS, JACQUELINE. Memory in reading and listening to discourse. *Memory and Cognition*, 1974, *2*, 95–100.

_____. Recognition memory for syntactic and semantic aspects of connected discourse. *Perception and Psychophysics*, 1967, *2*, 437–442.

SEARLE, JOHN. Indirect speech acts. In P. Cole & J. Morgan (Eds.), *Syntax and semantics, Vol. 3: Speech acts*. New York: Academic Press, 1975.

_____. *Speech acts*. Cambridge: Cambridge University Press, 1969.

SCHANK, ROGER. The role of memory in language processing. In Charles Norvale Cofer and Richard Atkinson (Eds.), *The nature of human memory*. San Francisco: W. H. Freeman Press, 1975.

SMILEY, SANDRA S., OAKLEY, DREW DAULPH, WORTHEN, DAVID, CAMPIONE, JOSEPH C. & BROWN, ANN L. Recall of thematically relevant material by adolescent good and poor readers as a function of written versus oral presentation. *Journal of Educational Psychology*, 1977, *69*, 381–387.

SPRAT, THOMAS. History of the Royal Society of London for the improving of natural knowledge. In Jackson I. Cope & Harold Whitmore Jones (Eds.). St. Louis: Washington University Press, 1966 (originally published London 1667).

STEIN, NANCY L. & GLENN, CHRISTINE G. An analysis of story comprehension in elementary school children. In R. Freedle (Ed.), *Discourse processing: Multidisciplinary perspectives, Vol. 2*. Hillsdale: N.J.: Ablex, Inc., 1978.

THORNDYKE, PERRY W. Cognitive structures in comprehension and memory of narrative discourse. *Cognitive Psychology*, 1977, *9*, 77–110.

VACHEK, JOSEF. *Selected writings in English and general linguistics by Joseph Vachek*. The Hague: Mouton, 1976.

WALLER, T. GARY. Children's recognition memory for written sentences: A comparison of good and poor readers. *Child Development*, 1976, *47*, 90–95.

WARREN, WILLIAM H., NICHOLAS, DAVID W. & TRABASSO, TOM. Event chains and inferences in understandiang narratives. In R. Freedle (Ed.), *Discourse Processes: Advances in Research and Theory Vol. 1*. Norwood, N.J.: Ablex Publishing Co. 1979, pp. 23–52.

3 Integration and Involvement In Speaking, Writing, and Oral Literature*

Wallace L. Chafe
University of California, Berkeley

Starting from what now seems to be an accepted fact—that typical written language and typical spoken language differ from each other in more ways than just the medium in which they are written—we would like to know more about what those ways are. Various studies have focused on particular differences or sets of related differences. Drieman (1962), for example, found that written texts are shorter, have longer words, have more attributive adjectives, and have a more varied vocabulary. Devito (1966, 1967) found written language to have fewer words that refer to the speaker, fewer quantifiers and hedges, and greater abstractness. Beginning with Harrell (1957), various studies have found that written language has more subordinate clauses than spoken language (e.g. O'Donnell, 1974; Kroll, 1977). Kroll made a particularly detailed study of this difference, distinguishing 24 types of clausal and seven types of phrasal subordination, as well as seven types of coordination.

These and other authors have been quick to admit that their work has been incomplete and exploratory. Kroll concludes her article by saying, 'There is still much that remains to be said about the distinction and the overlap between which structures are commonly used in speech and in writing' (p. 106). In the spirit that we are still very much in the age of exploration so far as these differences are concerned, I want here to suggest how certain differences in the processes of speaking and writing have led to specific differences in the two products, spoken and written language. I will focus on two differences in the speaking and writing processes:

*This work is part of a project to investigate differences between written and spoken language sponsored by Grant NIE-G-80-0125 from the National Institute of Education. I am extremely grateful to Jane Danielewicz for her indispensable collaboration in this project and for her many contributions to this chapter.

35

1) that speaking is faster than writing (and slower than reading),
2) that speakers interact with their audiences directly, whereas writers do not.

I will suggest some specific features of spoken and written language which I believe have arisen from these differences, and will illustrate them with data presently available to me, giving some counts of their occurrences in the two kinds of language. At the end I will try to show briefly how a language which has no written tradition may nevertheless have different styles which in some ways parallel the differences between spoken and written language; how 'oral literature', that is, may justifiedly be considered 'literary' (cf. Bright, this volume).

A word about the data I am using is in order. We have been collecting samples of four styles of language:

1) informal spoken language, from dinnertable conversations,
2) formal spoken language, from lectures,
3) informal written language, from letters,
4) formal written language, from academic papers.

Subjects have been academic people (faculty and graduate students) who are accustomed to producing language of these four kinds. We are in the process of analyzing these language samples for occurrences of a large number of features which we hypothesize to have significantly different distributions in the four styles. I will report here on only a few features which seem especially important, and on only the two maximally differentiated styles: informal spoken language and formal written language. Counts will be based on data from 14 subjects from an eventual total of 25, and on 9,911 words of informal spoken language and 12,368 words of formal written language. This will be no more than a partial and preliminary report from a project still in its early stages.

SPEAKING IS FASTER THAN WRITING (AND SLOWER THAN READING)

The average speed of spoken English, including pauses, is in the neighborhood of 180 words per minute.[1] The speed of writing depends on whether it is handwriting or typewriting, as well as on individual differences. It is at least in the right ballpark to say that handwriting characteristically takes place at slower than one-tenth the speed of speaking.[2] Presumably, most of the differences between written

---

[1]This is the rate we found in the pear stories data reported in Chafe, 1980.

[2]Matsuhashi (in press) gives speeds for one subject averaging 13 words per minute over four different discourse types.

and spoken language have resulted from the nature of handwriting rather than typing, but even typing takes place at, say, about one-third the speed of speaking, and that rate is for copying, not for the creation of new language. Writing, then, of whatever kind, is slower than speaking, and handwriting is much slower. It is also relevant that reading, the other end of the process, is faster. Reading speeds vary considerably, of course, but the average may be between 200 and 400 words per minute (Gibson & Levin, 1975, p. 539), a little faster than speaking and listening. Thus, while speaking and listening necessarily proceed together at the same speed, writing and reading deviate from that spoken language baseline in opposite directions, writing being much slower and reading somewhat faster.

Observation of spontaneous spoken language has led various investigators independently to the finding that it is produced in spurts, sometimes called idea units, with a mean length (including hesitations) of approximately two seconds or approximately six words each (Chafe, 1980). Idea units typically have a coherent intonation contour, they are typically bounded by pauses, and they usually exhibit one of a small set of syntactic structures. They are a striking, probably universal property of spoken language. It is useful to speculate that each idea unit represents a single 'perching' of consciousness (James, 1890, p. 243), or a single 'idea' in that sense. If that is true, then when we speak we are in the habit of moving from one idea to the next at the rate of about one every two seconds. Perhaps that is even our normal 'thinking rate', if language reflects the pace of thought. Whether or not this rate applies to all thinking, it is certainly a rate we are accustomed to while we are using language—probably while we are thinking in language to ourselves as well as when we are overtly vocalizing.

If that is our temporal baseline, the activity of writing presents a problem. If we write more than 10 times more slowly than we speak, what is happening in our thoughts during all that extra time? It is doubtful that very much of our cognitive capacity has to be devoted to the mechanical activity of writing itself, at least after we get beyond the first grade. In writing, it would seem, our thoughts must constantly get ahead of our expression of them in a way to which we are totally unaccustomed when we speak. As we write down one idea, our thoughts have plenty of time to move ahead to others. The result is that we have time to integrate a succession of ideas into a single linguistic whole in a way that is not available in speaking. In speaking, we normally produce one idea unit at a time. That is apparently about all we have the capacity to pay attention to, and if we try to think about much more than that we are likely to get into trouble (cf. the 'one-clause-at-a-time hypothesis' suggested by Frances Syder and Andrew Pawley). In writing we have time to mold a succession of ideas into a more complex, coherent, integrated whole, making use of devices we seldom use in speaking. It is probably also significant that a reader, proceeding at a greater speed than even a listener, can assimilate very quickly the larger span of ideas that the writer has taken time to integrate. In other words, the abnormal quickness of reading fits together with the abnormal slowness of writing to foster a kind of language in which ideas are combined to form more complex idea units and sentences. I will say that written language tends to have an 'integrated' quality which contrasts with the fragmented quality of spoken language.

FRAGMENTATION

The fragmentation of spoken language shows up partly in the stringing together of idea units without connectives:[3]

(1)   And my room was small.
       . . . It was like . . . nine by twelve or something.
       It seemed spacious at the time.
       . . . I came home,
       I was really exhausted,
       I was eating a popsicle,
       . . . I was sitting there in my chair,

But idea units are also frequently introduced with coordinating conjunctions, by far the most common of which is *and*:

(2)   A—nd it's . . . very well . . um equipped.
       . . . You know the kitchen,
       . . . and and it's got a dishwasher,
       and it's got . . . uh . . all kinds of . . . you know . . . mixers and . . . uh
       . . .plates
       and . . . you know every kind of equipment you need.
       And . . a—nd uh— . . staple . . things.

Other conjunctions which occur fairly often are *but, so,* and *because*:

(3a)   But of course to the audience sounded like. . . sort of a total nonsequitur.

(3b)   But the other thing too is she's always had a thing for older men.

(3c)   So they were having a fit.

(3d)   So it's . . you know really handy.

(3e)   Because the theory is prescribed in some way.

(3f)   Because the— uh starting date will be in October.

In the data at hand, the occurrences of these conjunctions at the beginnings of idea units were as follows, the figures being numbers of occurrences per thousand words:

---

[3]In these transcriptions two dots indicate a break in timing too brief to be measured as a pause, three dots indicate a measurable pause, and two hyphens show a lengthening of the preceding segment.

	Spoken	*Written*
and	44.2	10.1
but	9.8	4.1
so	7.4	0.0
because	4.7	1.5
combined	66.0	15.8

Thus in these spoken data there were about four times as many coordinating conjunctions which were initial in idea units.

INTEGRATION

Integration refers to the packing of more information into an idea unit than the rapid pace of spoken language would normally allow. In fragmented language, a typical idea unit consists of a single clause, containing one predicative element (a verb or predicate adjective) and the noun phrases which are directly associated with that element as subject, object, and the like:

(4a)   I was eating a popsicle.

(4b)   And my room was small.

Sometimes a fragmented idea unit may consist of nothing more than a noun phrase or prepositional phrase:

(5a)   And . . a—nd uh— . . staple . . things.

(5b)   At that point.

Integrated language, on the other hand, makes use of a variety of devices for incorporating additional elements into an idea unit. The following are some of the more conspicuous of these devices.

Nominalizations

The most characteristic integrative device in our samples of written language was nominalization, as in the use of *treatment* rather than *treat, development* rather than *develop, operation* rather than *operate,* and *use* (the noun) rather than *use* (the verb) in the examples immediately below. A nominalization allows a notion which is verbal in origin to be inserted into an idea unit as if it were a noun. Such an element then plays the role of a noun in the syntax of the idea unit, acting as one of the arguments of the main predication. Thus it adds another, intrinsically predicative, element to the idea unit in the guise of a nominal one.

(6a)   There appeared to be evidence of differential *treatment* of children.

(6b)   The historical *development* of proper names often deviates from regular processes of linguistic change.

(6c)   the meaning generated by the *operation* of productive algorithms which make
no *use* of context, inference, or past calculation.

There were about eleven and a half times as many occurrences of
nominalizations in our written data (the figures are again occurrences per thousand words):

Spoken	Written
4.8	55.5

Associated with nominalizations is the occurrence of prepositional phrases,
usually introduced by *of*, which express the subject or object of the nominalized
verb; for example, *treatment of children*, where the children are the object of treatment, or *development of proper names*, where the proper names are the subject of
development. We found these 'genitive subjects' and 'genitive objects' occurring
significantly in the written material, but hardly at all in the spoken:

	Spoken	Written
genitive subject	0.1	4.1
genitive object	0.1	12.3

Participles

Another frequently used integrative device was the use of participles, both present
and past. Participles allow verbs to be used syntactically as either nouns or adjectives, and thus to be integrated into idea units in either a nominal or a modifying
function. We have looked separately at the occurrences of present and past participles. For present participles we counted occurrences of the *-ing* suffix on verbs,
but omitted progressive constructions like 'he was reading' and clearly lexicalized
words like 'meaning' or 'interesting' which, whatever their origins, behave as frozen nouns or adjectives. We counted present participles used as nouns, or
gerunds:

(7)   Her realism is preoccupied with *establishing* the literary work's relation to the
world,

as well as those used adjectivally:

(8)   It was a *recurring* classroom activity.

We also included postposed modifiers like the following, which might alternatively be regarded as reduced relative clauses:

(9)   There are, for example, no slang terms for patients *suffering* from severe or painful forms of cancer,

Here the participle is an abbreviated way of saying, 'who are suffering'.

With past participles we omitted perfect constructions like 'he has read' and lexicalized forms like 'confused'. What we counted were preposed modifiers such as:

(10)   The sight of an object brings about *directed* looking.

and postposed modifiers which, again, might be interpreted as reduced relative clauses:

(11)   A frequent change *found* in proper names is syllable loss.

Here the participle is an abbreviated way of saying 'which is found'. Present participles were more common in our data and were more frequent in writing than in speaking. Past participles were overwhelmingly more frequent in writing (per thousand words):

	Spoken	Written
present	7.1	20.7
past	1.2	14.9
combined	8.3	35.6

Thus participles in general were more than four times as frequent in the written data.

Attributive Adjectives

We found predicate adjectives, as in 'the house was *old*', to occur with approximately equal frequency in spoken and written language: 15.8 occurrences per thousand words in speaking, and 20.2 in writing. Such predicate adjectives are the basic device for expressing states in English. The use of attributive adjectives, as in 'the *old* house', allows states to be expressed as modifiers rather than assertions and is thus another integrative device. Examples from our written data include:

(12a) and have produced *drastic* changes in previously *stable* facets of the language.

(12b) Now these are two *distinct* places.

Although attributive adjectives were fairly common even in speaking, they appeared about four times as often in writing:

Spoken	Written
33.5	134.9

Thus, while nominalizations show the greatest proportional difference across the two kinds of language, attributive adjectives are the single most prevalent feature of written language.

Conjoined Phrases

The possibility of conjoining verb phrases, adjective phrases, or noun phrases provides another device by which more information can be packed inside one idea unit. Thus *learn* and *use* are joined together in parallel in the following example:

(13) as well as for speaker's tendency to learn these names earlier and use them more frequently.

rather than:

(14) as well as for speaker's tendency to learn these names earlier, and for speaker's tendency to use them more frequently.

The same can be done with adjectives:

(15) The traders are greedy and gullible.

rather than:

(16) The traders are greedy, and the traders are gullible.

And with nouns:

(17) so that Dorothea Brooke can, eventually, find her proper husband and her proper task in the world.

rather than:

(18) so that Dorothea Brooke can, eventually, find her proper husband, and so that Dorothea Brooke can, eventually, find her proper task in the world.

The total count of conjoined phrases in our data shows about four times as many in writing as in speaking:

	Spoken	Written
verb phrases	1.2	1.5
adjective phrases	0.6	5.1
noun phrases	3.4	17.1
combined	5.8	23.8

Series

Series provide a similar device, in this case for integrating three or more items within an idea unit:

(19)   No capital letters, definite articles, or plural markers provide clues.

rather than:

(20)   No capital letters provide clues,
       no definite articles provide clues,
       no plural markers provide clues.

Series appeared eight times as often in our written data:

Spoken	Written
0.9	7.2

Sequences of Prepositional Phrases

Prepositional phrases may be chained in sequence within an idea unit to consolidate a larger amount of information than would typically be found in an idea unit in fragmented language:

(21a) I avoid the question *of* the nature *of* referential forms *in* any underlying linguistic structure.

(21b) and should serve as a set *of* criteria *for* evaluating theories *of* cognitive development *with regard to* their implications *for* education.

This device was, in our data, nine times more prevalent in writing than in speaking. The occurrences of such sequences per thousand words were:

Spoken	Written
1.8	16.2

Complement Clauses

So far we have looked at the integration of single words and phrases into idea units, but of course whole clauses may be embedded as well. So-called complement clauses provide an example. We have looked at occurrences of clauses introduced by *that* and *to*:

(22a) It is notable *that assimilation rules are not much in evidence.*

(22b) This is not to suggest *that there are unlikely to be terms of this kind.*

(22c) and a wish *to care for the most needy.*

(22d) It is essentially impossible *to consider one without the other in educational practice.*

These two kinds of complement clauses together occurred more than twice as often in our written data (per thousand words):

	Spoken	Written
that complements	6.0	10.4
to complements	2.9	8.8
combined	8.9	19.2

Relative Clauses

A similar proportion of about two to one in favor of written language was found for relative clauses, which constitute another device by which a whole clause can be inserted within an idea unit:

(23a) and of the cognitive constraints *which seem to be responsible for this distribution.*

(23b) English has a variety of sentence types *in which the illocutionary force of the sentence is shifted in mid-stream.*

The occurrences per thousand words of restrictive relative clauses were:

Spoken	Written
9.7	15.8

SUMMARY

In summary, we found formal written language to differ from informal spoken language by having a larger proportion of nominalizations, genitive subjects and objects, participles, attributive adjectives, conjoined phrases, series, sequences of prepositional phrases, complement clauses, and relative clauses. These are all devices which permit the integration of more material into idea units. I have suggested that such integration is fostered by the greater amount of time available in writing, and that speakers are less likely to use them because of the faster pace of spoken language.

SPEAKERS INTERACT WITH THEIR AUDIENCES, WRITERS DO NOT

Speakers and writers usually have different relations to their respective audiences. It is typically the case that a speaker has face to face contact with the person to whom he or she is speaking. That means, for one thing, that the speaker and listener share a considerable amount of knowledge concerning the environment of the conversation. It also means that the speaker can monitor the effect of what he or she is saying on the listener, and that the listener is able to signal understanding and to ask for clarification. It means furthermore that the speaker is aware of an obligation to communicate what he or she has in mind in a way that reflects the richness of his or her thoughts—not to present a logically coherent but experientially stark skeleton, but to enrich it with the complex details of real experiences—to have less concern for consistency than for experiential involvement. The situation of the writer is fundamentally different. His or her readers are displaced in time and space, and he or she may not even know in any specific terms who the audience will be. The result is that the writer is less concerned with experiential richness, and more concerned with producing something that will be consistent and defensible when read by different people at different times in different places, something that will stand the test of time. I will speak of 'involvement' with the audience as typical for a speaker, and 'detachment' from the audience as typical for a writer.

DETACHMENT

The detached quality of written language is manifested in devices which serve to distance the language from specific concrete states and events. Such a device in English is the passive voice, which suppresses the direct involvement of an agent in an action. Examples of the passive in our written data are:

(24a) Its use *was observed* on only a single occasion.

(24b) The resonance complex *has been studied* through experiments with an electronic violin.

There were about five times as many occurrences of the passive in our written sample as in our spoken:

Spoken	Written
5.0	25.4

Nominalization seems to be another device associated with detachment, besides functioning as an integrative device as described above. Not only does nominalization allow predications to be integrated within larger sentences; it also suppresses involvement in actions in favor of abstract reification. Examples were given above, along with counts showing the striking predominance of nominalizations in our written data.

INVOLVEMENT

First Person References

A speaker's involvement with his or her audience is manifested, for one thing, in a speaker's more frequent reference to him- or herself. Although such use is in part determined by the subject matter (one can of course write about oneself), first person reference is otherwise much less frequent in formal written language. Typical examples of such reference in our spoken data were:

(25a) I have a friend who's . . . about six foot and blond.

(25b) I was reading some of his stuff recently.

Occurrences per thousand words of first person references, including *I, we, me,* and *us* were:

Spoken	Written
61.5	4.6

Second person reference would seem to be also a symptom of involvement, but there were too few examples in our data to demonstrate anything of interest.

Speaker's Mental processes

References to a speaker's own mental processes were also not uncommon, but were conspicuously absent in our written data; some examples from spoken language follow:

(26a) and I had no idea how I had gotten there.

(26b) but . . . I can recall . . . uh . . .a big undergraduate class that I had.

(26c) and I thought . . . am I alive?

The occurrences of such references in our data were as follows:

Spoken	Written
7.5	0.0

Monitoring of Information Flow

Involvement includes monitoring by the speaker of the communication channel which exists with the listener, and attempts to make sure that the channel is functioning well. The speaker may do things to reassure him- or herself that the listener is assimilating what he or she is saying, or to prod the listener into noticing and acknowledging the flow of information. Colloquial expressions like *well, I mean,* and *you know* perform one or another of these functions:

(27a) Well I . . I took off four weeks.

(27b) But . . but as it is still I mean . . everybody knows everybody.

(27c) So we . . so we . . you know, we have this confrontation.

These expressions were significantly present in our spoken sample, and entirely absent in the written:

	Spoken	Written
well	7.0	0.0
I mean	2.5	0.0
you know	13.6	0.0

Emphatic Particles

Particles expressing enthusiastic involvement in what is being said, like *just* and *really*, are also diagnostic:

(28a) I just don't understand.

(28b) And he got . . really furious.

The occurrences were:

	Spoken	Written
just	7.5	0.4
really	5.1	0.0

Fuzziness

Vagueness and hedges are also more prevalent in speaking, and may also express a desire for experiential involvement as opposed to the less human kind of precision which is fostered by writing. The following are examples of spoken fuzziness:

(29a) schemes for striking, lifting, pushing, pulling, *and so on.*

(29b) moving the bridge or soundpost *a millimeter or two.*

(29c) Since this banker is *something like* forty-seven.

(29d) And he started *sort of* circling.

Counts of occurrences per thousand words of this kind of language were:

Spoken	Written
18.1	5.5

Direct Quotes

Finally, direct quotes also express an involvement in actual events which tends to be lacking in written language:

(30a) And uh . . she said, 'Sally can I have one of your papers?'

(30b) And I said, 'Well no I'm afraid I don't.'

The occurrences of direct quotes in our data were as follows:

Spoken	Written
12.1	4.2

SUMMARY

In summary, whereas written language fosters the kind of detachment evidenced in the use of passives and nominalizations, spoken language shows a variety of manifestations of the involvement which a speaker has with his or her audience. Among these evidences of involvement are references to the speaker, references to the speaker's mental processes, devices for monitoring the flow of information, the use of emphatic particles, fuzziness, and the use of direct quotes.

I should repeat that these seemingly categorical statements about spoken and written language apply in fact to extremes on a continuum. The figures I have given are from maximally differentiated samples: spontaneous conversational language on the one hand and formal academic prose on the other. There are other styles of speaking which are more in the direction of writing, and other styles of writing which are more like speech. With other data now being collected and analyzed, we will eventually be able to report on a fuller range of styles. At the same time, we are looking also at the speech and writing of children, with the hope of tracing the manner in which these differences are acquired.

ORAL LITERATURE

The term 'oral literature' seems, etymologically at least, to contain an internal contradiction. How can something be oral and written at the same time, if 'literature' implies writing? The term seems to unite in one concept the two kinds of language whose differences we have been exploring. But oral literature has proved to be an identifiable way of using language, and it may be interesting to consider briefly how language that fits that category relates to what I have been discussing.

For many years I have been involved with a language called Seneca, an Iroquois language spoken in western New York State. Seneca has no written tradition. A missionary named Asher Wright developed an excellent orthography for the language in the 19th century and published some religious materials in it, but no widespread use of writing developed out of his efforts. Within the last few years an interest in teaching the language has led to a new orthography and the preparation of written educational materials, but there is still no use of writing for other purposes. Seneca, on the other hand, has an extraordinarily rich and varied oral literature, some of it ironically accessible now only from written records of earlier speakers (e.g. Hewitt, 1903), but much of it still known and performed. Some years ago I worked extensively with certain ritual materials in this language (Chafe, 1961). In examining features which differentiate spoken and written language, I have noticed that features of a similar sort may differentiate colloquial Seneca from the language used in these rituals.

Why should that be? Why should the distinction between colloquial and RITUAL language in some ways parallel the distinction between colloquial and WRITTEN language? One reason, I suspect, is that ritual language, like written guage, has a permanence which colloquial language does not. The same oral ritual is presented again and again, not verbatim, to be sure, but with a content, style, and formulaic structure which remain constant from performance to performance. A piece of ritual language is something which is valued, and which is repeated because of its value. We may sometimes say, 'That was a good conversation,' but we are unlikely to repeat the conversation later because it was so good. Rituals, on the other hand, are performed and listened to over and over again. As a result they contain language that has been formalized and polished, even over many centuries, contrasting with the spontaneity and roughness of conversation. We might then expect to find in ritual language something like the integration of written language, as opposed to the fragmentation of spoken.

It is also the case that the performer of a ritual is removed from his audience in a way that parallels the solitude of a writer. In religious performance he stands before the assembled crowd and recites from memory, using stylized intonation patterns having little in common with the intonation contours of colloquial speech. What he performs is a monologue, with minimal feedback and no verbal interaction. Thus the situation is one which fosters detachment rather than involvement, just as we saw to be the case with writing.

It is impossible to compare, in colloquial and ritual Seneca, the occurrences of any of the features we found to differentiate spoken and written English. Seneca has no nominalizers performing the same function as the English nominalizers discussed above. It has no participles. It has no attributive adjectives either; adjectival meanings are expressed by stative verbs. It has neither prepositions nor postpositions. It has no complementizers like English 'that' or 'to', and no constructions which are like English relative clauses. To find these integrative devices missing in a language without a written tradition might suggest, of course, that they are features which arise in a language precisely because of writing. But such a conclusion would have to be treated with a large dose of skepticism, since there are numerous other unwritten languages in which at least some of these same features do exist. However that may be, we cannot simply count, in colloquial and ritual Seneca, the same integration features we counted in spoken and written English, since many of these features simply are not there.

Instead I will try to suggest the flavor of the difference in integration between the two styles of Seneca with a typical example. A speaker in a Seneca conversation, reminiscing about some events in his earlier life, said the following, for which I provide a free English translation:

(31)   *Da: ne:' di neh, ga:növögö: gaya:söh,*
       And so it's called *ga:növögö:h,*

       jöëdzë' syö' gë:s hadi:ya:s, nonëjih.
       jöëdzë'syö' they used to call it long ago.

       Ne:' ne'ho wa'agwanödayë:'.
       We camped there.

       Dedza:ögwa: nö'gëhödi wa:yanöge'.
       There are berries on both sides of the river.

This sequence surely has a fragmented quality. It consists of three intonationally separate sentences, and four syntactically independent clauses or idea units. In contrast we can look at the following sequence from a Seneca Thanksgiving Ritual (Chafe, 1961, p. 18):

(32)   *Da: ne:' wai ne tgaye:i'*,
       And so in fact it's true,

       ögwajä:'dahgöh,
       we are using it,

       ha'dewë:nishäge:h
       every day

       ha'dewahsödage:h,
       every night,

       ne'ho deyögwadawënye:h,
       we who are moving about,

       hë:öwe yöëdzade'.
       where the earth is.

Here the idea units are combined into an integrated whole. For one thing, the only sentence-final intonation occurs at the end of this sequence; the sequence of phrases or clauses is united into a single sentence. Beyond that, the phrases and clauses depend on one another. The first line establishes the validity of what is to follow. The second line can be regarded as the principal clause, with all that follows elaborating it in one way or another. The third and fourth lines provide a temporal modification of the second, the fifth line elaborates on the 'we' of the second, and the sixth line gives a spatial modification of the fifth. The entire passage hangs together with an internal cohesion that is absent from the earlier example.

Turning now to the distinction between involvement and detachment, we can look for features of Seneca which reflect this difference. For English we noted the occurrence of passives as a symptom of detachment. Seneca has nothing like the English passive. It does, however, have an impersonal reference marker, a verb prefix which means 'one' (French 'on'). As with the passive, this prefix allows the omission of specific reference to the agent of an action, and thus appears also to be evidence of detachment. In a thousand words of colloquial Seneca this 'one' prefix occurred only twice, whereas in a thousand words of ritual it occurred 36 times.

Seneca has a variety of particles which can be interpreted as expressing involvement, for example *agwas* 'really' and *do:gës* 'for sure', which occurred respectively five and four times in a thousand words of conversation, but not at all in the ritual data I looked at. More striking was the occurrence of particles expressing fuzziness or evidentiality, whose occurrences per thousand words were as follows:

	Colloquial	Ritual
nö:h I guess	18	0
a:yë:' it seems	10	0
gi'shëh-maybe	5	1
i:wi:h I think	4	0

To discuss more of these differences would carry us too far into the details of the Seneca language (see Chafe, 1981 for further discussion). I wish here only to leave the suggestion that oral literature may indeed be more like written than spoken language in some ways. The permanence, value, and polish of an oral text may lead to a more integrated, less fragmented kind of language than that found in spontaneous conversation, and the detachment of a reciter from his audience may produce a kind of language lacking the involvement of colloquial speech. Certainly the differences between colloquial language and oral literature do not in all ways parallel those between spoken and written language, but the extent to which the parallel does seem to hold is intriguing and worthy of more systematic attention.

CONCLUSION

I have tried to show that spoken and written language differ with regard to two sets of features. The features of one set can be assigned to an opposition of fragmentation and integration, which I suggested is a consequence of differences in the use of time in speaking and writing. The features of the other set reflect an involvement vs. detachment dichotomy, attributable to the different relations of a speaker or writer to the audience. Occurrences of specific features in conversation and academic prose were cited and illustrated. I concluded with a suggestion that some of the same differences may distinguish colloquial language and oral literature, even in a language that has never been written. The reasons may be that oral literature has a kind of permanence analogous to that of written language, and that the reciter of oral literature is, like a writer, detached from direct personal interaction.

REFERENCES

CHAFE, WALLACE L. 1961. Seneca thanksgiving rituals. Bureau of American Ethnology Bulletin 183. Washington: Smithsonian Institution.
———. 1980. The deployment of consciousness in the production of a narrative. The pear stories: cognitive, cultural, and linguistic aspects of narrative production, ed. by W. L. Chafe. Norwood, N.J.: Ablex.
——— 1981. Differences between colloquial and ritual Seneca or how oral literature is literary. Reports from the Survey of California and Other Indian Languages No. 1. Berkeley.
DEVITO, J. A. 1966. Psychogrammatical factors in oral and written discourse by skilled communicators. Speech Monographs 33:73–76.
———. 1967. Levels of abstraction in spoken and written language. Journal of Communication 17:354–361.
DRIEMAN, G. H. J. 1962. Differences between written and spoken languages: an exploratory study. Acta Psychologica 20:36–57, 78–100.
GIBSON, ELEANOR J., AND HARRY LEVIN. 1975. The psychology of reading. Cambridge, Mass.: The MIT Press.

HARRELL, L. E., JR. 1957. A comparison of oral and written language in school-age children. Monographs of the Society for Research in Child Development 22, No. 3. Lafayette, Ind.: Child Development Publications.

HEWITT, J. N. B. 1903. Iroquoian cosmology, first part. Bureau of American Ethnology Annual Report 21:127–339. Washington: Smithsonian Institution.

JAMES, WILLIAM. 1980. The principles of psychology. Reprinted by Dover Publications in 1950.

KROLL, BARBARA. 1977. Combining ideas in written and spoken English. Discourse across time and space, ed. by E. O. Keenan and T. L. Bennett. Southern California Occasional Papers in Linguistics 5:69–108.

MATSUHASHI, ANN. Pausing and planning: the tempo of written discourse production. Research in the teaching of English. In press.

O'DONNELL, R. C. 1974. Syntactic differences between speech and writing. American Speech 49:102–110.

4 Written and Spoken Style in Japanese Narratives*

Patricia M. Clancy
Brown University

To an American attempting to master Japanese, one of the most difficult features of the language is the bewildering variety of speech styles which must be learned. Each style has its own lexical, morphological, syntactic, and intonational properties, and it often seems that every situation one encounters calls for a different style. The selection of a style is typically determined by the relative status, age, and sex of speaker and hearer. Furthermore, men and women frequently speak differently, using not only distinctive intonation, but also characteristic grammatical and lexical forms. The combination of stylistic options appropriate to particular configurations of relative age, sex, and status in any speech context creates a multiplicity of speech styles. The situation is further complicated by the possibility of style shifting within a single context, or using stylistic features metaphorically to convey distance, sarcastically exaggerated respect, childishness, etc.

In Japanese, written and spoken language are also stylistically distinct. The differences between 'hanashikotoba' (speech) and 'kakikotoba' (writing) are, in fact, so great that native speakers are often shocked and dismayed when shown detailed verbatim transcripts of ordinary spoken Japanese. For example, one Japanese graduate student who saw the quite typical samples of adult speech used for the present paper initially believed that the speakers must have been children. Just

---

*I would like to express my sincere gratitude to Haruo Aoki, Masayoshi Hirose, Yoshiko Matsumoto, Pamela Downing, and John Hinds for their generous help in interpreting the data for this paper, and correcting and commenting on the first draft. I am grateful to Janet Akaike-Toste, Yukiko Kurihata, and Jean Keller, who worked on the transcription of the oral narratives, and to Masaharu Fujita for his help with the written stories. I would also like to thank Deborah Tannen and Knud Lambrecht for their many helpful comments and suggestions.

as there is no single spoken style in Japanese, so there are many types of written styles besides the formal expository prose which tends to be regarded as the norm for writing. Yet even in more casual forms of writing, the differences between written and spoken language are striking, and often seem to be mandated by the medium of communciation rather than any characteristics of the speaker, hearer, or topic. For example, the same speaker who will use plain verb forms in conversation to a particular friend may use polite forms when writing that friend a personal letter. Thus it is possible to analyze the effects of the communication medium, writing or speaking, upon the way in which a particular message is expressed linguistically.

The present discussion of written and spoken Japanese will be based upon a sample of 40 narratives, 20 written and 20 spoken, produced by young Japanese women in response to a short film. These narratives were collected as part of a research project conducted by Wallace Chafe at the University of California, Berkeley, investigating the verbalization of remembered experience. For this project, speakers in several different countries were shown a seven-minute film; they were then asked to tell what they had seen to a listener of the same age and sex. All the Japanese speakers, listeners, and writers in the present sample were female university students in their late teens and early twenties. The student who collected the written narratives was an American (also female, in her twenties), but subjects were told that their stories would be read by a native speaker of Japanese. No time limitations were placed upon either speakers or writers, and the length of the stories varied considerably.

Clearly, this sample of data will permit analysis of only a limited range of the many differences between written and spoken Japanese, which would be even more striking if, for example, the comparison were between ordinary conversation and formal expository prose. However, since the narratives were all based upon the same film, the data afford an ideal opportunity to examine those differences which appear in the communication of the same message in the two different media.

In the first section below, differences in verb morphology between written and spoken Japanese will be considered. The conventions for written Japanese include use of certain non-final verb endings which never occur in speech; for social reasons, sentence-final verbs are marked for different levels of politeness. In the second section, sentence-final particles, which function to facilitate face-to-face communication in Japanese, will be discussed. Next, the different ways of referring to story characters in written and spoken Japanese narratives will be taken up. The use of certain referential options, such as third person pronouns in writing, reflect formal conventions which are related to register; the frequency of options such as ellipsis may have a cognitive basis, reflecting the amount of time available for planning. Conventions for 'correct' Japanese are observed more strictly in writing, where word order, to be considered in the fourth section, follows the canonical verb-final pattern rather than the postposed patterns typical of spoken Japanese. In the final section, linguistic integration will be analyzed, (cf. Chafe, Chap. 3, this volume) and it will be seen that the less integrated structure of spoken Japanese serves both cognitive and social functions.

VERB MORPHOLOGY

Compared to languages like English, Japanese is particularly rich in morphologial markers of style. A major morphological difference between the written and spoken stories in the present sample was the form of the verb used at the ends of unembedded clauses, both within and at the ends of sentences. Although some overlap did occur, all of the written stories used at least one morphological choice which never occurred in the oral narratives, and all but two of the oral narratives used forms which never appeared in writing. Thus written and spoken style in Japanese are strongly differentiated by verb morphology.

In Japanese oral narratives, the most common connective between successive clauses is -te, a non-final verb ending which means 'and/and then,' and is used to recount events in temporal and often causal succession, as well as simultaneous events, and the speech, thoughts, and feelings which may accompany an action or event. In the written narratives in this sample, this form was frequently replaced by a different non-final form (called RENYOODOME in traditional Japanese grammar), which never occurred in the oral narratives. In spoken Japanese, this form is not common; it is heard, for example, in political speeches, television newscasts, and other formal speech which is actually being read aloud. Although there are slightly different semantic constraints upon the use of these two forms (cf. Kuno, 1973), there were no obvious differences in their usage in the present sample of narratives. In fact, it was often possible to find the same event sequence recounted with different non-final verb forms, as in example (1) from a spoken story and example (2) from a written one.[1]

---

[1]In the transcription of the spoken stories, three dots are used to indicate audible pauses, and two dots for brief disruptions of rhythm smaller than a pause. Commas mark the ends of non-final intonation contours, and periods mark points of sentence-final falling intonation. Apostrophes at the ends of lines indicate that the last syllable of the last word received heavy stress and higher pitch; this prosodic pattern was commonly used by speakers who did not end each intonation contour with the particles *ne* or *sa*. The listener's comments and questions are indented below the intonation group after which they occurred, usually either just after or simultaneously with the last syllable. In the transcription of the written narratives, each syntactic main clause is placed on a separate line, and commas are used only at points where the author actually placed them.

S(1)   . . . *u--nto ne,*
        . . . *jitensha ni notta onna no ko to surechigatte',*
        . . . *sore ni mitorete te,*
        . . . *sorede . . ishi ni tsumazuite,*
        taoshichatte',

        . . . Um,
        . . . he passed a girl who was riding on a bicycle,
        . . . and he was fascinated by that,
        . . . and then . . he bumped into a rock,
        and fell,

W(2)   *Tochuu,*
        semai michi de
        hantai gawa kara yahari jitensha ni notte yatte kuru onna no ko ni ki o
             torare,
        michi ni korogatte ita ooki na ishi ni butsukari
        tentoo shite shimau.

        On the way,
        the road is narrow
        and he is distracted by a girl who comes along riding on a bicycle from the
             opposite direction,
        and he bumps into a big rock which had fallen on the road
        and he falls over.

The subtle differences in nuance and the constraints governing the use of each form require further investigation. However, it is clear that since the renyoodome form in example (2) is not usually used in speaking, it serves as a marker of written style in Japanese.

To some extent, written Japanese shares features of formal spoken Japanese. In these narratives, for example, the conjunction *ga* 'but/however' was used by only one speaker; the more casual *keredomo,* which has the same meaning, was used by only one writer. Formality and politeness do not always coincide in Japanese, however, as a comparison of sentence-final verb forms in this sample of written and spoken narratives reveals. When there is no personal involvement with an addressee, formality may be appropriate, while politeness may be unnecessary or even inappropriate. In spoken Japanese, all verb forms are marked for some level of politeness. The 'plain' forms of the verb, *-ru* 'non-past' and *-ta* 'past' are used in addressing social equals and inferiors; the 'polite' forms *-masu* and *-mashita* are used to listeners of superior social status. Although polite forms are used on many formal occasions both in speech and in writing, they do not occur in types of writing in which there is no personal relationship between writer and reader. In newspapers and novels, for example, which are addressed to a vast unknown audience, plain forms are used.[2] In writing which is both formal and personal, such as wedding invitations, 'super-polite' expressions and lexical items, as well as polite verb endings, appear. In certain interesting cases, polite forms are used in writing even when there is no personal relationship with the reader. For example, the single unknown reader of labels on packages is often addressed with polite forms, especially in product descriptions, to convey a personal touch. Similarly, letters of request addressed to an office or department typically contain polite forms, as if a favor were being asked of a particular individual.

In these narratives all but four of the writers used plain verb endings, whereas eleven of the speakers used polite verb forms at least some of the time. The speakers who used a more casual style usually added after the plain verb form either *no* or *wake,* nominalizers which literally mean 'thing' and 'reason', respectively.[3] *No* is very common in the speech of women, making it sound less abrupt than if plain forms are used; however, both *no* and *wake* also occur in the relaxed, casual speech of men. The following table summarizes the use of the three types of sentence-final verb forms: plain (*ru/-ta*), casual (*-ru/-ta* + *no/wake*) and polite (*-masu/-mashita*).

As the table shows, there was a strong tendency for plain forms to occur in writing, and polite forms to occur in speech. The forms *no* and *wake* occurred exclusively in the spoken narratives.

It is apparent that narrators did not always make the same choices in a given medium; some writers used polite forms, while certain speakers used plain forms. In ordinary conversational Japanese, women's casual speech makes use of both the nominalizers *no* and *wake* and a certain frequency of plain forms, which may vary a good deal depending upon the context. Thus the seven speakers who used predominantly *no* and *wake* at the ends of sentences also used plain forms, as Table I shows, 25.6 percent of the time. Two speakers shifted during the course of narration from polite verb endings to *no/wake,* and several others intermixed these two options throughout their story. Thus the level of politeness is something that is negotiated between speakers and hearers during the course of an interaction.

In the narratives of several speakers, the level of politeness marked on verbs was related to the content of their speech; statements addressed directly to the listener tended to have polite verb forms, whereas during narration of the story per se, *no* and *wake* predominated. The following example illustrates this tendency:

---

[2]There is a special form of the copula, *de aru,* which occurs in formal writing but was not used in these written narratives, perhaps because it was felt to be too pedantic.

[3]Sentences ending in '*no*' and '*wake*' are actually abbreviations of constructions with the copula, such as . . . *wake desu* 'the reason/fact is that . . . '. Without the polite *desu,* which is the same stylistic level as *-masu,* the tone is more casual.

TABLE I
Distribution of Verb Forms in Written
and Spoken Narratives

	Plain	Casual	Polite
Written	85.0%	—	15.0%
Spoken	25.6	47.7	26.7

S(3)   . . . *Sono tochuu de,*
ano--. . . onna no ko ga tootta no ne.
Sono . . onna no ko o . . mite,
. . . *A--! nante ki o torarete iru uchi ni,*
5   . . . *ano . . ishi ni tsumazuite*
okkotoshichatta wake.
Suteki na no sono ko.
Sono onna no ko ga.
U--n wari to chaamingu datta n ja nai desu ka?
                Un.
10   *Anmari oboete inai n desu kedo.*

. . . On the way,
um--. . . a girl passed by.
He looked at . . that . . girl,
and while he was distracted (saying) "Ah!"
5   . . . he bumped into a rock
and fell over.
That child was cute.
That girl.
Uh-- wasn't she rather charming?
               Yes.
10   I don't remember too well.

On lines 2 and 6, *no* and *wake* are used at the ends of sentences recounting the plot, but when the speaker addresses a question to the listener on line 9, and then adds a personal introspection on line 10, she uses the polite *desu* form. Questions, personal opinions, and other commentary evoke the speaker/hearer relationship more directly than does the narration of events in which neither speaker nor hearer participated. The switch to polite endings in these utterances supports the view that morphological politeness in Japanese is strongly responsive to the dimension of 'involvement' which Chafe (Chap. 3, this volume) has proposed as one of the chief characteristics of spoken language. In Japanese, the morphological choices of speakers indicate that there is variation in the degree of involvement within a single speech context. And when a speaker addresses an unfamiliar and/or socially superior listener, greater involvement evokes the overt expression of distance in the use of polite forms.

In writing, there were only two options for sentence-final verb forms, plain or polite, and only four writers used polite verb morphology. In these cases, the writers seemed to be affecting a special 'jidoo bungaku' (children's literature) style, typical of storybooks meant to be read to very young children or to be read by elementary school children. One characteristic of this genre is the use of polite verb endings, which creates a less impersonal flavor than plain forms. It is interesting that two of the writers who used polite forms introduced a personal relationship between the two main characters of the film, who were not supposed to be related, calling them *ojiisan/mago* 'grandfather/grandson' and *otoosan/musuko* 'father/son'. Apparently, for certain viewers the simple story of the film evoked a storybook style, and they wrote their narratives as if for young children, with the polite forms that are more typical of spoken than written language.

In general, the choice of verb forms in spoken vs. written Japanese reflects the presence or absence of personal contact between narrator and addressee. Many types of written Japanese are formal, impersonal, and neutral with respect to social status. Spoken Japanese, whether formal or informal, tends to be more personal or 'involved', is highly sensitive to differences in relative speaker/hearer status, and therefore exhibits different levels of politeness reflecting different degrees of solidarity or distance between speaker and hearer. Further research should help to establish the morphological options typical of different types of written vs. spoken language in Japanese, and to clarify the sources of each style and the influence which one style has upon the others.

PARTICLES

The personal contact between speaker and hearer in Japanese triggers not only morphological markers of politeness, but also a number of different particles which express the speaker's attitude, the illocutionary force of the message, and concern for the listener's comprehension. Again, this is a question of 'involvement'. Uyeno (1971) points out that sentence-final particles occur in personal letters or books for small children, but not in most written material; their use in spoken communication is limited when the listener(s) are not direct participants, as in public lectures. As Chafe (Chap. 3, this volume) has pointed out, one manifestation of involvement is speakers' monitoring of the communication channel. In Japanese, speakers frequently indicate their concern for the listener by using the particle *ne,* which is similar to a tag question or 'you know?' with rising intonation in English. The particle *ne* is essentially a request for confirmation, either that the listener agrees with the speaker's statement, has understood it, or merely is continuing to listen attentively to what is being said. Seventeen of the speakers in this sample used *ne,* both in recounting the events of the story, and in addressing the listener personally. In Japanese listeners usually react to an occurrence of *ne* with some verbal or non-verbal response such as a nod; in these narratives the listener often responded with *hai* (polite), *ee,* or *un* (casual), which mean approximately 'yes,' 'mm,' or 'uh-huh' in English. In the following example, the speaker uses *ne* at the ends of the intonation groups on lines 1, 3, and 4.

S(4)   *Ano . . tabenagara ne,*
                ‾*Un.*
       . . . *ano-- . . . . ojisan no mae o ne,*
                        ‾*Un.*
       aso . . . sono toki ojisan ga sa,
                     Un.
4   *shita ni orite kite ne,*
           ‾*Un.*
       . . . uh . . . while they were eating them,
                        Yes.
       . . . uh-- . . . in front of the man,
                    Yes.
       . . . at that time the man,
              Yes.
4   climbed down to the ground,
           Yes.

Thus one way in which speakers can monitor the success of their communication is to use *ne,* which will elicit a reassuring response of some kind from the listener.

As line 3 of the example shows, speakers also sometimes used the particle *sa* in these narratives. This particle, which is common in Tokyo dialect, is used in the same syntactic environments as *ne,* but conveys a somewhat different feeling, sometimes compared with English 'of course'. It is extremely casual, and was used by only three speakers in these narratives, who also never used polite verb endings. As example (4) shows, *ne* and *sa* were freely used in the same narrative, but never occurred in immediate succession.[4] Although *ne* more consistently calls for some kind of response, listeners also frequently respond at the ends of intonation groups with *sa.* Like *ne, sa* never appeared in these written narratives; it is a manifestation of the speaker's attitude or feeling in a communicative context and is elicited by the presence of a listener.

The other particle in these narratives which depends upon the interaction between speaker and hearer was *yo.* Use of this particle tends to be emphatic and/or to imply that the speaker is presupposing that the listener does not already know the information being communicated. *Yo* was used most frequently in imparting new information in these narratives when something was being asserted somewhat more strongly than usual, either because it was unexpected or because it had been

---

[4]The sequence *ne sa* is unacceptable, but *sa ne* can occur. In that case, *sa* is linked with the preceding phrase, and *ne* has a different intonation contour.

elicited by the listener. In the following case, *yo* is used to assert information which should have been presented earlier in the story, but which the narrator suddenly remembers at the point where it is about to become important to the plot.

S(5)   . . . *jitensha de notte ikoo to,*
         . . . *hashitte,*
                   Un.
         . . . <u>*booshi o otoshite shimatta n desu yo.*</u>
         Sono toki ni.
                   A!

         . . . when he started to ride off on his bicycle,
         . . . he rode off,
                   Yes.
         . . . <u>his hat had fallen off.</u>
         At that time.
                   Oh!

The use of *yo* at this point emphasizes that it is important for the listener to know this information, and the listener's response is accordingly somewhat stronger than usual.

Uyeno (1971) has pointed out that the closer and less formal the relationship between speaker and hearer, the more sentence-final particles they will use. In the present case, different speakers apparently defined their relationship with the listener differently, and there was extensive individual variation in the use of sentence-final particles. Two speakers never used *ne, sa,* or *yo,* whereas others used several of these particles per syntactic clause. However, there was total agreement among the writers; none of the 20 ever used *ne, sa,* or *yo.* Clearly, these particles are elicited by the communicative context, and serve as a means of supporting and maintaining a face-to-face interaction and assuring the adequacy of the communication.

REFERENCE

In telling a story, one important task for the narrator is to communicate to the listener at each point in the action which story characters are participating in the events being recounted. There were certain striking differences between speakers and writers in their selection of forms referring to story characters, and these differences seem to be based upon the different stylistic conventions and cognitive demands involved in writing and speaking.[5]

---

[5]A more detailed analysis of reference in this sample of Japanese oral narratives, and a comparison with American narratives based on the same film, are presented in Clancy, 1980a.

With very few exceptions, new characters were introduced into both oral and written narratives with noun phrases, usually accompanied by relative clauses, adjectives, and other modifiers providing information about the age, appearance, or activity of the character in question. There were major differences, however, in the way speakers and writers referred to characters after their introduction into the story. In Japanese it is common for a noun phrase to be used for the second mention of a character before switching to ellipsis, or non-mention, which is the most common form of reference, more or less functionally equivalent to English pronouns. In the written narratives, the same noun phrase used to introduce a character was often repeated in the second mention of that character, as in the following example, where the writer repeats *otoko no ko* 'boy, lit. male child'.

W(6)   *Jitensha ni notta otoko no ko ga noofu ga nashi tsumi o shite iru ki no shita o toorikakaru.*
Otoko no ko wa nashi o hitotsu toroo to suru ga

A boy who was riding a bicycle passes beneath the tree where the farmer is gathering pears.
The boy goes to take one pear but

In contrast, in the oral narratives the second mention of a character was frequently a reduced form of the noun phrase used to introduce that character. In the following example the speaker shifts from *otoko no hito* 'man, lit. male person' to *sono hito* 'that person' in referring to a newly introduced story character.

S(7)   *. . . saisho ni,*
. . . yagi o tsureta otoko no hito toorikakatte,
sono hito wa,
. . . yagi . . . o tsureta mama
tada tootta dake de,

. . . at first,
. . . a man who was leading a goat passed by,
and that person,
. . . pulling . . . the goat
just passed by,

This kind of reduced noun phrase for subsequent mentions of story characters occurred much more frequently in the spoken than in the written narratives.

In the written narratives, pronouns rather than reduced noun phrases were often used to refer to characters after their introduction into the story. In ordinary Japanese conversation, third person 'pronouns' imply a personal relationship between the speaker and the referent, and convey much more than the number and gender of a referent. In fact, in certain contexts *kare* 'he' implies 'boyfriend' and *kanojo* 'she', 'girlfriend' (cf. Hinds, 1978 for a more complete discussion of Japanese 'pronouns' and their noun-like properties). Third person pronouns function as reduced referential indices, like English pronouns, only in certain types of written Japanese and in a particular register of spoken Japanese which has been influenced by Western languages. They do not occur, for example, in written versions of traditional Japanese folktales. In Japanese, *kare* 'he', *kanojo* 'she', and *karera* 'they' are the forms used to translate the third person pronouns in European languages; native speakers of Japanese tend to feel that they are unfamiliar and unnatural in ordinary conversation. These pronouns usually occur in a quasi-academic style, such as might be used in debates, critiques, or college discussions. Use of these third person pronouns is a sign of education, and this style may carry negative connotations, conveying the impression that the speaker is being pretentious or pedantic.

The association of third person pronouns with this register probably accounts for the finding that the present sample of speakers, telling the simple story of the film which they had seen to a classmate, never used third person pronouns to refer to story characters. However, in writing, third person pronouns were apparently felt to be appropriate. Seven of the 20 writers in this sample used one or more third person pronouns, typically for the second mention of a character just introduced or reintroduced with a nominal reference. If these pronouns in the written stories are regarded as reduced noun phrases roughly equivalent to expressions such as *sono hito* 'that person' or *sono ko* 'that child' in the spoken narratives, then speakers and writers used reduced noun phrases for recently mentioned referents with about the same frequency.

Since by far the most common form of reference for previously mentioned characters in Japanese is ellipsis, i.e. complete omission, understanding reference can sometimes become problematic. Prior research (Clancy, 1980a) has shown that in these oral narratives speakers frequently changed the identity of the referent in subject position without explicitly mentioning the new referent, thus creating a rather high rate of potential ambiguity. The following table compares the frequency of different referential options used in subject position of main clauses in the written and spoken stories.[6]

As Table II shows, when the same subject was preserved from the prior main clause, both writers and speakers tended to use ellipsis, speakers somewhat more frequently. Writers tended to use pronouns for preserved subject referents rather than for new subjects; since most of the main characters in this story were male, the pronoun *kare* 'he' frequently would not clarify reference any more explicitly than ellipsis. Clearly, the greatest difference between the written and spoken narratives was the referential form chosen for a new subject referent. When the subject referent was changed, writers made the switch explicit with a noun phrase much more frequently than speakers, who continued to rely heavily on ellipsis despite the potential ambiguity for their listener. In many cases this ambigu-

---

[6]Only subjects of main clauses have been included in these percentages, since elliptical switch reference is more likely to lead to ambiguity, at least temporarily, in main than in embedded clauses.

TABLE II
Referential Choices in Subject Position

	SAME SUBJECT			NEW SUBJECT			
	NP	PRO	Ø	NP	PRO	Ø	NP (postposed)
Written	7.6%	4.0%	88.4%	86.6%	2.9%	10.5%	—
Spoken	6.8	—	93.2	61.8	—	32.5	5.7

ity was either quickly resolved by the nature of the events being recounted, or else was not important enough to concern the listener, but there were times when the listener did interrupt the speaker to clarify reference, as in the following example:

S(8)　. . . *tochuu . . . sono-- . . . hakobu tochuu ni',*
　　　　to . . . mukoo-- kara kita ano,
　　　　. . . *jitensha de kite,*
　　　　. . . *onna no ko da to omotta n desu kedo,*
　　　　. . . *to butsukatte,*
　　　　. . . *ishi ni tsumazuite,*
　　　　　　　　　　　Dotchi ga?
　　　　. . . *Otoko no ko.*

　　　　. . . while . . . uh--. . . while (he) was carrying it,
　　　　then . . . coming from . . . the other side uh,
　　　　. . . coming on a bicycle,
　　　　. . . I thought it was a girl but,
　　　　. . . (he) bumped into (her),
　　　　　　　　　　　Who?
　　　　. . . The boy.

(Note that the pronouns appearing in parentheses in the English translation are not present at all in the original Japanese.)

In contrast, writers tended to make such changes in subject reference explicit, as in the following example:

W(9)　*Suru to,*
　　　　kare no hantai hookoo kara jitensha ni notta onna no ko ga kite,
　　　　surechigau toki,
　　　　kare wa booshi o tobasare,
　　　　jitensha to issho ni taore,

　　　　And then,
　　　　a girl who was riding a bicycle came from the opposite direction from him,
　　　　and when (they) passed,
　　　　he had his hat blown off,
　　　　and fell over with his bicycle,

As the category of 'postposed NP' on the table indicates, sometimes speakers did make subject changes explicit, but with a slight time lag, first producing a predication without an explicit subject, and then clarifying reference by placing a noun phrase after the main verb. The following example is typical:

S(10)   *Sorede,*
        . . . sono . . . hitori no ko ni,
        . . . mittsu agete,
        . . de minna ni wakete ageru wake ne,
5   *. . sono moratta ko ga.*

        And then,
        . . . (he) gives three (pears),
        . . . to one of the boys,
        . . . and (he) divides (them) up for everyone,
5   . . . *the boy who received (them).*

When the subject referent changes on line 4 from the boy who gives away three pears to the boy who takes them to divide among his friends, the speaker mentions the new referent only after the clause is syntactically complete. In the spoken narratives in this sample, postposed subjects never occurred when the same subject was being preserved from the prior clause; in the written narratives postposed subjects never occurred in any context. At times this pattern seems to represent a form of self-correction, a temporary failure in monitoring the narration for referential clarity from the listener's point of view. Writers have more time to plan, and therefore can decide before beginning a clause whether to use an explicit subject. Writers can also simply look back at what they have written to check their own prior referential choices. Speakers, who cannot so easily monitor entire stretches of discourse, sometimes revert to egocentric referential choices, elliptying referents which the hearer cannot easily identify at that moment in the narration. As Ochs (1976) has pointed out, adults as well as children may slip into this kind of egocentrism when performing very difficult tasks. Since it is simple enough in the course of an interaction for the listener to request clarification where necessary, it makes sense for the speaker, while performing the difficult task of narration, to devote less attention to reference, and allow the listener to assume part of this burden in ensuring the success of the communication.

WORD ORDER

One of the major differences between the written and spoken narratives in this sample was word order. The cannonical word order in Japanese is subject-object-verb, and modifiers precede their heads (cf. Kuno, 1973). In the written narratives, SOV order was consistently maintained, but the word order in the oral narratives was much more flexible, with subjects, objects, and many other constituents appearing after the verb. Similarly, the writers always placed relative clauses and other modifiers before head nouns, whereas speakers sometimes produced a noun first, and then added one or more modifiers. The postposed word orders which appeared in this sample of oral narratives are typical of conversational Japanese, which rather frequently fails to exhibit canonical verb-final word order.

Some examples of postverbal constituents will illustrate the nature of postposing in spoken Japanese, and give insight into its discourse functions. Postposed subjects often occurred when the speaker changed the subject referent, and served to clarify this change for the listener, as in example (10). Kuno (1978) interprets such cases as "afterthoughts", added to make certain that the listener has understood. Relative clauses which were verbalized after, rather than before, their head nouns also served to clarify reference.

Rather frequently, the information presented after the verb merely added a detail to complete the image of a scene. These cases seem to fit Kuno's (1978) category of "supplementary" postverbal elements. The following postposed locative illustrates this usage.

S(12)   *Soshitara ne,*
         mugiwara booshi ga oite atta wake,
                                        Un.
         michibata ni.
         ‾‾‾‾‾‾‾‾‾‾‾‾‾
                  Un.

         Then,
         the straw hat was lying there,
                                    Yes.
         at the side of the road.
         ‾‾‾‾‾‾‾‾‾‾‾‾‾‾‾‾‾‾‾‾‾‾‾‾
                        Yes.

As Chafe (Chap. 3, this volume) has pointed out, one aspect of the 'involvement' characteristic of spoken discourse is that speakers feel they should try to convey some of the rich, experiential detail which they have in mind, rather than simply communicating a bare outline of events. In Japanese, this kind of detail often is given after the main events have been communicated, in post-verbal position.

Similarly, entire clauses with non-final verb forms or conjunctions were sometimes produced after a sentence-final verb describing the main event. These postposed clauses added on after the final verb often gave the narrator's interpretation or explanation of the event. The following example is typical:

S(13)   . . . *Watashi wa ne,*
          sono ko tachi ga
          ishi o oita n da to omotte ta no.
          . . . *Ri ringo o toru tame ni.*

          . . . I,
          . . . thought that those boys,
          . . . had put the rock there.
          . . . In order to take the ap apples.

As the above examples show, flexible word order is an important feature of spoken Japanese. In these narratives postverbal constituents or postposed clauses were used by 16 of the 20 speakers, with one speaker making use of postposing in as many as 20 percent of her clauses. An analysis of the content and contexts in which postposing occurred suggests that it serves important discourse functions in Japanese. Many postposings in the oral narratives were clearly afterthoughts (cf. Kuno, 1978), produced after sentence-final falling pitch and an audible pause. Others were produced quite fluently with no pause and an unbroken intonation contour with lower, level pitch on the postposed constituent. In these cases postposing was apparently used to defocus either familiar or easily deducible information which was in some way semantically subordinate to the material preceding the main verb. This seems natural, since the type of material which speakers might momentarily forget is precisely the type of material which they might plan from the beginning to defocus. Thus the use of postposing in spoken Japanese conveys subtle information concerning the speaker's attitude toward the material in question and its status in the discourse.

In the written narratives, word order was never used to convey such subtle distinctions between focused and defocused material. The writers did occasionally forget information, which they added in the margins or above the original words with arrows showing where the new material was to be included, invariably the correct position in standard word order. It seems that since writing takes more time than speaking, writers occasionally face the problem of being unable to keep pace with their thoughts, and may end up omitting even crucial parts of the story at points where the events took place in rapid succession or simultaneously. In contrast, speakers did not usually forget to verbalize important parts of the scene they were describing; their only 'flashbacks' were to present information which was unimportant at the time it occurred but became crucial to the plot line at some later point. Thus, while the greater speed of verbal production restricts the amount of time speakers can devote to planning, it also allows them to verbalize their thoughts and mental images as they narrate, in a way in which writers cannot.

Postverbal constituents can be found in certain types of personal, informal writing in Japanese, such as friendly letters. However, in formal written Japanese, postposing after a sentence-final verb form is not permitted. To the extent that postverbal constituents represent self-corrections or afterthoughts, they may be inappropriate for writing. Although they provide the listener with information about the speaker's process of organizing and planning the verbalization which may enrich overall understanding, writing does not generally seek to convey the author's process of self-expression, but rather just the finished product. Insofar as postposing functions as a deliberate defocusing device, there does not seem to be any reason why it should be prohibited in writing, since variations in word order preceding the verb to effect different degrees of highlighting or focus are permitted. Thus avoidance of postposing seems to be a matter of formal convention for 'correct' usage in written Japanese.

LINGUISTIC INTEGRATION

Chafe (Chap. 3, this volume) has proposed that one of the important differences between written and spoken language is the degree of syntactic integration typically achieved in each medium. Written language is, in general, more integrated than spoken language, Chafe claims, since writing allows more time to combine a succession of ideas into a single linguistic whole. In contrast, Chafe found that in speaking each "idea unit" tends to be produced separately, with individual clauses connected by coordinating conjunctions, usually *and*. Syder and Pawley (in preparation) and Labov (1972) have also found that spoken language tends to be fragmented into a series of separate main clauses rather than into complex units integrating clauses through embedding and subordinating conjunctions, which appear in writing. In written vs. spoken Japanese there are differences in linguistic integration at several levels of structure. In the present sample of narratives, writers and speakers integrated sequences of clauses into sentences differently, embedded clauses with different frequencies, and organized the constituents within single clauses with differing degrees of cohesion. These structural differences seem to be based upon the greater amount of time available to writers for planning the structure of their message.

At the level of the sentence, the writers in this sample structured their stories into multi-clause sentences with much greater consistency than did the speakers. The median number of main clauses[7] per sentence in the written narratives was 2.5, with a range of variation from an average of 1.5 to 3.9 across writers. In contrast, speakers had a median number of 8.3 main clauses per sentence, with an average range of from 1.8 to 34 clauses per sentence in individual stories. Only half of the speakers produced sentences which were similar to those of the writers, that is, fewer than four main clauses in length.

---

[7]Any clause which was not an embedded complement or relative clause was counted as a main clause, despite the syntactic similarity between certain types of temporal clauses, such as those with *toki* 'time/when', and relative clauses in Japanese.

Chafe (1980) states that the placement of sentence boundaries to create an intermediate level of closure between the syntactic clause and the entire story is something which speakers must learn, and which even adults may have difficulty doing successfully. In this sample of Japanese narratives, four of the 20 speakers did not make any attempt to create a sentential level of structure distinct from that of the narrative as a whole; for example, one speaker told her entire 34-clause story in a single long sentence. These four speakers all told very brief stories; their equation of the sentence and narrative levels seems to be based on the intention of producing a summary rather than a full story. Apparently, a speaker's overall plan for telling a story includes a set of priorities for which linguistic tasks will be attended to in the course of narration; in this sample, only those who intended to tell a long story devoted a considerable amount of attention to the creation of an intermediate level of linguistic structure, expressed by sentence boundaries.[8] This did not seem to be true for the writers in this sample, perhaps because they were not under the same pressures of time and of conducting a face-to-face interaction. None of the writers, no matter how long or short her story, chose to ignore the task of sentence construction at an intermediate level between clause and story.

Writers also created more highly structured narratives at the level of the clause. In keeping with the findings of Chafe (Chap. 3, this volume) and Ochs (1976), the writers in this sample tended to produce 'denser' main clauses incorporating a greater number of embeddings.[9] The following examples illustrate this contrast in syntactic integration between the written (example 16) and the spoken (example 17) stories:

W(16)   *Mite ita hito tachi ga tasuke ni kuru.*
         Booshi o hirotte kureta otoko no ko ni kodomo wa nashi o ikutsuka ageru.

         Some people who were watching come over to help.
         The child gives several pears to a boy who picked up his hat for him.
S(17)   *. . . De otoko no ko ga choodo sannin toorikakarimashite,*
                                                              Hai.
         . . . sore o . . . ano hirotte agete',
         . . . sore kara ato,
         . . . booshi ga ochite ita n de,
         sore mo ato kara hirotte ageta n desu kedo ne.
         Sono toki ano sono . . . nusunda otoko no ko ga',
                                                              Hai.

---

[8]Sentence length in Japanese oral narratives is sensitive to a variety of factors including, for example, the recounting of dialogue, which tends to elicit shorter sentences. In a different sample of Japanese narratives based on a videotape, the average sentence length across ten adult speakers, many of whom used a considerable amount of dialogue, was only 2.4 main clauses (cf. Clancy, 1980b).

[9]Note that adjectives in *-i* or *na,* and nominal modifiers with *no,* were not counted as relative clauses. (Past tense adjectives did not occur.)

> . . . *ano . . . nashi o . . . mittsu bakashi agemashite,*
> . . . And just then three boys came by,
> > Yes.
> . . . and they picked . . . that . . . up for him,
> . . . and after that later,
> . . . his hat was on the ground,
> so afterwards they also picked that up for him.
> Then uh uh . . . the boy *who stole (them),*
> > Yes.
> . . . uh . . . gave about three . . . pears . . . (to them),

The actual frequency of relative clauses in written and spoken stories varied from narrator to narrator. In the written stories, 17.7 percent of all clauses across narrators were relative clauses, whereas the corresponding figure was 11.1 percent in the oral narratives. In both writing and speaking, relative clauses were used to identify referents, to provide descriptive information, especially about newly introduced story characters, and to refer to events which were predictable from the narration presented in main clauses. Thus, for example, in both written and spoken stories narrators referred to 'the hat that had fallen' after recounting that the hero fell from his bicycle and his pears fell to the ground.

The main difference between the relative clauses in the written vs. spoken narratives was that, in writing, relative clauses were used much more frequently to present entirely new, unpredictable information. For example, in (16) the information that people were watching the hero's accident and that one of them picked up his hat for him is unpredictable, yet is presented in relative clauses. In contrast, the relative clause in example (17) is typical of those in the oral narratives in that it is very short, is used to clarify the identity of an already well-known character, and presents only information which has already been recounted in main clauses. The use of relative clauses illustrated in example (16) 'sneaks' new events into the narration in the guise of modifiers identifying or describing story characters, and thus integrates separate ideas into a single main clause. It is probably more difficult both for a listener to comprehend such 'dense' clauses and for a speaker to construct them under the time pressure of oral communication. Thus in Japanese, as in English, the written/spoken contrast influences the degree of syntactic integration used in narration.

Although the cognitive constraints of spoken communication may result in less integrated syntactic construction in any language, in Japanese there are significant differences in the degree of integration in written and spoken language within a single unembedded clause. In spoken Japanese, a syntactic clause is frequently broken down into a number of smaller units, each of which is preceded by an audible pause and/or other hesitations, has a distinct intonation contour, and often ends with heavy stress and higher pitch on the final syllable of the last word

---

[10]In these narratives, only *ne* and *sa* were used in this way, although *yo* can occur as well within clauses.

or with a particle such as *ne* or *sa*.[10] These intonation groups are frequently followed by some kind of response from the listener, even when the speaker does not use *ne*. The following example is typical of the oral narratives:

S(18)   . . . *u--nto* . . *ano kondo,*
           sono mango o totte ita ojisan ga',
                                           Hai.

           ko zuutto tootte itte,
           . . . *shita ni modot* . . . *ki no shita ni orite mitara,*
                                                 Hai.

           sono . . . *hito kago goto ga,*
           . . . *zembu dokka ni,*
           . . . *nakunatte ite,*
                               Ee--.
           . . . *soo yuu* . . . *okashii naa to omotte',*
                                           Hai.

           . . . U--m . . . uh next,
           the old man who was picking these pears,
                                           Yes.

           uh was still picking them,
           . . . and when he came back down . . . climbed down to the bottom of
                 the tree,
                       Yes.
           that . . . whole basket,
           . . . had disappeared,
           . . . somewhere,
                         Oh--.
           . . . 'that's . . . strange' he thought,
                                           Yes.

This highly fragmented quality of spoken Japanese, in which a single clause is communicated in several distinct intonation groups, is perhaps the greatest difference between oral and written communication in that language. The use of such small intonation groups during narration means that a speaker can pause frequently within a single clause to plan the rest of the clause without lapsing into disfluent hesitating, false starts, and self-corrections. In this sample of oral narratives, 67.4 percent of all intonation groups were shorter than a syntactically complete clause; that is, they did not include the predicate of the case frame being verbalized. Temporal, locative, and adverbial phrases, arguments of the predicate, modifiers, verbal complements, conjunctions, and even hesitations such as the common . . . *ano ne* 'well uh', were frequently produced as separate units having their own intonation contour. Conjunctions such as *sorede* 'and then', which accounted for 26 percent of the syntactically incomplete intonation groups, and subjects (24%), were the most common constituents produced separately. Thus it is possible for the speaker of Japanese to first verbalize just the temporal or locative setting for an event, then give the subject, next express any other arguments in the case frame and finally produce the predicate. It seems likely that syntactic planning often spans more than one intonation group, since the correct case particles must be used with nominal arguments of the predicate as they are verbalized. However, the fragmented pattern of verbal production in spoken Japanese probably allows speakers to plan more of their utterances during the actual verbalization than is the case with languages such as English, which do not have intonation patterns conducive to silent pauses in mid-clause. The syntactic fragmentation of spoken Japanese may also simplify the task of the listener, who can process the verbal input little by little.[11]

The cognitive advantages for the speaker's planning and the listener's comprehension are not the only reasons for the fragmented nature of spoken Japanese; this pattern of speaking serves social functions as well. As example (18) reveals, the listener plays an important role in a verbal interaction in Japanese, and participates in the creation of the fragmented rhythm of oral communication by giving some kind of verbal feedback at the end of most intonation groups. Speakers' use of *ne, sa,* or heavy stress and higher pitch on the last syllable makes the intonation contours more perceptually salient; the listener usually times her responses to coincide either with the last syllable of an intonation group or with the pause preceding the next group. It is clear that these responses do not always indicate actual comprehension of what the listener is saying, but often merely serve to indicate that the listener is still paying attention and not experiencing any problems in understanding. The listener's constant participation creates a more intensely cooperative interaction than is typical of conversation in American English. In fact, speakers of Japanese tend to feel rather insecure when Americans fail to respond overtly as they speak, especially on the telephone, where non-verbal signs of continuing attention are lacking. On the other hand, some English speakers addressing Japanese listeners may find themselves reduced to paralyzed silence by the barrage of verbal response and nodding which greet their words and seems to indicate that they have already been understood when they have scarcely begun to speak.

In writing there is, of course, no direct contact with the reader, and therefore the social reasons for the fragmented rhythm of spoken Japanese are absent. The commas and periods used in modern Japanese writing only partially reflect the intonation patterns of the spoken language. In this sample of narratives, writers varied tremendously in their use of commas, although the frequency of sentence boundaries was fairly consistent across writers. Some writers used commas very sparingly, marking only the ends of main clauses, whereas others used commas even after constituents smaller than a single clause, much like the intonation groups of spoken Japanese. On the average, however, units lacking a predicate

---

[11]Grimes (1975) has pointed out that languages make use of various devices to control 'the rate of injection of unpredictable information'. In spoken Japanese, avoidance of embedding and use of short intonation groups are two such devices.

were produced separately three times as frequently in speech as in writing. Moreover, in writing, main clauses were often not separated from each other by commas, although in the spoken stories almost every main clause had at least one distinct intonation contour. Thus extreme syntactic fragmentation at the clausal level seems to be limited to spoken Japanese, where it serves both social and cognitive functions.

SUMMARY AND CONCLUSIONS

In this paper some of the differences between written and spoken Japanese have been analyzed in terms of the different stylistic conventions, social factors, and cognitive processes which govern communication in the two media. In general, written style in Japanese institutionalizes the typical effects of the cognitive and social differences between writing and speaking. For example, in many types of writing the writer and reader do not know one another, and since the appropriate level of politeness cannot be determined, morphological expressions of politeness on verb endings are not used. Except for certain types of letters, writing tends to be impersonal by definition, and those features of spoken Japanese which represent a personal contribution of the speaker or a reaction to the addressee are eliminated.

Word order, for instance, is much more flexible in spoken Japanese, where it expresses the speaker's attitude toward the information being communicated, and defocuses material which is less important or easily deducible in context. These subtle shades of emphasis on the part of the speaker are neutralized in writing, where the message is communicated in standard word order. Similarly, the particles *ne, sa,* and *yo,* which express various feelings and attitudes of the speaker, such as assertiveness or concern for the listener's comprehension, are eliminated from writing. In reference, the ordinary connotations of a personal relationship between speaker and referent are ignored in using pronouns, which become reduced, neutral referential symbols. The extensive ellipsis characteristic of spoken Japanese is avoided, since writer and reader cannot resolve ambiguities through personal interaction.[12] Maintaining the formal conventions for written Japanese may require somewhat greater cognitive effort than ordinary conversation, since certain linguistic features of written style, such as third person pronouns, are less familiar and acquired later in life (cf. Ochs, 1976). This is compensated for, however, by the greater time available to the writer for linguistic planning. Thus the conventions for written Japanese are based upon and also serve to perpetuate certain cognitive and social differences between writing and speaking.

---

[12]The frequency and nature of ellipsis in written Japanese varies, of course, with the genre. Thus in artistic works such as traditional novels, extensive ellipsis with its attendant ambiguities and vagueness may be used quite frequently, whereas reference in the expository prose characteristic of academic articles, for example, tends to be much more explicit.

In the analysis of discourse, cognitive and social factors may often seem to be separate forces affecting the nature and success of communication rather independently. A comparison of syntactic integration in written vs. spoken Japanese has shown that, at least in this area, cognitive and social functions are interdependent. In writing, neither author nor reader must be concerned with the social burdens of maintaining an interaction, both have more time for linguistic planning and processing, and syntactic fragmentation does not appear. In contrast, in spoken Japanese, verbalizing short, simple syntactic constituents one at a time limits the flow of information to the listener, making it easier to understand what is being said. This type of communication also reduces the cognitive burden upon the speaker, who must only plan very brief spurts of output at once, and can use the moments of silence at the ends of intonation groups for linguistic planning. From a social point of view, this style of spoken communication reinforces many values, such as consideration for others, mutual support, and cooperation, which are very important in Japanese society. In spoken Japanese, a speaker tends to communicate information gradually, unintrusively, allowing plenty of opportunity for the listener to assimilate the input, ask questions if necessary, and indicate comprehension. The listener, in turn, is concerned that the speaker feel supported, understood, and appreciated, and times feedback so that at the conclusion of each separate unit of production, the speaker is reassured of the listener's continuing cooperation and participation in the interaction. Thus the cognitive and social functions of syntactic fragmentation are inseparable, operating together to ensure the success of spoken communication in Japanese.

REFERENCES

CHAFE, WALLACE L. (1982) Integration and involvement in speaking, writing, and oral literature. Chapter 3 of this volume.

──────. 1980. The deployment of consciousness in the production of a narrative. The pear stories: cognitive, cultural, and linguistic aspects of narrative production, ed. by W. Chafe, Norwood, NJ: Ablex.

CLANCY, PARTICIA M. 1980a. Referential choice in English and Japanese narrative discourse. The pear stories: cognitive, cultural, and linguistic aspects of narrative production, ed. by W. Chafe, Norwood, NJ: Ablex.

──────. 1980b. The acquisition of narrative discourse: a study in Japanese. Unpublished doctoral dissertation, University of California, Berkeley.

GRIMES, JOSEPH E. 1975. The thread of discourse. The Hague: Mouton.

HINDS, JOHN. 1978. Anaphora in Japanese conversation. Anaphora in discourse. Edmonton, Canada: Linguistic Research, Inc.

KUNO, SUSUMU. 1973. The structure of the Japanese language. Cambridge: MIT Press.

──────. 1978. Japanese: a characteristic OV language. Syntactic typology: studies in the phenomenology of language, ed. by W. P. Lehmann, Austin: University of Texas Press.

LABOV, WILLIAM. 1972. The transformation of experience in narrative syntax. Language in the inner city (Chap. 9). Philadelphia: University of Pennsylvania Press.

OCHS, ELINOR. 1979. Planned and unplanned discourse. Discourse and syntax, ed. by T.Givon, New York: Academic Press.

SYDER, FRANCES AND ANDREW PAWLEY, (In preparation.) English conversational structures.

UYENO, TAZUKO. 1971. A study of Japanese modality: a performative analysis of sentence particles. Unpublished doctoral dissertation, University of Michigan, Ann Arbor.

5 The Gulf Between Spoken and Written Language: A Case Study in Chinese

Charles N. Li
University of California, Santa Barbara
Sandra A. Thompson
University of California, Los Angeles

INTRODUCTION

Any discussion of the relationship between spoken and written Chinese would begin with the well-known fact that the Chinese writing system is unique among modern writing systems in being semantically, rather than phonologically grounded. That is, in Chinese each 'character', or LOGOGRAPH,[1] represents a semantic or grammatical unit. It does not convey phonological information except in certain composite logographs where the pronunciation of the composite is similar or identical to one of its component logographs. Thus, even in those cases, the phonological information conveyed by the composite logographs is based on other logographs, whose forms provide no clue to their pronunciation.

What is perhaps less well-known is that there is a considerable discrepancy between the grammar and the lexicon of modern spoken Mandarin and those of modern written Chinese. In this paper we will explore the role that this logographic writing system has played in creating and maintaining this gulf. Before we can begin this exploration, however, we must consider classical Chinese.

---

[1]We use the term 'logograph' in this paper although we are aware of its inadequacies. For example, as we will see below, a 'logograph' does not generally represent a 'word' in modern Mandarin. No other term, however, seems to us to be superior.

CLASSICAL CHINESE

It is generally assumed that classical Chinese literature, known as WÉN YÁN, corresponded fairly closely to the spoken language of northern China of the early Qín period in the 3rd Century B.C. (See Wáng Lì, 1979). This assumption that a written language corresponds to its contemporary spoken form may seem so natural and sensible that it hardly needs any justification as a universal principle. Yet anyone who has had the opportunity to examine classical Chinese literature can attest to the extreme brevity and telegraphic nature of the written language, which borders on being cryptic. One wonders, then, to what extent such a written language is truly rooted in a spoken language. To illustrate, we present a paragraph from a short story written in the wén yán style. We wish to make it clear that within the great body of classical Chinese literature there are considerable variations in style. Certain esoteric styles were created at different historical periods as literary innovations. The following sample paragraph chosen for the purpose of illustration, however, is a representative of the typical, ordinary wén yán style prevalent in classical Chinese literature. It is the first paragraph of a short story entitled *Lǎo shān dàoshì*, 'The Taoist of Lao Mountain', by Pu´ Sōnglíng. In the English rendition of each classical Chinese sentence, we place in parentheses those words that are not represented in the Chinese text.

(1a)   *yì*   *yǒu*   *Wáng*   *shēng*
     town   exist   Wang   youngster
     The town has a young man (by the name of) Wang.

(1b)   *xíng*   *qī*
     in:line   seven
     (He) is the seventh (child)

(1c)   *gù*   *jiā*   *zǐ*
     old   family   son
     (He) is a son in an old (well-established) family.

(1d)   *sháo*   *mù*   *dào*
     young   admire   Taoism
     (He) admired Taoism (since he was) young.

(1e)   *wén*   *Láo*   *shān*   *duō*   *xiān-rén*
     hear   Lao   mountain   many   immortal
     (He) heard Lao mountain (had) many immortals.

(1f)   *fù*   *jǐ*   *wǎng*   *yóu*
     carry:on:back   satchel   go   travel
     (He) put on (his) back a satchel (and) went (there to) travel.

(1g)   *dēng*   *yī*   *dǐng*
     ascend   one   summit
     (He) ascended a summit.

(1h)　*yǒu*　　*guàn-yù*
　　　exist　　Tao:temple
　　　There was a Tao temple.

(1i)　*shèn*　　*yōu*
　　　very　　elegant
　　　(It was) very elegant.

(1j)　*yī*　　*dàoshì*　　*zuò*　　*pútuán*　　*shàng*
　　　one　　Taoist　　sit　　rush:mat　　on
　　　(There was) a Taoist sitting on a rush mat.

(1k)　*sù*　　*fǎ*　　*chuí*　　*lǐng*
　　　white　　hair　　hang　　neck
　　　(He had) white hair falling over (his) neck.

(1l)　*ér*　　*shén*　　*guān*　　*shuǎng*　　*màn*
　　　but　　god　　feature　　relaxed　　superior
　　　But (he had) heavenly features, (and looked) relaxed (and) superior.

(1m)　*kòu*　　*ér*　　*yù*　　*yǔ*
　　　salute　　then　　with　　speak
　　　(Wang) saluted (him) and then spoke with (him).

(1n)　*lǐ*　　*shèn*　　*xuán-miào*
　　　logic　　very　　profound-abstruse
　　　The logic (of the Taoist words) was profound (and) abstruse.

(1o)　*qǐng*　　*shī*　　*zhǐ*
　　　request　　be:master　　him
　　　(Wang) asked (the Taoist) to be his master.

(1p)　*dàoshì*　*yuè:*　　'*kǒng*　　*jiāo*　　*duò*　　*bù*　　*néng*　　*zuò*　　*kǔ'*
　　　Taoist　　say　　afraid　　spoiled　　lazy　　not　　can　　do　　hardship
　　　The Taoist said: '(I am) afraid (that you are) spoiled (and) lazy (and) (you)
　　　　　　cannot endure the hardship.'

(1q)　*dá*　　*yuè:*　　'*néng*　　*zhǐ'*
　　　answer　　say　　can　　it
　　　Wang said in response: '(I) can (endure) it.'

　　　The extreme brevity and telegraphic nature of the classical language manifests itself in several ways:

Rampant Zero Anaphora

In the seventeen clauses of the paragraph given in (1), the young man Wang is introduced in the first sentence, and the Taoist is introduced in the tenth sentence. The paragraph involves descriptions of Wang, the Taoist, and the temple as background information, and narrates in the form of foreground information on-going events of the story, such as Wang traveling to Lao mountain, finding the Taoist, asking to be taken as a disciple, and engaging in conversation with the Taoist. Throughout the entire paragraph, however, Wang, after being presented in the first clause, is referred to by zero-anaphora, except in clause (1o) where an object pronoun refers to him. The Taoist, after being introduced in the clause (1j), is referred to by zero-anaphora, except in the next to last clause where the subject noun refers to him. Yet every clause in this paragraph, with the exception of (1h) and (1i), which introduce and describe the temple, involves either Wang or the Taoist. Let us examine the zero anaphora in a section of (1) in more detail.

Clause (1j) introduces the Taoist, and (1k) and (1l) describe the Taoist. It is not surprising that zero pronouns are used for the Taoist in (1k) and (1l), as they offer background information about him immediately after he has been presented. The next clause (1m), however, returns to the main line of the narrative: 'Wang saluted the Taoist and then spoke with him.' In (1m), zero anaphora is used for both Wang and the Taoist. It is only through the early part of the narrative, as in sentence (1d), which tells us that Wang admires Taoism, that we can infer in (1m) that it is Wang who is saluting the Taoist, and not the other way around. Zero anaphora, however, is not confined to noun phrases only. Observe the last clause (1q). Wang said: 'I can endure it.' The Chinese text of what Wang said contained only two morphemes: *néng* 'can', and *zhĭ*, 'it'. The transitive verb 'endure' is represented by zero anaphora.

The Scarcity of Grammatical Morphemes

In the 17 clauses of (1), there are only five occurrences of four grammatical morphemes: a postposition *shàng* 'on' in clause (1j), a clause linker *ér* 'but, then' in clause (1l) and (1m), a preposition *yù* 'with' in clause (1m), and *bù* 'not' in clause (1p). Impressionistically, this is a very low number of grammatical morphemes for a paragraph of 17 clauses. There are no tense and aspect markers, no articles or demonstratives, no number, gender, or case markers, and no complementizers or subordination markers. In Li & Thompson (1978) and (1981) we discussed the scarcity of grammatical signals in modern Mandarin Chinese. The ratio of grammatical signals to clauses in classical Chinese, however, is significantly lower. In a modern Mandarin clause-to-clause translation of this paragraph provided by a textbook, as shown in (2), we find 28 grammatical morphemes, including aspect markers, sentence particles, nominalizers, ordinal number markers, genitive markers, classifiers, co-verbs, clause linkers, and postpositions. The discrepancy between modern Mandarin and classical Chinese in this regard is almost as impressive as that between modern English and modern Mandarin. In the following Mandarin rendition of (1), the grammatical morphemes are underlined:

(2a) *zái* *Zīchuān* *xiàn-chéng* *yǒu* *yi-* *ge* *xìng* *Wáng*
      at   Zichuan   county-town   exist   one   classifier   have:surname   Wang
      de *niánqīng* *rén*
      nominalizer   young   person
      In the town Zichuan there is a young man who has the surname Wang.

(2b) *pái-xíng* *dì* *qī*
      in:line   ordinal:number:marker   seven
      (He) is the seventh (child).

(2c) *shì* *dāngdì* *guānlì* *rénjiā* *de* *érzi*
      be   local   official   family   genitive:marker   son
      (He) is a son in a local official family.

(2d) *tā* *cóng* *xiǎo* *jiù* *hěn* *xiànmù* *dàojiā de* *fǎshù*
      3sg   from   young   then   very   admire   Taoism associative:marker   principle
      Since he was young (he) admired the principles of Taoism.

(2e) *tīng-shuō* *Láo* *shān* *yǒu* *hěn* *duō* *xiān-rén*
      hear   Lao   mountain   exist   very   many   immortals
      (He) heard the Lao mountain had many immortals.

(2f) *jiù* *bèi* __ *le* *shū-xiāng* *qián - wǎng*
      then   carry:on :back-   perfective:aspect   book-case   forward-toward
      qiú-jiào
      ask-teach
      (He) then put on (his) back a satchel (and) went (there) to learn.

(2g) *dēng-shàng* *yi - ge* *gāo* *shān* *dǐng-shang*
      ascend-on   one-classifier   high   mountain   top- on
      (He) ascended a high mountain.

(2h) *jiàn* *yǒu* *yi - zuò* *dào-guān* *zài* *nàr*
      see   exist   one-classifier   Taoist:temple   at   there
      (He) saw that there was a Taoist temple.

(2i) *fēichǎng* *yōu-jìng*
      very   elegant-quiet
      (It was) very elegant.

(2j) *yǒu* *yi - ge* *dàoshì* *zuò* *zài* *pútuán-shàng*
      exist   one-classifier   Taoist   sit   at   rush:mat-on
      There was a Taoist sitting on a rush mat.

(2k) *bái* *fǎ* *chuí* *jǐng*
      white   hair   hang   neck
      (He had) white hair falling over (his) neck.

(2l) *dànshi* *shéntài* *què* *qīngjiàn* *chūzhòng*
      but   feature   instead   healthy   superior
      But (he) looked healthy and superior.

(2m) *Wáng   qī   <u>jiù</u>   shàng-jiān   bàijiàn   <u>ér</u>   yù   tā   jiāotán*
      Wang   seven   then   move - up   salute   and   with   3sg   talk
      Wang the seventh then went up to salute (him) and talked with him.

(2n) *tā   shuō   <u>de</u>   lǐlùn   dōu   hěn   àomiào*
      3sg   speak   nominalizer   logic   all   very   profound
      The logic of what the Taoist said was profound.

(2o) *<u>yīncǐ</u>   <u>jiù</u>   qǐngqiú   bài   tā   wéi   shī*
      hence   then   request   beseech   3sg   be   master
      Hence (Wang) asked the Taoist to be (his) master.

(2p) *dàoshì shuō-dao: 'kǒngpà   nǐ   jiāoyǎng   xièdài   guàn   <u>le,</u>*
      Taoist   say   afraid   you   spoiled   lazy   accustomed asp.
      bu   néng   láodòng   chī - kǔ'
      not   can   labor   bear-hardship
      The Taoist said: '(I am) afraid you are accustomed to being spoiled and lazy, (and)
          (you) cannot do manual labor and endure hardship.'

(2q) *huídá-dào: 'kěyǐ'*
      answer   O.K.
      (Wang) answered: '(I) can (do) (it)'.

Brevity of Clauses

With the exception of clause (1p), the average length of the clauses in (1) is approximately four morphemes. Yet clauses (1e), (1l), (1m), (1o), and (1q) are all
multi-predicate constructions. In order to demonstrate the brevity of clauses in
classical Chinese, we carried out a statistical survey of four randomly selected
paragraphs from a collection of short stories written in classical Chinese. In this
collection, each classical Chinese story is also translated into modern Mandarin.
The translation emphasizes fidelity to the classical Chinese original, and the translator has striven for a clause-to-clause rendition. Our statistical survey provides a
count of the total number of clauses and the total number of logographs for each
paragraph in classical Chinese and in modern Mandarin. The results are given in
Table I.
    Table I shows that the average paragraph of modern Mandarin writing em-
ploys approximately twice as many logographs as does the corresponding paragraph of classical Chinese writing. There are many reasons for this remarkable
difference in the number of logographs used in classical Chinese and modern
Mandarin. One is the scarcity of grammatical words we discussed previously. Another reason is the monosyllabic nature of classical Chinese words: most words
were just one syllable in length and therefore represented by one logograph,
whereas compounds are common in Mandarin, many nominal or verbal notions
being expressed by two-syllable words.

TABLE I

	Classical Chinese		Modern Mandarin	
	Number of Clauses	Number of Logographs	Number of Clauses	Number of Logographs
Paragraph 1	23	121	25	222
Paragraph 2	8	37	10	86
Paragraph 3	6	22	7	49
Paragraph 4	21	86	23	163

These differences, however, do not completely account for the discrepancy; we must still reckon with the telegraphic nature of the classical Chinese style of writing. Consider, for example, clauses (1l), (1m), and (1n). (1l) describes the demeanor of the Taoist without mentioning the Taoist. The next clause, (1m), switches to a narrative scene where Wang salutes the Taoist and converses with him; neither Wang nor the Taoist are mentioned in this clause. The next clause, (1n), then states: 'The logic is profound and abstruse' without clarifying what logic or whose logic is being referred to. Thus, in order to extract the correct message of (1l), the reader has to rely heavily on inference based on his/her knowledge of the world and the information provided by the earlier clauses of the paragraph. It is his/her knowledge of the world together with the information that Lao mountain has many immortals, a piece of background information provided by clause (1e), that allows the reader to infer that the profound and abstruse logic concerns the Taoist.

Another example that illustrates the style of brevity is found in the very first word of the initial sentence of the short story quoted in (1). This word is yì which means 'town.' Thus, the story begins with the sentence (1a) whose meaning is, 'The town has a young man by the name of Wang'. But the author never explained in the story what the town was that he was referring to. He left it to the reader to extrapolate that the town was his home-town, where he resided when he wrote the story. In the Mandarin translation of the story, (2), the translator made it clear that the town was Zichuan. In order to provide this piece of information to the reader, however, the translator had to research the life of the author and add a footnote to point out that Zichuan was the home-town of the author and that the author was referring to his home-town when he used the term yì 'town'.

Classical Chinese, then, as exemplified by the paragraph in (1), can be seen to have been written in a highly condensed and telegraphic style. There are three reasons for surmising that this literary language was not very close to any contemporary spoken language. The first reason has to do with the obvious difference between an auditory and a visual mode: oral presentation is temporal and evanescent, whereas written presentation is spatial and stable. From the point of view of perception, the hearer must rely on his/her memory to retain information already presented by the speaker, but the reader can take a sequence of sentences into his/her visual field at any point in time. Thus, the reader has a distinct advantage over the hearer in being able to make use of a much larger section of discourse information at any given time. In addition, the reader can always halt his/her reading and turn back to earlier passages or sentences for the sake of clarification, a perceptual aid denied to the hearer in oral communication. Given this difference between the auditory and the visual mode one wonders if a spoken language can be as condensed and telegraphic as the language of classical Chinese literature is.

The second reason for being suspicious of classical Chinese as a direct reflection of a contemporary spoken style has to do with the logographic writing system. As pointed out earlier, each unit in the written language is a logograph, which represents, not a phonological unit, but a semantic unit. This means that ambiguity that arises out of homophony is not carried over from speech to writing. The relatively low level of ambiguity of the logographs seems to have been a crucial factor in the development of the highly telegraphic style of classical writings. This lack of ambiguity, however, is a feature of the writing system; hence our suspicion of any direct relationship between classical Chinese writing and any spoken form.

A third reason to doubt a close correspondence between classical Chinese and any spoken language relates to the characteristic paucity of grammatical markers as we discussed above. While we cannot be certain that the language(s) spoken in China during the classical period had more grammatical morphemes than are found in the classical literature, the large number of descriptive studies of languages of the world suggests that a spoken language with so few grammatical markers would be quite out of line.

CLASSICAL CHINESE AND MODERN CHINESE

Classical Chinese plays a significant role in accounting for the gulf which exists between spoken Mandarin, the official language of China, and the current written language, since practically all contemporary Chinese writing involves a mixture of the classical style and spoken Mandarin. The mixture is reflected at both the lexical and the structural level. Certain contemporary Chinese writings, especially the political literature designed to be read by the public in the People's Republic of China, contain very little of the classical language. Other contemporary Chinese writings, such as certain literary pieces, draw extensively on the classical language. Hence, the issue is not whether or not modern written Chinese is a heterogeneous language composed of the classical written language and spoken Mandarin; modern written Chinese is definitely a heterogeneous language. The issue is, in a given piece of modern Chinese writing, how much of it is classical Chinese and how much of it is spoken Mandarin?

We have just mentioned that the political literature of the PRC tends to be most colloquial. The PRC government has been explicit in requiring all written material, no matter whether it is literature, science, journalism, or propaganda, to follow as closely as possible the official spoken language, known as Putonghua, which is based on Beijing Mandarin. But traces of the classical language can be found even in political propaganda writing in the PRC. We randomly examined selected pages of *Xuéxí*, 'Learning', a monthly magazine of political propaganda for popular consumption, and found words and phrases taken from classical Chinese, not used in colloquial Mandarin, on every page. For instance:

(3) *háo*   *wú*   *yíwèn*   *(p. 42, 1955, #7)*
     iota   not   doubt
     There isn't a bit of doubt.

Wú, 'not', is a negative particle in classical Chinese which is not used in spoken Mandarin. The expression *háo wú* 'not a bit' is thus classical Chinese in both structure and lexicon. The equivalent of (3) in modern Mandarin would be (4):

(4) *yì-diǎn*   *dōu*   *méiyou*   *yíwèn*
     one-bit   all   not   doubt.
     There isn't one bit of doubt.

Consider another example from the same page of the magazine:

(5) *kěshì*   *Húfén*   *bìng*   *bù*   *yīn*   *cǐ*   *shāo*   *yǒu*   *suǒ*   *wù*
     but   Hufen   but   not   because this slight exist nominalizer aware
     But Hufen did not gain even a little bit of awareness (of his mistake) because
     of this.

This sentence provides a good illustration of a mixture of classical and colloquial writing styles. The words from the classical language in this sentence are: *yīn* 'because'; *shāo* 'slight'; and *wù* 'awareness'. Their modern Mandarin equivalents are all bisyllabic expansions: *yīnwèi* 'because'; s *hāowéi* 'slight'; and *juéwù* 'aware'. In addition, the demonstrative pronoun *cǐ* 'this' is no longer used in modern Mandarin. The most natural Mandarin equivalent of the expression *yīn cǐ* as it occurs in (5) would be:

(6) *yīnwèi*   *zhèi - ge*   *yuángù*
     because   this-classifier   reason
     because of this reason

The morpheme *suǒ* occurring near the end of the sentence remains as an optional nominalizing particle in Mandarin; but it cannot serve as the sole nominalizer in

Mandarin. The obligatory nominalizer in Mandarin is *de*. For example, (7) is a nominalization in Mandarin. Notice that *suǒ* is optional but *de* is obligatory:

(7)   *tā*   *(suǒ)*   *xǐhuan*   *de*
       3sg   nominalizer   like   nominalizer
       what s/he likes

Hence the structure of the phrase *shāo yǒu suǒ wù* at the end of sentence (5) is completely in the mold of classical Chinese. Its Mandarin equivalent would be (8):

(8)   *shāowéi*   *yǒu*   *yī-diǎn*   *juéwù*
       slight   exist   one-bit   awareness
       (He) has become slightly aware (of his mistake).

In other genres of contemporary Chinese writing, the presence of the classical language is much more prominent than in political propaganda literature. We examined a small booklet entitled *Běijīng rén*, 'Peking Man', an item in a serial entitled 'Common Knowledge in History' published in the PRC for public consumption. On the very first page, the chapter title is:

(9)   *Běijīng*   *rén*   *zhī*   *jiā*
       Peking   person   genitive   home
       The home of Peking man.

The genitive particle, *zhī*, in (9) is lifted right out of classical Chinese. *Zhī* is no longer used Mandarin except in special formulas like (10), its Mandarin equivalent being *de*.

(10)   *bā*   *fēn*   *zhī*   *sān*
        8   parts   genitive   3
        three-eighths

In descriptive writing by creative writers, the presence of classical Chinese becomes even more obvious. In a collection of literary sketches, the title of the very first piece is a classical Chinese phrase: *yǎ shè* 'elegant abode'. The Mandarin equivalent of *yǎ* 'elegant', would be *yōuyǎ*, while the Mandarin equivalent of *shè* would be *wūzi*. Thus, the title rendered in modern Mandarin would be *yōuyǎ de wūzi* 'elegant nominalizing-particle house' = 'elegant abode.' The first page of this sketch contains twenty-five occurrences of classical Chinese phrases and lexical items.

In order to understand why the written language of modern China is such a mixture of the classical written language and spoken Mandarin, we must briefly delve into the literary history of China. Beginning with the establishment of Confucianism and the civil service examination system, more than two millennia ago, the only acceptable style of writing had been that of the classical literature. It was not until the late teens of the twentieth century that a movement to replace the classical style of writing with a vernacular style based on spoken Mandarin began to gather strength. This cultural upheaval was an important aspect of the historical 'May 4th Movement' that occurred in Beijing in 1919. Y. R. Chao, the distinguished linguist, was one of the leaders pushing for the change in the written language. Thus, the yoke of the classical style in written Chinese was not broken until the twentieth century.

Since the May 4th Movement, vernacular styles of writing have become acceptable. The classical style, however, as we have seen, could by no means be said to have disappeared. Beginning in grade school, Chinese students learn and memorize a considerable amount of classical Chinese literature. Command of the classical style of writing, and elegance of calligraphy with the brush, remain deeply admired qualities of an intellectual in China. Thus, Mao is revered for his poetry, which is written completely in the classical style. In addition, educated Chinese are bi-dialectal; most of them share the feeling that the succinctness of the classical style carries with it an elegance and pithiness not found in the colloquial style, and inevitably slip into the classical tradition in their writing. Thus, the heavy influence of the classical style on modern written Chinese helps to maintain a considerable gulf between the written and the spoken language of modern China.

Another factor keeping modern written Chinese quite distinct from spoken Mandarin, however, is again the nature of the logographs themselves. Modern Mandarin has slightly more than four hundred segmentally distinct syllables. Since there are four lexical tones, we would expect the number of phonetically distinct syllables to be about 1600. Actually, since not every syllable occurs on all four tones, the number of distinct syllables is somewhat over 1300. Now, in the most recent dictionary of the Chinese language, *Cí Hǎi,* published in the PRC in 1979, which includes both classical and colloquial entries, there are 106,578 entries, of which 14,872 are single logographs. Since a logograph always represents one syllable, if we divide 14,872 by 1200, we find that each distinct syllabic unit must be associated with an average of 12 different logographs! As a ratio of the correspondence between phonologically and semantically distinct units, this figure of 12 : 1 is exaggerated in two directions: first, the number of logographs any given educated individual knows is much closer to 6000 than to 14,000; second, there is synonymy among the logographs. It is still the case, however, that in the written language the relationship between the semantic unit and the written unit (the logograph) is essentially one-to-one, while in the spoken language, the relationship between the semantic unit and the phonological unit (the syllable) is many-to-one.

How could such a situation arise? On the basis of the highly 'monosyllabic' nature of the other 'dialects' of Chinese, we make the uncontroversial assumption that the ancestor of all the modern dialects was essentially a monosyllabic language; that is, we assume that it was a language in which the vast majority of words were one syllable in length. Comparative dialect research shows that Mandarin has lost many of the segmental and tonal distinctions preserved in the other dialects. As a response to the intolerable amount of homophony that would result if it had remained a monosyllabic language with only 400+ distinct syllable types, modern Mandarin has dramatically increased its inventory of bisyllabic words through compounding and affixation. The written language, of course, has had to resort to no such measures: since it is not tied to the phonology, there is, in written Chinese, no analog to the threat of massive homophony. Thus, where a bisyllabic compound is used in spoken Mandarin, a monosyllabic morpheme represented by one logograph is often used in written Chinese, as we have seen in our discussion of example (5), and where a suffix is necessary in spoken Mandarin, it may not appear in written Chinese, e.g., *wū* versus *wūzi* 'house'. The net result is a written language which can 'afford' to be terse and condensed in a way that the spoken language cannot, since in context there is rarely any question as to what the semantic unit is to which a given logograph corresponds.

Given these facts, we can suggest a partial explanation for why the logographic writing system has not been abolished, despite the burden it places on the memories of its users, and despite the existence of an official spelling system, Pinyin, introduced in the PRC in the early '50's, though not used to any extent outside of schools as an aid to Mandarin pronunciation. Since written Chinese could not be directly transliterated into any phonologically-based script without losing most of its comprehensibility, abolishment of the logographs in favor of a spelling system would imply not only translating the entire written literature into something approximating Mandarin, but also developing a new writing style. A decision to implement such radical changes would clearly not be an easy one to arrive at.

REFERENCES

JIǍ, LÁNBŌ. (No date of publication available). *Běijīng Rén* (Peking Man). Beijing: Zhōnghuá Shūjú.

LI, CHARLES N. AND SANDRA A. THOMPSON. 1978. "An exploration of Mandarin Chinese", in Lehmann, Winfred, ed., *The Typology of Language*, University of Texas Press, 223–266.

LI, CHARLES N. AND SANDRA A. THOMPSON. 1981. *Mandarin Chinese: A Functional Reference Grammar.* Berkeley and Los Angeles: University of California Press.

LIANG, SHIH-CHIU. 1963. "*yǎ shè*" (Elegant Abode), in *Yǎ shè xiǎo píng* (Sketches in an Elegant Abode), by Liang, Shih-chiu, pp. 1–4. Taiwan: Yuandong Book Company.

PÚ, SŌNGLÍNG. 1970. "*Láo shān dàoshì*" (The Taoist of Lao Mountain). In *Lìdài Duǎnpiān Xiǎoshuō Xūn* (Selected Short Stories of Differ ent Historical Periods), pp. 87–89, edited by Huáng, Wénxīn. Singapore: Shanghai Book Company.

WÁNG, Lì. 1979. *Gǔdài Hànyǔ* (Classical Chinese). Vol. 1, No. 1. Beijing: Zhōnghuá Shūjú.

Cí Hǎi (Dictionary of the Chinese Language) (3 Volumes). 1979. Shanghai, China.

Xuéxí (Learning). p. 42, No. 7, 1955. Beijing.

II TRAVELING ALONG ORAL AND WRITTEN CONTINUUA

6

Protean Shapes in Literacy Events: Ever-shifting Oral and Literate Traditions

Shirley Brice Heath
Stanford University

> 'the Proteus-nature. . .of ever-shifting language'
> John Upton, *Critical Observations on Shakespeare*, 1747

Since the mid-1970s, anthropologists, linguists, historians, and psychologists have turned with new tools of analysis to the study of oral and literate societies. They have used discourse analysis, econometrics, theories of schemata and frames, and proposals of developmental performance to consider the possible links between oral and written language, and between literacy and its individual and societal consequences. Much of this research is predicated on a dichotomous view of oral and literate traditions, usually attributed to researchers active in the 1960s. Repeatedly, Goody & Watt (1963), Ong (1967), Goody (1968), and Havelock (1963) are cited as having suggested a dichotomous view of oral and literate societies and as having asserted certain cognitive, social, and linguistic effects of literacy on both the society and the individual. Survey research tracing the invention and diffusion of writing systems across numerous societies (Kroeber, 1948) and positing the effects of the spread of literacy on social and individual memory (Goody & Watt, 1963; Havelock, 1963, 1976) is cited as supporting a contrastive view of oral and literate social groups. Research which examined oral performance in particular groups is said to support the notion that as members of a society increasingly participate in literacy, they lose habits associated with the oral tradition (Lord, 1965).

The language of the oral tradition is held to suggest meaning without explicitly stating information (Lord, 1965). Certain discourse forms, such as the parable or proverb (Dodd, 1961), are formulaic uses of language which convey meanings without direct explication. Thus, truth lies in experience and is verified by the experience of listeners. Story plots are said to be interwoven with routine formulas,

91

and fixed sayings to make up much of the content of the story (Rosenberg, 1970). In contrast, language associated with the literate tradition is portrayed as making meaning explicit in the text and as not relying on the experiences of readers for verification of truth value. The epitome of this type of language is said to be the formal expository essay (Olson, 1977). The setting for learning this language and associated literate habits is the school. Formal schooling at all levels is said to prescribe certain features of sentence structure, lexical choice, text cohesion, and topic organization for formal language—both spoken and written (Bourdieu, 1967). An array of abilities, ranging from metalinguistic awareness (Baron, 1979) to predictable critical skills (reported in Heath, 1980a) are held to derive from cultural experiences with writing.

In short, existing scholarship makes it easy to interpret a picture which depicts societies existing along a continuum of development from an oral tradition to a literate one, with some societies having a restricted literacy, and others having reached a full development of literacy (Goody, 1968:11). One also finds in this research specific characterizations of oral and written language associated with these traditions.

But a close reading of these scholars, especially Goody (1968) and Goody and Watt (1963), leaves some room for questioning such a picture of consistent and universal processes or products—individual or societal—of literacy. Goody pointed out that in any traditional society, factors such as secrecy, religious ideology, limited social mobility, lack of access to writing materials and alphabetic scripts could lead to restricted literacy. Furthermore, Goody warned that the advent of a writing system did not amount to technological determinism or to sufficient cause of certain changes in either the individual or the society. Goody went on to propose exploring the concrete context of written communication (1968:4) to determine how the potentialities of literacy developed in traditional societies. He brought together a collection of essays based on the ethnography of literacy in traditional societies to illustrate the wide variety of ways in which TRADITIONAL, i.e. pre-industrial but not necessarily pre-literate, societies played out their uses of oral and literate traditions.

Few researchers in the 1970's have, however, heeded Goody's warning about the possible wide-ranging effects of societal and cultural factors on literacy and its uses. In particular, little attention has been given in MODERN complex industrial societies to the social and cultural correlates of literacy or to the work experiences adults have which may affect the maintenance and retention of literacy skills acquired in formal schooling. The public media today give much attention to the decline of literacy skills as measured in school settings and to the failure of students to acquire certain levels of literacy. However, the media pay little attention to occasions for literacy retention—to the actual uses of literacy in work settings, daily interactions in religious, economic, and legal institutions, and family habits of socializing the young into uses of literacy. In the clamor over the need to increase the teaching of basic skills, there is much emphasis on the positive effects extensive and critical reading can have on improving oral language. Yet there are scarcely any data comparing the forms and functions of oral language with those of written language produced and used by members of social groups within a complex society. One of the most appropriate sources of data for informing discussions of these issues is that which Goody proposed for traditional societies: the concrete context of written communication. Where, when, how, for whom, and with what results are individuals in different social groups of today's highly industrialized society using reading and writing skills? How have the potentialities of the literacy skills learned in school developed in the lives of today's adults? Does modern society contain certain conditions which restrict literacy just as some traditional societies do? If so, what are these factors, and are groups with restricted literacy denied benefits widely attributed to full literacy, such as upward socioeconomic mobility, the development of logical reasoning, and access to the information necessary to make well-informed political judgments?

THE LITERACY EVENT

The LITERACY EVENT is a conceptual tool useful in examining within particular communities of modern society the actual forms and functions of oral and literate traditions and co-existing relationships between spoken and written language. A literacy event is any occasion in which a piece of writing is integral to the nature of participants' interactions and their interpretive processes (Heath, 1978).

In studying the literacy environment, researchers describe: print materials available in the environment, the individuals and activities which surround print, and ways in which people include print in their ongoing activities. A literacy event can then be viewed as any action sequence, involving one or more persons, in which the production and/or comprehension of print plays a role (Anderson, Teale, & Estrada 1980:59). There are rules for the occurrence of literacy events, just as there are for speech events (Hymes, 1972). Characteristics of the structures and uses of literacy events vary from situation to situation. In addition to having an appropriate structure, a literacy event has certain interactional rules and demands particular interpretive competencies on the part of participants. Some aspects of reading and/or writing are required by at least one party, and certain types of speech events are appropriate within certain literacy events. Speech events may describe, repeat, reinforce, expand, frame, or contradict written materials, and participants must learn whether the oral or written mode takes precedence in literacy events. For example, in filling out an application form, should applicants listen to oral instructions or complete the form? On many occasions, an interview consists of participating orally with someone who fills out a form based on the oral performance, and access to the written report is never available to the applicant in the course of the interview. Oral comments often contradict the usual assumption that written materials are to be read: You don't have to read this, but you should have it.

The having of something in writing is often a ritualistic practice, and more often than not, those who hold the written piece are not expected to read what they have. In other cases, the actual reading of the piece of written material may be possible, but not sufficient, because some oral attestation is necessary. A church congregational meeting may be an occasion in which all must read the regulations of applying for a loan or a grant for church support (this is usually done by having the minister read them aloud). But the entire congregation must orally attest that they have read and approved the regulations. On other occasions, the written material must be present, but the speech event takes precedence. A Girl Scout comes to sell cookies at the door; she passes out a folder asserting who she is, to which troop she belongs, and to which project her fund will go. After handing over this piece of paper, the Girl Scout talks about the cookies and the project which the sale will benefit. Few individuals read the folder instead of listening to the Girl Scout. Here, the speech event takes precedence at the critical moments of the interaction. It is important to know what the framing situations for literacy events are in a variety of contexts, for situations may differ markedly from each other and may, in fact, contradict such traditional expectations of literacy as those taught in school or in job training programs. For example, ways of asking clarification of the USES of written materials are often far more important in daily out-of-school life than are questions about the content. What will be done with forms submitted to the Department of Motor Vehicles after an accident is of as much consequence as, if not more consequence than, the actual content of the forms. Thus it may be hypothesized that examination of the contexts and uses of literacy is communities today may show that THERE ARE MORE LITERACY EVENTS WHICH CALL FOR APPRO-PRIATE KNOWLEDGE OF FORMS AND USES OF SPEECH EVENTS THAN THERE ARE AC-TUAL OCCASIONS FOR EXTENDED READING OR WRITING.

Furthermore, the traditional distinctions between the habits of those characterized as having either oral or literate traditions may not actually exist in many communities of the United States, which are neither non-literate nor fully literate. Their members can read and write at least at basic levels, but they have little occasion to use these skills as taught in school. Instead, much of their daily life is filled with literacy events in which they must know how to use and how to respond in the oral mode to written materials. In short, descriptions of the concrete context of written communication which give attention to social and cultural features of the community as well as to the oral language surrounding written communications may discredit any reliance on characterizing particular communities as having reached either restricted or full development of literacy or as having language forms and functions associated more with the literate tradition than with the oral, or vice versa.

THE COMMUNITY CONTEXT

Some testing of these ideas is possible from data collected in a Piedmont community of the Carolinas between 1969 and 1979. The community, Trackton, is a working-class all-Black community, whose adults work in the local textile mills and earn incomes which exceed those of many public school teachers in the state. All adults in this community can read and write, and all talk enthusiastically about the need for their children to do well in school. Ethnographic work in the primary networks within the community, the religious institutions, and work settings documented the forms and functions written and spoken language took for individual members of Trackton. The literacy event was the focus of descriptions of written language uses in these contexts.

At Home in Trackton

In the daily life of the neighborhood, there were numerous occasions when print from beyond the primary network intruded; there were fewer occasions when adults or children themselves produced written materials. Adults did not read to children, and there were few pieces of writing produced especially for children. Sunday School books, and single-page handouts from Sunday School which portrayed a Biblical scene with a brief caption, were the only exceptions. Adults, however, responded to children of all ages, if they inquired about messages provided in writing: they would read a house number, a stop sign, a name brand of a product, or a slogan on a T-shirt, if asked to do so by a child. In September, children preparing to go to school often preferred book bags, pencil boxes, and purses which bore labels or slogans. Adults did not consciously model, demonstrate, or tutor reading and writing behaviors for the young. Children, however, went to school with certain expectancies of print and a keen sense that reading is something one does to learn something one needs to know. In other words, before going to school, preschoolers were able to read many types of information available in their environment. They knew how to distinguish brand names from product descriptions on boxes or bags; they knew how to find the price on a label which contained numerous other pieces of written information. They knew how to recognize the names of cars, motorcycles, and bicycles not only on the products themselves, but also on brochures about these products. In these ways they read to learn information judged necessary in their daily lives, and they had grown accustomed to participating in literacy events in ways appropriate to their community's norms (see Heath, 1980 for a fuller description). They had frequently observed their community's social activities surrounding a piece of writing: negotiation over how to put a toy together, what a gas bill notice meant, how to fill out a voter registration form, and where to go to apply for entrance to daycare programs.

There were no bedtime stories, children's books, special times for reading, or routine sets of questions from adults to children in connection with reading.[1]

---

[1]Preschool literacy socialization is a growing field of research heavily influenced by studies of social interactions surrounding language input to children learning to talk. For a review of this literature and especially its characterizations of how mainstream school-oriented families prepare their children for taking meaning from print, see Heath, 1982. The most thorough study of literacy socialization in a comparative perspective is Scollon and Scollon, 1981.

Thus, Trackton children's early spontaneous stories were not molded on written materials. They were derived from oral models given by adults, and they developed in accordance with praise and varying degrees of enthusiasm for particular story styles from the audience. In these stories, children rendered a context, or set the stage for the story, and called on listeners to create jointly an imagined background for stories. In the later preschool years, the children, in a monologue-like fashion, told stories about things in their lives, events they saw and heard, and situations in which they had been involved. They produced these stories, many of which can be described as story-poems, during play with other children or in the presence of adults. Their stories contained emotional evaluation of others and their actions; dialogue was prevalent; style shifting in verbal and nonverbal means accompanied all stories.

All of these features of story-telling by children call attention to the story and distinguish it as a speech event which is an occasion for audience and storyteller to interact pleasantly to a creative tale, not simply a recounting of daily events. Story-telling is very competitive, especially as children get older, and new tricks must be devised if one is to remain a successful story-teller. Content ranges widely, and there is truth only in the universals of human experience which are found in every story. Fact as related to what really happened is often hard to find, though it may be the seed of the story. Trackton stories often have no obvious beginning in the form of a routine; similarly, there is no marked ending; they simply go on as long as the audience will tolerate the story (see Heath, 1980 and chapter 5 of Heath, forthcoming, for a fuller description).

In response to these stories, Trackton adults do not separate out bits and pieces of the story and question the children about them. Similarly, they do not pick out pieces of the daily environment and ask children to name these or describe their features. Children live in an on-going multiple-channeled stream of stimuli, from which they select, practice, and determine the rules of speaking and interacting with written materials. Children have to learn at a very early age to perceive situations, determine how units of these situations are related to each other, recognize these relations in other situations, and reason through what it will take to show their correlation of one situation with another. The specifics of labels, features, and rules of behaving are not laid out for them by adults. The familiar routines described in the research literature on mainstream school-oriented parents are not heard in Trackton. They do not ask or tell their children: What is that? What color is it? Is that the way to listen? Turn the book this way. Let's listen and find out. Instead, parents talk about items and events of their environment. They detail the responses of personalities to events; they praise, deride, and question the reasons for events and compare new items and events to those with which they are familiar. They do not simplify their talk about the world for the benefit of their young. Preschoolers do not learn to name or list the features of items in either the daily environment or as depicted through illustration in printed materials. Questions addressed to them with the greatest frequency are of the type What's that like? Where'd that come from? What are you gonna do with that? They develop connections between situations or items not by specification of labels and features in these situations, but by configuration links.

Recognition of similar general shapes or patterns of links seen in one situation and connected to another pervade their stories and their conversations, as illustrated in the following story. Lem, playing off the edge of the porch, when he was about two and a half years of age, heard a bell in the distance. He stopped, looked at his older siblings nearby, and said:

Way
Far
Now
It a church bell
Ringin'
Dey singin'
Ringin'
You hear it?
I hear it
Far
Now.

Lem here recalls being taken to church the previous Sunday and hearing a bell. His story is in response to the current stimulus of a distant bell. He recapitulates the sequence of events: at church, the bell rang while the people sang the opening hymn. He gives the story's topic in the line It a church bell, but he does not orient the listeners to the setting or the time of the story. He seems to try to recreate the situation both verbally and non-verbally so it will be recognized and responded to by listeners. Lem poetically balances the opening and closing in an INCLUSIO, beginning Way, Far, Now. and ending Far, Now. The effect is one of closure, though he doesn't announce the ending of his story. He invites others to respond to his story: You hear it? I hear it. All of these methods call attention to the story, and distinguish it as a story. The children recall scenes and events through nonverbal and verbal manipulation. They use few formulaic invitations to recall, such as You know, You see, etc. Instead, they themselves try to give the setting and the mood as they weave the tale to keep the audience's attention. The recall of a setting may depend on asking the listener to remember a smell, a sound, a place, a feeling, and to associate these in the same way the storyteller does. A smiliar type of recall of relevant context or set of circumstances marks children's memories or reassociations with print. When they see a brandname, number, etc., they often recall where and with whom they first saw it, or call attention to parts now missing which were there previously. Slight shifts in print styles, decorations of mascots used to advertise cereals, or alterations of television advertising mottos are noticed by children.

Trackton children's preschool experiences with print, stories, and talk about the environment differ greatly from those usually depicted in the literature for children of mainstream school-oriented parents. Similarly, adults in Trackton used written materials in different ways and for different purposes than those represented in the traditional literature on adult reading habits and motivations (cf. Staiger, 1979; Hall & Carlton, 1977). Among Trackton adults, reading was a social activity which did not focus on a single individual. Solitary reading without oral explanation was viewed as unacceptable, strange, and indicative of a particular kind of failure, which kept individuals from being social. Narratives, jokes, sidetracking talk, and negotiation of the meaning of written texts kept social relations alive. When several members of the community jointly focused on and interpreted written materials, authority did not rest in the materials themselves, but in the meanings which would be negotiated by the participants.

New instructions on obtaining medical reports for children about to enter school provoked stories of what other individuals did when they were confronted with a similar task; all joined in talk of particular nurses or doctors who were helpful in the process. Some told of reactions to vaccinations and troubles they had had getting to and from the doctor's office. In the following conversation, several neighbors negotiate the meaning of a letter about a daycare program. Several neighbors were sitting on porches, working on cars nearby, or sweeping their front yards when a young mother of four children came out on her porch with a letter she had received that day.

> Lillie Mae   :You hear this, it says Lem [her two-year-old son] might can get into Ridgeway [a local neighborhood center daycare program], but I hafta have the papers ready and apply by next Friday.
>
> First female neighbor (mother of three children who are already in school): You ever been to Kent to get his birth certificate?
>
> Second female neighbor (with preschool children): But what hours that program gonna be? You may not can get him there.
>
> Lillie Mae: They want the birth certificate? I got his vaccination papers.
>
> Third female neighbor: Sometimes they take that, 'cause they can 'bout tell the age from those early shots.
>
> First female neighbor: But you better get it, 'cause you gotta have it when he go to school anyway.
>
> Lillie Mae: But it says here they don't know what hours yet. How am I gonna get over to Kent? How much does it cost? Lemme see if the program costs anything [she reads aloud part of the letter].

Conversation on various parts of the letter continued for nearly an hour, while neighbors and Lillie Mae pooled their knowledge of the pros and cons of such programs. They discussed ways of getting rides to Kent, the county seat

thirty miles away, to which all mothers had to go to get their children's birth certificates to prove their age at school entrance. The discussion covered the possibility
of visiting Lillie Mae's doctor and getting papers from him to verify Lem's age,
teachers now at the neighborhood center, and health benefits which came from the
daycare programs' outreach work. A question What does this mean? asked of a
piece of writing was addressed to any and all who would listen; specific attention
to the text itself was at times minimal in the answers which followed.

Adults read and wrote for numerous purposes, almost all of them social.
These were:

1) Instrumental—to provide information about practical problems of daily
   life (bills, checks, price tags, street signs, house numbers)

2) Interactional—to give information pertinent to social relations with individuals not in the primary group (cartoons, bumper stickers, letters,
   newspaper features, greeting cards)

3) News-related—to provide information about secondary contacts or distant events (newspaper items, political flyers, directives from city
   offices)

4) Confirmation—to provide support for attitudes or ideas already held
   (reference to the Bible, brochures advertising products, etc.)

5) Provision of permanent records—to record information required by external agencies (birth certificates, loan notes, tax forms). Trackton residents wrote most frequently for the following reasons:

6) Memory-supportive—to serve as a memory aid (addresses, telephone
   numbers, notes on calendars)

7) Substitutes for oral messages—to substitute for oral communication on
   those occasions when face-to-face or telephone contact was not possible
   or would prove embarrassing (thank-you letters to people in distant cities, notes about tardiness to school or absence at school or work, a request to local merchants for credit to be extended to a child needing to
   buy coal, milk, or bread for the family).

On all of these occasions for reading and writing, individuals saw literacy as
an occasion for social activities: women shopped together, discussed local credit
opportunities and products, and sales; men negotiated the meaning of tax forms,
brochures on new cars, and political flyers. The evening newspaper was read on
the front porch, and talk about the news drifted from porch to porch. Inside, during the winter months, talk about news items interrupted on-going conversations
on other topics or television viewing. The only occasions for solitary reading by
individuals were those in which elderly men and women read their Bible or Sunday School materials alone, or school-age children sat alone to read a library book
or a school assignment. In short, written information almost never stood alone in

Trackton; it was reshaped and reworded into an oral mode. In so doing, adults and children incorporated chunks of the written text into their talk. They also sometimes reflected an awareness of a different type of organization of written materials from that of their usual oral productions. Yet their literacy habits do not fit those usually attributed to fully literate groups: they do not read to their children, encouraging conversational dialogue on books; they do not write or read extended prose passages; reading is not an individual pursuit nor is it considered to have intellectual, aesthetic, or critical rewards. But Trackton homes do not conform to habits associated with the oral tradition either. Literacy is a resource; stories do not fit the parable model; children develop very early wide-ranging language skills; and neither their language nor their parents' is marked by a preponderance of routine formulaic expressions.

At Church

Trackton is a literate community in the sense that its members read and write when occasions within their community demand such skills. Outside the community, there are numerous occasions established by individuals and institutions in which Trackton residents must show their literacy skills. One of these situations is in the church life of the Trackton people. Most residents go to country churches for Sunday services, which are usually held twice a month. In these churches, the pastor serves not one, but several churches, and he also holds another job as well during the week. A pastor or reverend is always a man, usually a man who in his younger days was known as wild and had come to the Lord after recognizing the sins of his youth. Many pastors had been musicians entertaining in clubs before their conversion to religion. Few had formal theological training; instead they had gone to Black colleges in the South and majored in religion. Most had at least a four-year college education, and many had taken additional training at special summer programs, through correspondence courses, or in graduate programs at nearby integrated state schools. In their jobs outside the church, they were businessmen, school administrators, land-owning farmers, or city personnel.

The country churches brought together not only residents of Trackton, a majority of whom worked in textile mills, but also school-teachers, domestic workers, hospital staff, clerks in local retail businesses, and farmers. Levels of formal education were mixed in these churches, and ranged from the elderly men and women who had had only a few years of grammar school in their youth, to the minister and some school administrators who had graduate-level education. Yet, in the church, all these types and levels of literacy skills came together in a pattern which reflected a strong reliance on the written word in both substance and style. Everyone wanted others to know he could read the Bible and church materials (even if he did not do so regularly). Church was an occasion to announce knowledge of how to handle the style of written language as well as its substance. Numerous evidences of formal writing marked every church service, and on special occasions, such as celebration of the accomplishments of a church member, formal writing was very much in evidence. For these celebration services, there were brochures which contained a picture of the individual, an account of his or her life, lists of members of the family, and details of the order of service. Funeral services included similar brochures. All churches had hymn books, and a placard on either side of the front of the church announced the numbers of the hymns. Choir leaders invited the congregation to turn to the hymn and read the words with him; he announced the number of the verses of the hymn to be sung. The minister expected adults to bring their Bibles to church along with their Sunday School materials and to read along with him or the Sunday School director. Mimeographed church bulletins dictated the order of the service from the opening hymn to the benediction. The front and back covers of the bulletin contained drawings and scripture verses which illustrated either the sermon topic or the season of the year. Announcements of upcoming events in the recreational life of the church or political activities of the Black community filled one page of the bulletin. Reports of building funds and missionary funds were brief and were supplemented by the pastor's announcements in church service.

Yet many parts of the service move away from the formality of these written sources. The congregation often begins singing the hymn written in the book, but they quickly move away from the written form to 'raise' the hymn. In this performance, the choir leader begins the hymn with the written words and the congregation follows briefly; however, another song leader will break in with new words for a portion of the hymn; the audience waits to hear these, then picks up the words and follows. The hymn continues in this way, with different members of the congregation serving as song leader at various points. Some of the words may be those which are written in the hymnbook, others may not be. A member of the congregation may begin a prayer at a particular juncture of the hymn, and the congregation will hum until the prayer is completed. The ending of the hymn is to an outsider entirely unpredictable, yet all members of the congregation end at the same time. Hymns may be raised on the occasion of the announcement of a hymn by the choir leader, spontaneously during a story or testimonial by a church member, or near the end of a semon. In the raising of a hymn, written formulas are the basis of the hymn, but these are subject to change, and it is indeed that change which makes the congregation at once creator and performer. The formulas are changed and new formulas produced to expand the theme, to illustrate points, or to pull back from a particular theme to pick up another which has been introduced in a prayer or in the sermon. Every performance of a particular hymn is different, and such performances bear the mark of the choir leader and his interactional style with the congregation.

A similar phenomenon is illustrated in oral prayers in church. These are often written out ahead of time by those who have been asked by the minister to offer a prayer at next Sunday's service. The prayer as follows was given orally by a 45-year old female school teacher.

1   We thank thee for watchin' over us, kind heavenly Father
2   Through the night.
3   We thank thee, oh Lord.
4   For leadin' 'n guidin' us
5   We thank thee, kind heavenly Father
6   For your strong-arm protection around us.
7   Oh Lord, don't leave us alone.
8   We feel this evenin', kind heavenly Father, if you leave us
9   We are the least ones of all.
10   Now Lord, I ask thee, kind heavenly Father,
11   to go 'long with my family,
12   I ask thee, kind heavenly Father, to throw your strong-arm protectors around
13   Oh Lord, I ask thee, oh Lord,
14   to take care of my childrens, Lord, wherever they may be.
15   Oh Lord, don't leave us, Jesus.
16   I feel this morning, kind heavenly Father, if you leave me,
17   Oh, Lord, please, Lord, don't leave me
18   in the hands of the wicked man.
19   Oh Lord, I thank thee kind heavenly Father
20   for what you have done for me.
21   Oh Lord, I thank thee, kind heavenly Father
22   Where you have brought me from.
23   Oh Lord, I wonder sometime if I didn't have Jesus on my side,
24   Lord, have mercy now,
25   what would I do, oh Lord?
26   Have mercy, Jesus.
27   I can call on 'im in the midnight hour,
28   I can call on 'im, Lord, in the noontime, oh Lord,
29   I can call on 'im anytime o' day, oh Lord.
30   He'p me, Jesus,
31   Oh Lord, make me strong
32   Oh Lord, have mercy on us, Father
33   When we have done all that you have 'signed our hands to do, Lord,
34   Have mercy, Lord,
35   I want you to give me a home beyond the shinin' river, oh Lord,
36   Where won't be no sorrowness,
37   Won't be no shame and tears, oh Lord.
38   It won't be nothing, Lord, but glory, alleluia.
39   When we have done all that you 'signed our hands to do, kind heavenly Father,
40   And we cain't do no mo',
41   We want you to give us a home in thy kingdom, oh Lord.
42   For thy Christ's sake. Amen.

After the service, when I asked the schoolteacher about her prayer, she gave me the following text she had composed and written on a card she held in her hand during the prayer:

> Kind heavenly Father, we thank thee for watching over us through the night.
> We thank thee for thy guidance, kind heavenly Father, for your strong protection.
> We pray that you will be with us, Lord, be with our families, young and old, near and far.
> Lead us not into temptation, Lord. Make us strong and ever mindful of your gifts to us all. Amen.

A comparison of the oral and the written prayer indicates numerous differences, but the major ones are of four types.

Use of formulaic vocatives. *Oh Lord, kind heavenly Father,* and *Jesus* appear again and again in the prayer once the woman has left the printed text. In the written text, all but the final sentence contains such a vocative, but in the oral text, there are often two per sentence. In descriptions of folk sermons, such vocatives are said to be pauses in which the preacher collects his thoughts for the next passage (Rosenberg, 1970). Here, however, the thoughts have been collected, in that the entire text was written out before delivery, but the speaker continues to use these vocatives and to pause after these before moving on to another plea.

Expression of personal involvement. Throughout the written version, the woman uses *we,* but in the expanded oral version, she shifts from *we* to *I,* and uses *my* and *me* where the plural might have been used had she continued the pattern from the written version. She shifts in line 10 to a singular plea, speaking as the weak sinner, the easily tempted, and praying for continued strength and readiness to being helped by her Lord. The written prayer simply asks for guidance, (orally stated as *'leadin''* and *'guidin''*) strong protection ('strong-arm protection' and 'protector' in the oral version). The plea that the sinner not be faced with temptation is expressed in the written version in a familiar phrase from the Lord's Prayer, and is followed by a formulaic expression often used in ministers' prayers Make us ever mindful of. . .At line 22, she stops using *thee, thy,* and *thou,* archaic personal pronouns; thereafter she uses second person singular *you.*

Expression in a wide variety of sentence structures. The written version uses simple sentences throughout, varying the style with insertion of vocatives, and repetitions of paired adjectives ('young and old', 'near and far'). The spoken version includes compound-complex sentences with subordination, and repetition of simple sentences with variation (e.g., 'I can call on 'im'. . .). There are several incomplete sentences in the spoken version (line 16–18), which if completed would have been complex in structure.

Use of informal style and Black English vernacular forms. The opening of the spoken version and the written version uses standard English forms, and the first suggestion of informality comes with the dropping of the *g* in line 4. As the prayer progresses, however, several informal forms and features associated with the Black English vernacular are used: *'long(* = along), childrens, *'im(* = him), anytime *o'day, he'p(* = help), *'signed(* = assigned), omission of *there* (in lines 36, 37) and use of *it* for standard English in line 38, double negative (lines 36, 37, 38, 40), *cain't(* = can't), and *mo'(* = more).

There is no way to render the shifts of prosody, the melodic strains, and the changes in pace which accompany the spoken version. The intonation pattern is highly marked, lilting, and the speaker breaks into actual melody at the end of line 10, and the remainder of the prayer is chanted. (Note that at this point she also shifted to the singular first person pronoun.) Sharp pitch modulations mark the prayer, and on one occasion (end of line 35), a member of the congregation broke in with a supporting bar of the melody, lasting only 3.5 seconds). All vocatives after line 6 are marked by a lilting high rise-mid fall contour.

It is possible to find in numerous studies of the religious life of Afro-Americans lengthy discussions of the historical role of the spoken word (see, for example, Levine, 1977:155ff for a discussion of literacy and its effects on Black religion). Current research with preachers (e.g. Mitchell, 1970; Rosenberg, 1970) and gospel songwriters (e.g. Jackson, 1966; Heilbut, 1971) in Black communities underscore and pick up numerous themes from historical studies. Repeatedly these sources emphasize the power of words as action and the substantiating effect a dynamic creative oral rendering of a message has on an audience. Preachers and musicians claim they cannot stick to a stable rendering of written words; thoughts which were once shaped into words on paper become recomposed in each time and space; written words limit a performance which must be created anew with each audience and setting. Though some of the meaning in written words remains stable, bound in the text, the meaning of words people will carry with them depends on the integration of those words into personal experience. Thus the performance of words demands the calling in of the personal experience of each listener and the extension by that listener of the meanings of those words to achieve the ultimate possibility of any message.

In terms of the usual expectations of distinctions between the oral and literate mode, practices in the church life of Trackton residents provide evidence that neither mode is in control here. Members have access to both and use both. Oral spontaneous adjustments from the written material result in longer, more complex sentences, with some accompanying shifts in style from the formal to the more informal. Clearly in the oral mode, the highly personalized first person singular dominates over the more formal collective first person. Pacing, rate of speech, intonation, pitch, use of melodic phrases, and finally a chant, have much fluctuation and range from high to low when written materials are recomposed spontaneously. Spoken versions of hymns, prayers, and sermons show the speaker's attempt to identify with the audience, but this identification makes use of only some features usually associated with the oral tradition (e.g. high degree of involvement of speaker, extensive use of first person). Other features associated with oral performance (e.g. simple sentences linked together by simple compounds, and highly redundant formulaic passages which hold chunks of information together) are not found here. The use of literate sources, and even literate bases, for oral performances does not lead to a demise of many features traditionally associated with a pure oral tradition. In other words, the language forms and uses on such occasions bear the mark of both oral and literate traditions, not one or the other.

At Work

In their daily lives at home and in church, Trackton adults and children have worked out ways of integrating features of both oral and written language in their language uses. But what of work settings and contacts with banks, credit offices, and the employment office—institutions typical of modernized, industrial societies?

Most of the adults in Trackton worked in the local textile mills. To obtain these jobs, they went directly to the employment office of the individual mills. There, an employment officer read to them from an application form and wrote down their answers. They were not asked if they wanted to complete their own form. They were given no written information at the time of their application, but the windows and walls of the room in which they waited for personal interviews were plastered with posters about the credit union policy of the plant and the required information for filling out an application (names of previous employers, Social Security number, etc.). But all of this information was known to Trackton residents before they went to apply for a job. Such information and news about jobs usually passed by word of mouth. Some of the smaller mills put advertisements in the local paper and indicated they would accept applications during certain hours on particular days. Interviewers either told individuals at the time of application they had obtained jobs, or the employment officer agreed to telephone in a few days. If applicants did not have telephones, they gave a neighbor's number, or the mill sent a postcard.

Once accepted for the job, totally inexperienced workers would be put in the particular section of the mill in which they were to work, and were told to watch experienced workers. The foreman would occasionally check by to see if the observer had questions and understood what was going on. Usually before the end of the first few hours on the shift, the new worker was put under the guidance of certain other workers and told to share work on a particular machine. Thus in an apprentice-like way new workers came on for new jobs, and they worked in this way for only several days, since all parties were anxious for this arrangement to end as soon as possible. Mills paid in part on a piece-work basis, and each machine operator was anxious to be freed to work at his or her own rapid pace as soon as possible. Similarly, the new worker was anxious to begin to be able to work rapidly enough to qualify for extra pay.

Within each section of the mill, little written material was in evidence. Safety records, warnings, and, occasionally, reports about new products, or clippings from local newspapers about individual workers or events at the mill's recreational complex, would be put up on the bulletin board. Foremen and quality control personnel came through the mill on each shift, asking questions, noting output, checking machines, and recording this information. They often asked the workers questions, and the information would be recorded on a form carried by the foreman or quality control engineer. Paychecks were issued each Friday, and the stub carried information on Federal and state taxes withheld, as well as payments for health plans or automatic payments made for credit loans from the credit bureau. Millworkers generally kept these stubs in their wallets, or in a special box (often a shoe box, sometimes a small metal filebox) at home. They were rarely referred to at the time of issuance of the paycheck, unless a recent loan had been taken out or paid off at the credit bureau. Then workers would check the accuracy of the amounts withheld. In both the application stage and on the job, workers had to respond to a report or a form being filled out by someone else. This passive performance with respect to any actual reading or writing did not occur because the workers were unable to read and write. Instead, these procedures were the results of the mill's efforts to standardize the recording and processing of information. When asked why they did not let applicants fill out their own employment form, employment officers responded:

> It is easier if we do it. This way, we get to talk to the client, ask questions not on the form, clarify immediately any questions they have, and, for our purposes, the whole thing is just cleaner. When we used to have them fill out the forms, some did it in pencil, others had terrible handwriting, others gave us too much or too little information. This way, our records are neat, and we know what we've got when someone has finished an application form.

In the past, job training at some of the mills had not been done 'on the floor', but through a short session with manuals, an instructor, and instruction 'by the book'. Executives of the mills found this process too costly and inefficient, and those who could do the best job of handling the written materials were not necessarily the best workers on the line.

Beyond the mill, Trackton adults found in banks, credit union offices, and loan offices the same type of literacy events. The oral performance surrounding a written piece of material to which they had little or no access was what counted or made a difference in a transaction. When individuals applied for credit at the credit union, the interviewer held the folder, asked questions derived from information within the folder, and offered little or no explanation of the information from which he derived questions. At the end of interviews, workers did not know whether or not they would receive the loan or what would be done with the information given to the person who interviewed them. In the following interview (see figure 1), the credit union official directs questions to the client primarily on the basis of what is in the written documents in the client's folder.[2] She attempts to reconcile the written information with the current oral request. However, the client is repeatedly asked to supply information as though she knows the contents of the written document. Referents for pronouns (*it* in 4, *this* in 7, *this* in 10, and *they* in 16) are not clearly identified, and the client must guess at their referents without any visual or verbal clues. Throughout this literacy event, only one person has access to the written information, but the entire oral exchange centers around that information. In (4) the credit union employee introduces new information: *it* refers to the amount of the current loan. The record now shows that the client has a loan which is being repaid by having a certain amount deducted from her weekly paycheck; for those in her salary range, there is an upper limit of $1700 for a loan.

But this information is not clear from the oral exchange, and it is known only to the credit union employee and indicated on documents in the client's folder. The calculation of a payment of $50 per month (10) is based on this information, and the way in which this figure was derived is never explained to the client. In (10) the official continues to read from the folder, but she does not ask for either confirmation or denial of this information. Her ambiguous statement, 'We're gonna combine this', can only be assumed to mean the current amount of the load with the amount of the new loan, the two figures which will now equal the total of the new principal $1700. The statement of gross weekly salary as $146.66 is corrected by the client (11), but the official does not verbally acknowledge the correction; she continues writing. Whether she records the new figure and takes it into account in her calculations is not clear. The official continues reading (12) and is once again corrected by the client. She notes the new information and shortly closes off the interview.

In this literacy event, written materials have determined the outcome of the request, yet the client has not been able to see those documents or frame questions which would clarify their contents. This pattern occurred frequently for Trackton residents, who argued that neighborhood center programs and other adult education programs should be aimed not at teaching higher level reading skills or other subjects, but at ways of getting through such interviews or other situations (such as visits to dentists and doctors), when someone else held the information which they needed to know in order to ask questions about the contents of that written material in ways which would be acceptable to institution officials.

---

[2]This transcript was first included in Heath, 1979, a report on several types of literacy events in the work settings of Trackton residents. In these events, neither customarily expected literacy behaviors nor general conversational rules were followed.

A-CU5 Heath 1979
C1: Client
Off: Credit Union Official
(enters office where client is seated)

(1) Off: okay, hh, what kind of a loan did your ⌐hh wanna see about now?
                                          (pause)

(2) C1:   ⌐ well, hh, I wanna   wanted it for my hhh personal reserve.
              (exits)

(3) Off: let me get your folder. I'll be right back.
    (reenters)   (looking at folder)

(4)   and you want to increase it to seventeen.
    (looking toward client)

(5)   and your purpose?
               (pause)

(6) C1: I hhh need a personal   uh, I got some small bills.

Total units of discourse: 16
4 elicitations directed to C1, 4 responses by C1
4 utterances directed to folder by Off
2 responses by C1 to folder information
2 announcements of exits by Off

(7) Off: because when I did this, I, hhh, didn't know, but you were telling me both had to sign.

(looking at client)

(8) what kind of bills?

(9) C1: water, gas, clothes, hhh, water department.

(flips through folder, writing figures on pad)

(10) Off: okay, now you're paying fifty a month, and you want, you, hhh, ummmmm
you want your payments to stay at that, okay, you live at 847 J. O. Connell,

(pause)

and you've been there three years, okay   um, let's see, we're gonna combine this,
gross weekly salary is $146 ⎡46, forty-hour week
                           ⎣no, about $170

(11) C1:   (pause)

(looking at folder)

(12) Off: you don't have a car and your rent is $120, and you still owe Sears, hhh   it's twenty=

(13) C1: =no, it's more than that=

(looking at client)

(14) Off: =what is it now?

(15) C1: I think it's about $180 ⎡some

(16) Off: ⎣is that everything, yea, all we've got to do is apply to the credit bureau,
they decide, you can come back tomorrow.

FIGURE 1

109

CONCLUSIONS

Trackton is a literate community in the sense that the residents are able to read printed and written materials in their daily lives, and on occasion they produce written messages as part of the total pattern of communication in the community. Residents turn from written to spoken uses of language and vice versa as the occasion demands, and the two modes of expression seem to supplement and reinforce each other in a unique pattern. However, the conventions appropriate for literacy events within the community, in their worship life, and in their workaday world call for different uses of speech to interpret written materials. In a majority of cases, Trackton adults show their knowledge of written materials only through oral means. On many occasions, they have no opportunity to attend directly to the written materials through any active use of their own literacy skills; instead, they must respond in appropriate speech events which are expected to surround interpretation of these written materials.

It is impossible to characterize Trackton through existing descriptions of either the oral or the literate traditions; seemingly, it is neither, and it is both. Literacy events which bring the written word into a central focus in interactions and interpretations have their rules of occurrence and appropriateness according to setting and participants. The joint social activity of reading the newspaper across porches, getting to the heart of meaning of a brochure on a new product, and negotiating rules for putting an antenna on a car produce more speaking than reading, more group than individual effort, repeated analogies and generalizations, and fast-paced, overlapping syntactically complex language. The spontaneous recomposing of written hymns, sermons, and prayers produces not parables, proverbs, and formulas, but re-creations of written texts which are more complex in syntactic structure, performance rules, and more demanding of close attention to lexical and semantic cues, than are their written counterparts. For these recomposing creations are, like community literacy events, group-focused, and members of the group show their understanding and acceptance of the meaning of the words by picking up phrases, single words, or meanings, and creating their own contribution to a raised hymn or a prayer.

In work settings, when others control access to and restrict types of written information, Trackton residents have to learn to respond to inadequate meaning clues, partial sentences, and pronouns without specified referents. In these latter situations, especially those in financial and legal institutions, Trackton residents recognize their deficiency of skills, but the skills which are missing are not literacy skills, but knowledge about oral language uses which would enable them to obtain information about the content and uses of written documents, and to ask questions to clarify their meanings. Learning how to do this appropriately, so as not to seem to challenge a person in power, is often critical to obtaining a desired outcome and maintaining a job or reputation as a 'satisfactory' applicant, or worker.[3]

Descriptions of these literacy events and their patterns of uses in Trackton do not enable us to place the community somewhere on a continuum from full literacy to restricted literacy or non-literacy. Instead, it seems more appropriate to think of two continua, the oral and the written. Their points and extent of overlap, and similarities in structure and function, follow one pattern for Trackton, but follow others for communities with different cultural features. And it is perhaps disquieting to think that many of these cultural features seem totally unrelated to features usually thought to help account for the relative degree of literacy in any social group. For example, such seemingly unrelated phenomena as the use of space in the community and the ways in which adults relate to preschool children may be as important for instilling literacy habits as aspirations for upward mobility or curiosity about the world. In Trackton, given the uses of space and the ways in which adults interacted with preschool children, no amount of books suddenly poured into the community, or public service programs teaching parents how to help their children learn to read, would have made an appreciable difference. The linkage between houses by open porches, the preference of young and old to be outdoors rather than inside, the incorporation of all the community in the communication network of each household, and the negative value placed on individual reading, reinforced the social group's negotiation of written language. Formal writing always had to be renegotiated into an informal style, one which led to discussion and debate among several people. Written messages gave residents something to talk about; after they talked, they might or might not follow up on the message of the written information, but what they had come to know had come to them from the text through the joint oral negotiation of meaning.

Trackton children do not learn to talk by being introduced to labels for either everyday objects or pictures and words in books. Instead, without adjusted, simplified input from adults, they become early talkers, modeling their ways of entering discourse and creating story texts on the oral language they hear about them. They tell creative story-poems which attempt to recapture the settings of actions as well as the portrayal of actions. They achieve their meaning as communicators and their sense of their own worth as communicators through the responses they obtain to their oral language, not in terms of responses in a one-to-one situation of reading a book with an adult. Words indeed must be as

---

[3]Current work by linguists, sociologists, and anthropologists in medical, legal, and business settings repeatedly emphasizes the hazards of inappropriate behavior in these situations. See, for example, Cicourel, 1981, for a survey of research in medical settings; O'Barr, 1981, for a similar overview of legal studies. Gumperz, 1976, 1977, and to appear, and Gumperz and Cook-Gumperz, 1981, provide numerous theoretical and methodological perspectives on interethnic communication in professional contexts.

'behavioral' as any other form of action (Carothers, 1959). They carry personal qualities, have a dynamic nature, and cannot become static things always retaining their same sense. As one mother said of her ways of teaching her two-year old son to talk: Ain't no use me tellin' 'im: "learn this, learn that, what's this, what's that?" He just gotta learn, gotta know; he see one thing one place one time, he know how it go, see sump'n like it again, maybe it be the same, maybe it won't. In each new situation, learning must be reevaluated, reassessed for both the essence of meaning that occurs across contexts and for the particular meaning obtained in each new and different context.

What does this mean for the individual readers in Trackton? How different is their way of comprehending literate materials from that more commonly ascribed to literate individuals? For example, current research in reading suggests three ways or levels of extracting meaning from print: attending to the text itself, bringing in experiences or knowledge related to the text, and interpreting beyond the text into a creative/imaginative realm or to achieve a new synthesis of information from the text and reader experience (see Rumelhart, 1976; Rumelhart & Ortony, 1977; Adams, 1980 for technical discusssions of these processes). Trackton residents as a group do use these methods of getting information from print. One person, reading aloud, decodes the written text of the newspaper, brochure, set of instructions, etc. This level of extracting meaning from the text is taken as the basis for the move to the next level, that of relating the text's meaning to the experience of members of the group. The experience of any one individual has to become common to the group, however, and that is done through the recounting of members' experiences. Such recountings attempt to recreate the scenes, to establish the character of the individuals involved, and, to the greatest extent possible, to bring the audience into the experience itself. At the third level, there is an extension beyond the common experience to a reintegration. For example, what do both the text and the common relating of text's meaning to experience say to the mother trying to decide how best to register her child for a daycare program? Together again, the group negotiates this third level. The process is time-consuming, perhaps less efficient than one individual reading the information for himself and making an individual decision. But the end result has been the sharing of information (next year's mother receiving a similar form will hear this discussion re-created in part). Furthermore, the set of experiences related to the task at hand is greater than a single individual would have: the mother has been led to consider whether or not to enlist the doctor's help, which information to take for registration, and a host of other courses of action she might not have considered on her own. Thus Trackton residents in groups, young and old, are familiar with processes for comprehending text similar to those delineated for individual readers by reading teachers and researchers. Major differences between their experiences with literacy and those generally depicted in the mainstream literature are in the degree of focus on specific decoding skills (such as letter-sound relationships), the amount of practice at each level of extracting meaning available for each individual in the community, and the assignment of interpretive responsibility to the group rather than to any one individual.

There are still other questions which could be asked of the uses of oral and literate skills in Trackton. What of the social consequences of their uses of literacy? Because they do not frequently and intensively engage in reading and writing extended prose, is their literacy 'restricted', and what has this meant for them in socioeconomic terms? Work in the textile mills provided an income equal to or better than that of several types of professionals in the region: schoolteachers, salesmen, and secretaries. Successful completion of composition and advanced grammar classes in high school would not have secured better paying jobs for Trackton residents, unless very exceptional circumstances had come into play in individual cases. Improved scores on tests of reading comprehension or the Scholastic Aptitude Tests would not necessarily have given them access to more information for political decision-making than they had through the oral medium of several evening and morning television and radio news broadcasts. They tended to make their political judgments for local elections on the basis of personal knowledge of candidates or the word of someone else who knew the candidates. In national and state elections, almost all voted the party, and they said no amount of information on the individual candidates would cause them to change that pattern.

These behaviors and responses to what Goody might term 'restricted literacy' echo similar findings in the work of social historians asking hard questions about the impact of literacy on pre-industrial groups. For such diverse groups as the masses of seventeenth-century France (Davis, 1975), sixteenth and seventeenth-century England (Cressy, 1980), and colonial New England (Lockridge, 1974), social historians have examined the functions, uses, degrees, and effects of literacy. All agree that the contexts and uses of literacy in each society determined its values, forms, and functions. The societal changes which came with the advent of literacy across societies were neither consistent nor universal. Cressy (1980) perhaps best summarizes the conclusions of social historians about the universal potentialities of literacy:

1) People could be rational, acquire and comprehend information, and make well-founded political, social, and religious decisions without being able to read or write.
2) Literate people were no wiser or better able to control their universe than were those who were illiterate.

In short, in a variety of times and places, 'Literacy unlocked a variety of doors, but it did not necessarily secure admission' (Cressy, 1980:189).

Cressy and other social historians underscore the fact that, in some societies, literacy did not have the beneficial effects often ascribed to it. Davis found that, for the unlettered masses of seventeenth century France, printing made possible new kinds of control from the top segments of the society. Before the printing press, oral culture and popular community-based social organizations seemed strong enough to resist standardization and thrusts for uniformity. With literacy, however, people began to measure themselves against a widespread norm and to doubt their own worth. In some cases, this attitude made people less politically active than they had been without print or opportunities for literacy. Lockridge (1974), in his study of colonial New England, concluded that literacy did not bring new attitudes or move people away from the traditional views held in their illiterate days. Eisenstein (1979) suggested that shifts in religious traditions enabled print to contribute to the creation of new notions of a collective morality and to an increased reliance on rhetoric in the verbal discourse of sermons and homiletics.

But these are studies of pre-industrial societies; what of literacy in industrial societies? Stone (1969) proposed the need to examine in industrial groups the FUNCTIONS of literacy in a variety of senses ranging from the conferring of technical skills to an association with self-discipline. Stone further suggested that each society may well have its own weighted checklist of factors (e.g. social stratification, job opportunities, Protestantism, and sectarian competition) which causes literacy to serve one or another function. Sanderson (1972), building on Stone's work, showed that the economic development of the English industrial revolution made low literacy demands of the educational system. His argument points out the need to examine closely job demands for literacy; changes in mechanization may call for shifts of types of literacy skills. Indeed, in the English industrial revolution, the increased use of machinery enabled employers to hire workers who were less literate than were those who had previously done the hand work. Successful performance in cottage industries, for example, required a higher level of literacy for a larger proportion of workers than did mechanized textile work.

Research by economic and educational historians of the late nineteenth century United States has examined the effects of literacy not only on the economic laws of supply and demand of job opportunities, but also on the values society placed on a correct oral reading style and acceptable performance on standardized tests. Reading for comprehension and an expansion of creative thinking were less frequently assessed in the late nineteenth century than they had been earlier (Calhoun, 1973). Soltow and Stevens (1977) point out the extent to which standardized measures of performance were lauded by parents, and they suggest that acceptable performance on these tests convinced parents their children would be able to achieve occupational and social mobility. Whether or not the schools taught children to read at skill levels that might make a real difference in their chances for upward occupational mobility is not at all clear. Nevertheless, if students acquired the social and moral values and generalized 'rational' and 'cultured' behaviors associated with literate citizens, occupational mobility often resulted.

This social historical research raises some critical questions for the study of communities in today's complex society. A majority of communities in the modern world are neither preliterate, i.e. without access to print or writing of some kind, nor fully literate (Goody, 1968). They are somewhere inbetween. Some individuals may have access to literacy and choose to use it for some purposes and not for others. Some communities may restrict access to literacy to some portions of the population (Walker, 1981); others may provide a climate in which individuals choose the extent to which they will adopt habits associated with literacy (Heath, 1980). As Resnick and Resnick (1977) have shown, the goal of a h igh level of literacy for a large proportion of the population is a relatively recent phenomenon, and new methods and materials in reading instruction, as well as particular societal and economic supports, may be needed to achieve such a goal.

Furthermore, in large complex societies such as the United States, the national state of technological development and the extent of intrusion of governmental agencies in the daily lives of citizens may have combined to set up conditions in which literacy no longer has many of the traditional uses associated with it. Understanding and responding to the myriad of applications, reporting forms, and accounting procedures which daily affect the lives of nearly every family in the United States bears little resemblance to the decoding of extended prose passages or production of expository writing, the two literacy achievements most associated with school success. Furthermore, television and other media have removed the need to rely on reading to learn the basics of news and sports events, how to dress properly for the weather, and what to buy and where to find it. Increasingly industry is turning to on-the-job training programs which depend on observation of tasks or audio-visual instruction rather than literate preparation for job performance; specialists handle reports related to production, quality control, inventory, and safety. In industry, the specialized demands of reporting forms, regulations and agency reports, and programming requirements call for a communications expert, not simply a 'literate' manager. In a recent survey of employer attitudes toward potential employees, employers called not for the literacy skills generally associated with school tasks, but instead for an integration of mathematical and linguistic skills, and displays of the capability of learning 'on one's own', and listening and speaking skills required to understand and give instructions and describe problems (RBS, 1978).

These shifts in larger societal contexts for literacy are easily and frequently talked about, but their specific effects on communities such as Trackton, though occasionally inferred, are very rarely examined. It is clear that, in what may be referred to as the post-industrial age, members of each community have different and varying patterns of influence and control over forms and uses of literacy in their lives. They exercise considerable control within their own primary networks. In institutions, such as their churches, they may have some control. In other institutions, such as in their places of employment, banks, legal offices, etc., they may have no control over literacy demands. The shape of literacy events in each of these is different. The nature of oral and written language and the interplay between them is ever-shifting, and these changes both respond to and create shifts in the individual and societal meanings of literacy. The information to be gained from any prolonged look at oral and written uses of language through literacy events may enable us to accept the protean shapes of oral and literate traditions and language, and move us away from current tendencies to classify communities as being at one or another point along a hypothetical continuum which has no societal reality.

REFERENCES

ADAMS, M. J. Failures to Comprehend and Levels of Processing in Reading, *In* Theoretical Issues in Reading Comprehension, R. J. Spiro, B. C. Bruce, and W. F. Brewer, eds. Hillsdale, N.J.: Erlbaum, 1980

ANDERSON, ALONZO B., WILLIAM B. TEALE, AND ELETTE ESTRADA 1980 Low-income Children's Preschool Literacy Experiences: Some naturalistic observations. The Quarterly Newsletter of the Laboratory of Comparative Human Cognition 2.3:59—65.

BARON, NAOMI 1979 Independence and Interdependence in Spoken and Written Language. Visible Language. 1.1.

BOURDIEU, PIERRE 1967 Systems of Education and Systems of Thought. International Social Science Journal 19.3:338—58.

CALHOUN, DANIEL 1973 The Intelligence of a People. Princeton, N.J.: Princeton University Press.

CAROTHERS, J. C. 1959 Culture, Psychiatry, and the Written Word. Psychiatry 307-20.

CICOUREL, AARON V. 1981 Language and Medicine. *In* Language in the USA. Charles A. Ferguson and Shirley Brice Heath, eds. Cambridge: Cambridge University Press.

CRESSY, DAVID 1980 Literacy and the Social Order: Reading and writing in Tudor and Stuart England. Cambridge: Cambridge University Press.

DAVIS, NATALIE 1975 Printing and the People. *In* Society and Culture in Early Modern France. Stanford, CA: Stanford University Press.

DODD, C. H. 1961 The Parables of the Kingdom. New York: Charles Scribner's Sons.

EISENSTEIN, ELIZABETH L. 1979 The Printing Press as an Agent of Change. 2 Vols. Cambridge: Cambridge University Press.

GOODY, JACK, ED. 1968 Literacy in Traditional Societies. Cambridge: Cambridge University Press.

GOODY, JACK AND IAN WATT 1963 The Consequences of Literacy. Comparative Studies in Society and History 5:304–45.

GUMPERZ, JOHN J. 1976 Language, Communication, and Public Negotiation. *In* Anthropology and the Public Interest: Fieldwork and theory. P. Sanday, ed. New York: Academic Press.

———. 1977 Sociocultural Knowledge in Conversational Inference. *In* Georgetown Round Table on Languages and Linguistics 1977. M. Saville-Troike,ed. Washington, D. C., Georgetown University Press.

———. To appear Conversational Strategies.

GUMPERZ, JOHN J. AND JENNY COOK-GUMPERZ 1981 Ethnic Differences in Communicative Style. *In* Language in the USA. Charles A. Ferguson and Shirley Brice Heath, eds. Cambridge: Cambridge University Press.

HALL, OSWALD AND RICHARD CARLTON 1977 Basic Skills at School and Work: The study of Albertown, an Ontario community. Toronto, Ontario: Ontario Economic Council.

HAVELOCK, ERIC 1963 Preface to Plato. Cambridge, MA: Harvard University Press.

———. 1976 Origins of Western Literacy. Toronto: Ontario Institute for Studies in Education.

HEATH, SHIRLEY BRICE 1978 Outline Guide for the Ethnographic Study of Literacy and Oral Language from Schools to Communities. Philadelphia: Graduate School of Education.

————. 1979 Language Beyond the Classroom. Paper prepared for the Delaware Symposium on Language Studies, University of Delaware.

————. 1980 The Functions and Uses of Literacy. Journal of Communication 29.2:123–33.

————. 1982 What No Bedtime Story Means: Narrative skills at home and school. Language in Society 11.1.

————. Forthcoming Ways with Words: Ethnography of Communication in Communities to Classrooms.

HYMES, DELL H. 1972 Models of the Interaction of Language and Social Life. *In* Directions in Sociolinguistics. John J. Gumperz and Dell Hymes, eds. New York: Holt, Rinehart and Winston.

JACKSON, MAHALIA 1966 Movin' On Up. New York: Random House.

KROEBER, ALFRED 1948 Anthropology, New York: Harcourt, Brace.

LEVINE, LAWRENCE W. 1977 Black Culture and Black Consciousness: Afro-American folk thought from slavery to freedom. New York: Oxford University Press.

KOCKRIDGE, KENNETH A. 1974 Literacy in Colonial New England. New York: Norton.

LORD, ALBERT B. 1965 The Singer of Tales. Cambridge, MA: Harvard University Press.

MITCHELL, HENRY H. 1970 Black Preaching. Philadelphia: Lippincott.

O'BARR, WILLIAM M. 1981 The Language of the Law. In Language in the USA. Charles A. Ferguson and Shirley Brice Heath, eds. Cambridge: Cambridge University Press.

OLSON, DAVID 1977 From Utterance to Text: The bias of language in speech and writing. Harvard Educational Review 47.3:257–81.

ONG, WALTER 1967 The Presence of the Word. New Haven: Yale University Press.

RESEARCH FOR BETTER SCHOOLS 1978 Employer Attitudes toward the Preparation of Youth for Work. Philadelphia: Research for Better Schools.

RESNICK, DANIEL P. AND LAUREAN B. RESNICK 1977 The Nature of Literacy: A historical exploration. Harvard Educational Review 43: 370–85.

ROSENBERG, BRUCE A. 1970 The Art of the American Folk Preacher. New York: Oxford University Press.

RUMELHART, D. E. 1976 Toward an Interactive Model of Reading (Technical Report; 56) Center of Human Information Processing, University of California, San Diego.

RUMELHART, D. AND A. ORTONY 1977 The Representation of Knowledge in Memory. *In* Schooling and the Acquisition of Knowledge. R. C. Anderson, R. J. Spiro, and W. E. Montague, eds. Hillsdale, N.J.: Erlbaum Associates.

SANDERSON, MICHAEL 1972 Literacy and Social Mobility in the Industrial Revolution in England. Past and Present 56:75–103.

SCOLLON, RON AND SUZANNE B. K. SCOLLON 1981 Narrative, Literacy, and Face in Interethnic Communication. Norwood, N.J.: Ablex.

SCOLTOW, LEE AND EDWARD STEVENS 1977 Economic Aspects of School Participation in Mid-nineteenth-century United States. Journal of Interdisciplinary History 7:221–43.

STAIGER, RALPH C. 1979 Motivation for Reading: An international bibliography. *In* Roads to Reading. Ralph C. Staiger, ed. Paris: UNESCO.

STONE, LAWRENCE 1969 Literacy and Education in England, 1640–1900. Past and Present 42:70–139.

WALKER, WILLARD 1981 Native Writing Systems. *In* Language in the USA. Charles A. Ferguson and Shirley Brice Heath, eds. Cambridge: Cambridge University Press.

7 Colloquial and Literary Uses of Inversions*

Georgia M. Green
University of Illinois

Inversion constructions such as those in (1) and (2) have been largely neglected in the recent study of English syntax, with the conspicuous exception of some descriptive Scandinavian studies, and scattered remarks in the transformational literature.

(1a)   Here comes the bus.

(1b)   Was he mad!

(1c)   So does Chomsky.

(2a)   'It's just the same old wolf at the door,' said Mary, soberly. (TLCC:84)[1]

(2b)   Such is the terrible man against whom Peter Pan is pitted. (PP:72)

(2c)   No man, be he good or bad, can make his memoirs unfailingly interesting without embroidering the facts.

Apparently the assumption has been that inversions are all 'literary', and, therefore, not a part of ''real language'' like comparatives or relative clauses, and thus of no particular interest to a descriptive linguistics with universal aspirations.

---

*I am grateful to Margi Laff for helping to track down misplaced and vague references for a number of examples, and to Prof. Ladislav Zgusta for comments.

*This work was supported by the National Institute of Education under Contract No. US-NIE-C-400-76-0116

[1]Source citations are given in parentheses after cited examples. A list of abbreviations used follows the bibliographical references.

One of my main intentions here is to show that the first premise in this argument is false—several inversions are basically colloquial in character, and not a few more may be used in a literary style of speech. I will take pains along the way to show that it is not on the basis of spoken versus written language that speakers discriminate contexts for inversions, but on the basis of colloquial versus literary language, a related, but by no means isomorphous, distinction. In addition, this study may be taken to indicate that the ordinary monolingual native speaker, in knowing what kinds of literary inversions can be used in colloquial language, and when, and vice versa, demonstrates a considerable knowledge of code-switching.

Although the title appears to be perfectly straightforward and descriptive, I will begin by explaining it, and attempting to relate this work to previous work on functions of inverted constructions. The third section discusses the sources for the inversions used here to exemplify the classes of constructions whose use is at issue. The two small sets of inversions that are characteristically found in literary and conversational discourse will be described in the fourth and fifth sections, respectively. Inversions after preposed comparative constructions (e.g. *so, such*); direct quotations; positive frequency, degree, and manner adverbs; and abstract prepositional phrases (e.g. *At issue*) are found to be characteristically literary inversions, while inversions after negated verbs, after a restricted class of constructions including *Here comes*, after pronominal *so* and *neither*, and in exclamations are shown to be basically colloquial constructions. The sixth section will be devoted to the larger set of inversions which, while characteristic of either literary writing or conversational speech, may also be found in literary speech or colloquial writing, respectively. The inversions that occur after *nor* and preposed negative adverbs; in *if*- less conditionals; after preposed adjective phrases, and locative and directional prepositional phrases; and after participial phrases are found in literary speech as well as in writing, and those that occur after preposed negated noun phrases (e.g. *not a N*), in a comparative temporal construction (e.g. *No sooner. . .than. . .*), after temporal adverbs and prepositional phrases, and after preposed directional adverbs, are as characteristic of colloquial writing as they are of speech. In the last section, I attempt to account for the colloquial or literary nature of the various inversions. Some inversions are argued to be basically literary (or colloquial) for reasons having to do with the discourse functions that the construction serves, supports, or presupposes. Others seem to have the distribution that they have as a function of the distribution of crucial components. Still others apparently are simply conventionally literary (or colloquial).

I. SCOPE OF THE DISCUSSION

By inversion, I mean simply those declarative constructions where the subject follows part or all of its verb phrase. However, to limit the scope of this discussion, I will not be treating presentational or existential *there*-constructions (Aissen, 1975; Bolinger, 1977) or inversion in yes-no questions. I will be distinguishing in this work between inversions like those in (1) and (2) as colloquial and literary, respectively.

On first glance the difference may seem to be one of oral versus written—that the constructions in (1) are characteristic of speech, while those in (2) are limited to written discourse. But, on reflection, that is clearly not true. The sentence in (1b) might occur in a novel or a short story, and (1c) might easily be found in an essay or even a scholarly article. The difference is not that of informal versus formal either, if formal is taken in the sense of 'rigidly prescribed, for ritual use', for there is nothing particularly formal about (2a). It happens to be an example of a formula that is simply, by cultural custom, restricted to literary narratives, just as constructions like (3) are formulae restricted to legislative contexts.

(3)   Be it resolved that copies of this resolution be sent to Professor Bardeen and Representative Satterthwaite.

Example (2a) is so far from being formal that it would sound very out of place indeed in a sermon or a commencement address or a scholarly article, if it were not in an anecdote being recounted for some rhetorical effect. The difference is not that of (relatively) unplanned versus (relatively) planned discourse (contra Ochs, 1979), for ALL DISCOURSE (with the possible exception of utterances like *Ow!* and *Oh, hell!*) must be considered to be planned if we are to account for the fact that the speaker must have had to make constituent order, construction type, and lexical CHOICES (Green, in press) to have expressed what she expressed the way she expressed it, no matter how elegantly or inarticulately. The alternative, saying that some discourse is unplanned, is a deterministic, behavioristic view of speech production which would fail entirely to account for the phenomena of revisions and hesitations. In any case, (2a) is surely as nearly an automatic choice for the novelist as (1a) or (1b) is for the conversationalist in the street.

One may, of course, question whether the sets in (1) and (2) constitute natural classes, but because the constructions in (1) seem so characteristic of conversation, and those in (2) so characteristic of certain literary genres, I will proceed on the assumption that they do, and will refer to those in (1) as colloquial, because they are typically found in conversational discourse or discourse that is AS IF conversational, such as letters and other first-person narratives, stream-of-consciousness style, and style indirect libre (cf. Banfield, 1973). Those inversions in (2) I will refer to as literary, because, if not confined to literary prose, they are characteristic of it, and are apparently used in conversation only when the intent is to sound literary.

II. PREVIOUS RESEARCH

Most of the published research on the use of inversions has been historically oriented and/or primarily taxonomic (e.g. Visser, 1963; Jacobsson, 1951). Fowler (1923) is also a taxonomy, with prescriptive notes on usage. Jacobsson and

Fowler, and also Hartvigson and Jakobsen (1974), are function-based taxonomies, and all or most of the examples are drawn from cited texts. (Fowler is the only native speaker of English, and the only one to devise additional examples). The taxonomies are based partly on syntactic structure and presumed derivation, and partly on discourse functions perceived by the researchers, but none of the examples are cited in context, nor are the contexts referred to. Writers on the syntax of inversion (e.g. Emonds, 1971, 1976; Green, 1976, 1977) have used constructed examples almost entirely, for justifiable reasons, although a look at examples collected from texts might have prevented a few of the more extreme claims that have been made, for example, that they do not occur in embedded clauses (Emonds, 1971).

Gary (1975) and Green (1980) attempt to provide evidence and explanation for certain claimed functions of inversions, though both are somewhat limited in scope. Green (1980), taking off from the exploratory work of Gary, discusses five or so distinct communicative goals served by a number[2] of syntactically and/or distributionally distinguishable main-verb inversion types: a delaying function (cf. Sec. Five) that gives a speaker time to decide on the proper characterization of the individual who is to be mentioned as the subject, a connective function for the initial phrase, an introductory function that allows an important subject NP to be in rhematic, final position, a puzzle-resolving function (the core of the so-called emphatic function), and related functions of quotation inversions. The examples are a mix of literary[3] citations and constructed variations on them. However, the colloquial-literary dimension of the usage of inversion types is not mentioned. The present work aims to explore a larger class of inversions along a different dimension—how the naturalness of only certain inversion types in both natural speech and established literary genres is related to the nature of colloquial and literary discourse.

III. SOURCES

The sources for the numerous literary inversion types I discuss are essays (serious, but mostly non-scholarly) by a number of contemporary writers—the least recent being Thurber and H. W. Fowler; news and feature stories from newspapers; modern American short stories; a few novels from the last one hundred years, and many children's picture books from the last forty years; plus assorted random in-

---

[2]Depending on whether inversions over *be* are counted separately from inversions over other non-copular verbs (from whose syntax theirs differs), and on whether phrasal adverbial triggers are distinguished from non-phrasal adverb triggers (again, the distributional properties are somewhat different), the number is between eight and fifteen.

[3]In the broadest sense. Sources there, as well as here, include newspapers, children's books, and instructions, as well as narratives and essays by Dorothy Parker, S. J. Perelman, James Thurber, Brendan Gill, Mark Twain, and P. J. Wodehouse.

structions, personal letters, and cereal boxes. The conversational examples are drawn from fabricated conversations in short stories and novels, and from edited transcripts of natural speech (e.g. Terkel, 1974). A few are 'found objects' I just happened to overhear, or discover in published analyses of interview transcripts (e.g. Labov, 1972). Unfortunately, these last are somewhat inferior as data as they were transcribed (or presented) without any significant portion of the context in which they occurred.

I do not apologize for not using exclusively verbatim transcripts of naturally occurring speech. In the first place, as argued (more articulately) by Lakoff and Tannen (1979) and Prince (1980), literary and cinematic presentations of conversation generally represent speech that strikes speakers as perfectly natural, unless the writer is patently mediocre. Readers like myself, with no pretensions of expertise at literary criticism, recognize and reject fabricated dialogue that does not ring true, does not sound as if it could have actually occurred. So, I believe, dialogue in well-written short stories and novels provides as adequate a source for what people think people say as their judgements of grammaticality on fabricated or natural sentences do.[4] One really can't ask for more.

In the second place, in natural speech inversions of most types are few and far between. Long ago, I thought that personal narratives would be a good source of a variety of inversions, and with the help of a colleague, obtained a ninety-minute tape of undergraduates telling each other about 'scary things' that had happened to them, or surprises they might have had. In fifteen anecdotes by nine or ten individuals, there was not a single inversion. So I abandoned natural speech as a primary source of inversions for syntactic studies; in ninety minutes, I could read enough Dorothy Parker to collect seven or eight inversions.

Finally, certain constructions are so natural in context that even interested linguists listening for them do not hear them when they occur. At least one colloquial inversion, the adjunctive tag as in (4), is of this sort, and I have noticed but two in reading 700 pages of interview transcripts (Terkel, 1974).

(4)   Inversions can be found on cereal boxes, and so can sentence fragments.

Consequently, a few of my colloquial examples, like (1c), are fabricated on the spot.

IV. POSITIVELY LITERARY INVERSIONS

By far the majority of inversions I have found, both in number and in type, are typical of written discourse, whether it be narrative, expository, or journalistic. A smaller proportion is found exclusively in written materials.

---

[4]This too has been attacked as a source of data, unfairly I think. Green (1978) elaborates on this.

Some of those found exclusively in written materials involve language that is very literary, for example the two classes of comparative inversions exemplified in (5) and (6).

(5a)   Such is the impact of work on some people. (W:xix)

(5b)   In so emphatic, consistent, and homogeneous a consensus was born the useful, if quixotic, institution of the professional matchmaker. (JOY:77)

(5c)   Thus sharply did the terrified three learn the difference between an island of make-believe and the same island come true. (PP:65)

(6a)   But you know, such was my respect for him, that even after I switched to martinis I still ordered sweet manhattans when Gus was behind the bar. (CUC—Groninger, 3-6-77)

(6b)   So prevalent has pornography become that sober-minded analysts are trying to get a financial handle on it. (SFC-Moskowitz)

(6c)   There came also children's voices, for so safe did the boys feel in their hiding place that they were gaily chatting. (PP:80)

(6d)   All its life it had been asleep, but now it hardly got a chance to nod, so swiftly did big events and crashing surprises come along in one another's wake. . .(PW:91)

None of the nineteen examples in my files is from a conversational context. I am not claiming that the inversion is responsible for making these sentences sound literary; some of the vocabulary in these examples (e.g. (5b)), and some of the other constructions (e.g. the prenominal predicative adjectives *terrified* and *sober-minded* in (5c) and (6b)) are also basically literary. The point is that while one might use such constructions in writing, one would not use them in conversation and say things like (6e).

(6e)   I wish I could write better. I feel like I'm meandering around in the dark, so limited is my knowledge about writing.

On the other hand, the fact that these inversions occur pretty much exclusively in written materials is not a fact about the medium of transmission. One might expect to find examples of these constructions in orally delivered sermons or political speeches, even ones given from notes, rather than fully prepared texts. Rather, they are typical, symptomatic even, of an impersonal, declamatory style that is foreign to the conventions of interpersonal behavior in our culture. They seem to imply an address to a large, impersonal audience (such as the intended readership of a book, remote in time and space from the author). If someone were to use one of these constructions in a conversation, one might suspect him of hallucinating about his audience.

As for quotation inversion, it is simply part of the conventions about communication in our culture that quotation inversion as in (2a) is available for framing exact, direct quotations in literary narratives, but not in conversational narratives. This restriction is part of what it means to be a literary convention. Inversion after preposed quotes is usual when the information in the subject NP is more important and less predictable than information in the verb (Green, 1980; Hermon, 1979), but even when such conditions prevail in an oral narrative, the use of an inversion like the one in (7) would be unidiomatic to say the least.

(7)   The most unnerving thing happened to me this morning. Robin and Dylan and I were at breakfast, eating our cereal, and idly staring at the cereal box, you know? 'Sugar is recommended in this cereal,' *announced/remarked/said Robin*. I asked her where it said that. She says, "Nowhere. I want some sugar. There isn't any in here."

Inversion here doesn't sound pompous or pretentious. It just sounds alien.

Pre-literate children learn this convention just as they learn other literary conventions—from hearing written materials read aloud. In dictating stories, or in pretending to read, they will use this construction along with *Once upon a time* and other formulae, but it does not carry over into their natural speech. No child would make a complaint with something like (8).

(8)   Mommy, 'You forgot your gym shoes. Nyaah, nyaah, nyaah, nyaah, nyaah,' said all the kids in my room.

Storytellers might use inverted quotations, but in this day and age, storytelling is for the most part no longer an independent oral tradition, but something derivative of written materials, and is more a recitation than creative art. Even in the creative, spontaneous storytelling that I have observed, stories are modelled on the style of written stories, and use all of their conventions. In any case, the fact that quotation inversion is restricted to written material is again not a fact about the medium, nor in this case about the audience, but about the tradition.

Two more inversion types that are stereotypically literary are inversion in comparative clauses (9) and inversion after positive frequency, degree, and manner adverbs (10a-c).

(9)   And the establishment of democracy on the American continent was scarcely as radical a break with the past as was the necessity, which Americans faced, of broadening this concept to include black men. (JB:358)

(10a) Often did she visit the inhabitants of that gloomy village.

(10b) Particularly did she commend its descriptions of some of those Italian places. (DP:346)

(10c) Bitterly did we repent our decision. (Hartvigson and Jakobsen (1974:46), citing Jacobsson 1951:16)

(10c′) Bitterly did he rue it. (Fowler (1923:11), who probably fabricated it)

Both of these types are relatively rare (the examples in my files number less than ten altogether). I will take them up in order. Fowler finds inversions like (9) generally unnatural and ungraceful (1923:14)[5], and it is hard to disagree with him. Yet, many people, he notes (1923:16), "would write if not say *I spend less than do 9 out of 10 people in my position.*" He speculates that inversion is used "for saving the verb from going unnoticed" at the end, but points out, quite rightly: "so little does that matter that if the verb is omitted, no harm is done." His prescription is to delete the auxiliary or put it in an appropriate place after its subject, which is precisely what people do in speech. An old TV commercial advised, "*Zest* makes you feel cleaner than soap." The exuberant voice might have said less ambiguously *Zest makes you feel cleaner than soap does,* but there could be no pretense of natural speech if it had intoned, *Zest makes you feel cleaner than does soap.*

The inversions after positive frequency, degree, and manner adverbs have a decidedly archaic flavor, as Hartvigson and Jakobsen note (1974:46). Jacobsson (1951:117) says that this inversion "is now hardly used outside the literary language." However, he cites examples from twentieth century sources, including two from a British mystery that point up the literary nature of this inversion by contrasting the (uninverted) speech of the scullery maid (11a), with the idle musings of the upperclass protagonist, Lord Peter Wimsey, in (11b).

(11a) 'He did,' said Hannah, 'and well I remember it, for Mr. Urquhart asked particular after the eggs, was they new-laid, and I reminded him they was some he had brought in himself that afternoon from that shop on the corner of Lamb's Conduit street where they always have them fresh from the farm, and I reminded him that one of them was a little cracked and he said, "We'll use that in the omelette tonight, Hannah," and I brought out a clean bowl from the kitchen (. . .)' (DS:78)

(11b) '(. . .) I even took a special course in logic for her sake.'
'Good gracious!'
'For the pleasure of repeating "Barbara celarent darii ferio baralipton." There was a kind of mysterious romantic lilt about the thing which was somehow expressive of passion. Many a moonlight night have I murmured it to the nightingales which haunt the gardens of St. Johns—though, of course, I was a Balliol man myself, but the buildings are adjacent.' (DS:97)

In contrast to the almost archaic inversion after positive frequency and degree adverbs, inversion after negative frequency and degree adverbs (*never, rarely, barely*) is, for inversions, common and unremarkable in conversation, on which more below.

---

[5]'On the other hand, it is hardly credible, after a look through the collection shortly to follow, that the writers can have chosen these inversions either as the natural way of expressing themselves or as graceful decoration; so unnatural and so ungraceful are many of them.' (Fowler 1923:14)

But not all 'literary' inversions sound like they came out of a dusty book published before 1880. Inversions after preposed direct quotations are fully contemporary, and found in all manner of written narratives, ranging from novels by Mary McCarthy and John Updike to pornographic novels to picture books and basal readers for children. Writers vary considerably in the advantage they take of this construction, but it is much more frequent in children's books than in books for adults.[6]

Another 'literary' inversion that is not particularly associated with an elevated or aesthetically valued style is inversion after preposed abstract prepositional phrases, as in (12).

(12a) Of more probable concern to Crane's followers is a feeling Crane didn't come off too well in the first debate. (CUC editorial 10-12-78)

(12b) Against these stories, however, can be set the lost and found columns of the same papers, which in almost every issue carry offers of rewards for the recovery of dogs that, apparently couldn't find their way back from the next block. (Bergen Evans, quoted in JT:114)

(12c) At issue is Section 1401(a) of the Controlled Substances Act. (CUC-Carol Alexander)

(12d) To this list may be added. . .

(12e) In this category belong. . .

I do not have very many examples of this construction (cf., however, Lawler, 1977 and Green, 1977 for syntactic argument that hinges entirely on it), but its use seems to be restricted to expository prose, typically journalistic or scholarly-academic prose. Still, if someone were to drop one of these into even a serious intellectual conversation (which seems highly unlikely), the effect woud be to make him sound like a stuffed shirt—as in B's (a) response to A in (13).

(13) A: Well, I just don't think any review board composed of non-specialists can have the expertise to pass judgement on research proposals from faculty members of the College of Medicine.
      B: (a) Look, at issue is protection of the subject's right to have all risks of the research disclosed before consenting to participate.
      (b) Look, what's at issue is protection of. . .

---

[6]Ten-page samples from five books for adults showed inversion being used for from 0 to 35 percent of the directly quoted utterances. (The extent to which low inversion counts were a result of the use of inversion-blocking pronominal subjects, or the absence of quote frames altogether, was not taken into account. Probably it would be impossible to rule this out fully as a factor, since it would have to involve being able to predict pronominal reference with absolute certainty.) Large and/or exhaustive samples from two basal readers and four picture books showed inversion for from 41 to 73 percent of the instances of direct quotation. (Similarly, this figure may be inflated as a result of the peculiar practice in basals of not using pronominal reference where it would be naturally used in other narrative genres.)

Finally, there are formulaic inversions like (14), that are used only in formal, written, legal or quasi-legal documents.[7]

(14a) Be it resolved that. . .

(14b) Be it known by all present. . .

Formulae like (2c): be-NP-X—or be-NP[+pro]-Y are typically literary, but might, like many other inversions to be discussed below, be intentionally used in conversation, to create a literary effect.

V. PERFECTLY COLLOQUIAL INVERSIONS

Probably the most colloquial inversion type—or, at least, the least literary—is the inversion after a negated verb which is documented in a variety of American dialects, as in (15).

(15a) Didn't nobody teach me this. (W:240 N.W., stockchaser)

(15b) It's against the rule; that's why don't so many people do it. (from Labov 1972:812)

(15c) Won't nobody catch us. (from Labov 1972:811)

(15d) I know a way that can't nobody catch us. (from Labov 1972:811)

The subject is usually morphologically negative, as well as the verb; the syntactic multiple negation is independently a colloquial construction. This inversion is not found in so-called standard dialects, and it is one of the few inversions which occurs after a negated verb; in almost all other inversions, the verb may not be negated, as shown in (16).

(16a) *"Come and get me!" didn't say Fred.

(16b) *In didn't walk the chairman.

I have seen no examples of inversions like (15) in print that were not reported speech; if one were to get past a copy-editor, say as in (17), I would infer that the author had used it for effect—specifically to create an effect of forceful SPEECH.

---

[7]Of course, they may be uttered in the process of composing them at official meetings. Thus, from a newspaper report:
'Be it further resolved that copies of this resolution be sent to no one,' Matijevich said.
(CUC)

(17a) Don't no A-over-A condition prevent the desired ambiguous application in this case.

(17b) Don't no chimpanzees appear to make use of these/no vowel possibilities.

Another positively colloquial inversion is a subclass of inversion after preposed locative adverbs, a formula really:

Here   comes   NP
There   {goes}
{Yonder}

as other adverbs and verbs do not occur, as illustrated in (18).

(18a) Here comes the bus. (G.G. p.c.)

(18b) Here goes another somersault.

(18c) There goes the bus.

(18d) (?)There comes Mrs. Romberg.

(18e) *There speeds the bus.

(18f) *Around comes the bus. (no true present reading)

Three out of the first four examples in (18) are constructed. Despite my firm conviction that these are an utterly colloquial form of speech, I have, in fact, collected only one example of this type (18a). So unremarkable are they that they seem almost invisible, so much so that someone looking for one can hear or see it, and not notice it.[8] This construction tends to have no past tense forms; with the possible exception of sentences like (19c), there is no way to report them even in STYLE INDIRECT LIBRE cf. Banfield, 1973).

(19a) *Here came the bus.

(19b) *Here went another somersault.

---

[8]The interesting properties of this construction first came to my attention when i needed, many years ago, to put a tag on (18a):

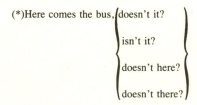

(*)Here comes the bus, doesn't it?

isn't it?

doesn't here?

doesn't there?

Some of their syntactic properties are discussed in Horn, Green, and Morgan, (ms.).

(19c) (?)There came the bus.

(19d) *There went the bus.

Examples like (19d) are not, strictly speaking, ungrammatical, but they cannot be used as a report of sentences like (18a) and (18c); (19d) could be used to describe a bus just disappeared from sight. The fact that they cannot be reported in the past tense suggests that they are non-literary constructions, for if they were literary, one would expect them to occur freely in the past tense, which is the normal and unmarked choice for written chronicles and narratives. In fact, the speech act deixis (*here, there*) implies that this is basically an oral language construction, though, of course, it is natural in personal letters as well, when writers write as if they were speaking.

In any case, in non-colloquial speech, this construction just sounds out of place. It seems unlikely, for instance, that the next president of the United States would say anything like (20a) in an inaugural address.

(20a) Here comes a time of great challenge for this country.

It seems more likely, that if s/he chose to use the ordinary words *come* and *here*, something like (20b) would be used instead.

(20b) We are coming to/upon opportunities here for the spirit of the American people to demonstrate to the rest of the world that (. . .)

Almost as invisible as the *Here comes* inversion, and at least as common in speech, is inversion after pronominal *so* and *neither*, as in (21).

(21a) It'll get your clothes pretty clean, but so will the others. (W:114 J.F., copy-chief)

(21b) A: You never clear your dishes off anymore.
       B: Neither do you.

I collected inversions for six years before I ever noticed one of these, which I probably use daily! They do not sound particularly colloquial in literary prose (cf. (22)), but they seem to be much more frequent in speech.

(22a) A well-accepted linguistic principle is that as culture changes, so will the language. (APN:134)

(22b) However, none of the examples in (13) are contrastive, as noted above, and neither are many of the other tokens in the corpus. (EP:22)

There is a literary counterpart, however: inversion after pronominal *as*, as in (23).

(23)   Two of his uncles had been on the force in New York City, as was his father, (. . .) (W:183 S.T.)

In speech, this sounds a bit stilted:

(24)   A: Why did you decide to become a policeman?
B: Well, two of my uncles were on the force, as was my father, until he lost his trigger finger in a railroad accident.

Another colloquial inversion type is the simple exclamatory inversion, as in (25).

(25a)   Boy! Did I have a lot of garbage to put up with. (W:60 S.A., receptionist)

(25b)   God, have I seen attitudes change! (W:728 L.D., priest)

(25c)   And boy, do I remember! (W:621 C.M., hospital aide)

This type is found exceedingly rarely, if at all, in literary contexts. The syntax of such constructions was described in N. McCawley (1973). Despite being highly visible (unlike the inversions just discussed), perhaps because they constitute a unique speech act type, they are fairly unremarkable. Nonetheless, they are very colloquial; it may be that rules of decorum that restrict display of emotion are responsible for inhibiting their use in certain kinds of speech situations. These inversions may occur in COLLOQUIAL WRITING, for example diaries (26) and personal letters, as well (as might inversion after negated verbs, though I haven't come across any).

(26)   Was the Mack's face red! (JT:323, 'Talk of the Town' piece for the *New Yorker*)

But I would be surprised to find an inversion like this in a piece of academic prose, or a nineteenth century novel, more or less as in (27).

(27a)   (And) would this treatment eliminate the potential, but apparently never realized, series of uvularized consonants which Chomsky and Halle cite!

(27b)   Tinker Bell at once popped out of the hat, and did she begin to lure Wendy to her destruction! (apologies to Sir James M. Barrie)

Before concluding this section on colloquial inversions, I want to touch briefly on an exclusively oral use of inversions to again demonstrate why colloquial language must not be confused with spoken language. In the context of play-by-play sportscasting—a linguistically demanding task requiring the identification of individuals in the course of a spontaneous description of a fast-moving, ongoing event—at least five different inversion types are used, as exemplified in (28).[9]

---

[9]All examples are from 1977 TV and radio broadcasts of games in a state high school basketball tournament.

(28a) Underneath is Smith. [Inversion after preposed locative adverb]

(28b) At the line will be Skowronski. [Inversion after preposed locative phrase]

(28c) Stealing it and then losing it was Dave Bonko. [Inversion after preposed present participle]

(28d) Down with the rebound comes Roan. [Inversion after directional adverb]

(28e) Into the ballgame is Dave Brenner. [Inversion after directional phrase]

Despite the fact that these inversions are quite frequent in play-by-play broadcasts (they are the rule, in fact, rather than the exception, when the named agent is a syntactic subject), they are not at all characteristic of ordinary spontaneous colloquial discourse. In fact, the one exemplified by (28e), is simply not found in forms of discourse other than sportscasting: while directional phrases with *into* do occur with a copular verb (as oppposed to a verb of motion like *come, run*), it is only in the idiom *be into,* meaning 'be involved in, interested in,' and it is never preposable.

(29a) Don Binner is into entomology.

(29b) *Into entomology is Don Binner.

While forms like those in (28a-d) may occasionally occur in colloquial speech, they are quite rare, and highly rhetorical, about which more below; I feel certain that transcripts of natural speech will show that even in an impassioned after-the-game account of a play, even a sportscaster is much more likely to use uninverted forms like those in (30) than inversions like those in (31).

(30a) Smith is/was underneath.

(30b) Skowronski is/was at the line.

(30c) Dave Bonko steals/stole it and then loses/lost it.

(30d) Roan comes/came down with the rebound.

(31a) Underneath is/was Smith.

(31b) At the line is/was Skowronski.

(31c) Stealing it and then losing it is/was Dave Bonko.

(31d) Down with the rebound comes/came Roan.

Indeed, it seems clear that there is little or no significance to the fact that these five inversions are found in this particular kind of spoken language. They merely provide convenient formulae for describing the action of the game, which have the double attraction (to a sportscaster) of 1) containing slots for the essential information (location of ball or ball-handler, action of player or ball, name of ball-handler) and 2) allowing naming the ball-handler to be postponed till the end of the sentence, so that the sportscaster has time to identify and recall the name of the ball-handler(s), while imparting the other essential information.

So far is their use in sportscasting from being an important fact about the use of inversions, that any construction which meets criterion 2) might be adopted as a sportscasting formula, and in fact, many other such constructions are employed in just this way. In addition to inversions, announcers use passives, extrapositions, and indirect object constructions, among others, to postpone identification of the ball-handler.

(32a) Here's a reverse lay-up—good—by Dave Skowronski.
(32b) The tip is good by Joe May, his second basket.
(32c) And the rebound goes to Joe May.

VI. LITERARY SPEECH AND COLLOQUIAL WRITING

So far I have described inversions that were particularly characteristic of written literary language or spoken colloquial usage. Most inversion types, however, are not rigidly restricted in their use, and can be found in both spoken and written contexts, though most are definitely more literary or more colloquial.

Perhaps I should explain here how I arrived at the classification presented here of inversion usage. Classification of an inversion as literary or colloquial was done partly on the frequency of occurrence in literary or colloquial contexts in my file of more than 360 inversions, and partly on a judgemental basis.

Some items (e.g. inversion after quotations, negated verbs) were on inspection of their distribution in my collection apparently restricted to either written literary or spoken colloquial contexts. Upon reflection, it was equally apparent that the restriction was absolute and representative, that they could not plausibly be used in the other kind of context. Other inversions (e.g. inversion in exclamations, after preposed adjective phrases) occurred overwhelmingly (i.e. as more than 50% of the collected examples) in one or the other kind of context. Here again, reflection on the plausibility of using such forms in the 'minority' context was convincing that such usage would be out of the ordinary, and have an especially strong literary tone in speech, or an especially colloquial tone in writing. This was also true of most types that had a substantial distribution in both kinds of contexts. For example, some inversion types sounded distinctly colloquial despite the fact that only 15–30 percent of the examples in my files were from overheard, reported, or fabricated spontaneous speech. Fifteen to thirty per cent is not such a small proportion when it is recalled that such colloquial contexts are vastly underrepresented in my collection. Even in such a work as Terkel (1974), which is more than 85 percent transcripts of speech, twenty out of the thirty-eight inversions are from Terkel's accompanying written exposition.

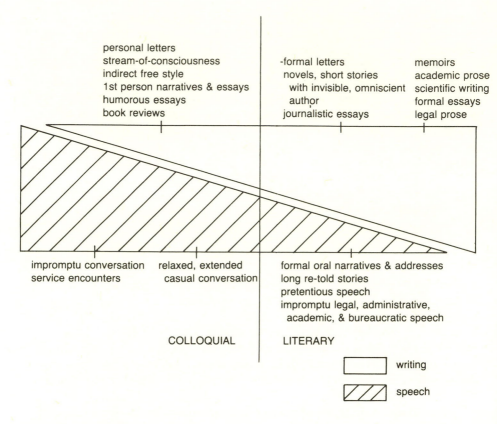

personal letters
stream-of-consciousness
indirect free style
1st person narratives & essays
humorous essays
book reviews

-formal letters
novels, short stories
 with invisible, omniscient
 author
journalistic essays

memoirs
academic prose
scientific writing
formal essays
legal prose

impromptu conversation
service encounters

relaxed, extended
casual conversation

formal oral narratives & addresses
long re-told stories
pretentious speech
impromptu legal, administrative,
 academic, & bureaucratic speech

COLLOQUIAL   LITERARY

☐ writing

▨ speech

Literary Speech

We have already looked at at least one inversion type (after positive degree adverbs) which while primarily literary, was not impossible in speech (cf. example (11b)). There are quite a few others that are even less marked in speech. Among the most literary-sounding inversions that are to be found in speech are two triggered by negative elements: inversion after *nor*, and inversion after negative adverbs. Examples are given in (33–34).

(33a) Nor would he have been at a loss if Edwin Potts had been some powerful thug. (PGW:197)

(33b) 'Nor can I deal with an account that says, "Get me a broad." ' (W:493 B.M., sports press-agent)

(34a) Rarely did I hear such overtones of gratitude as went into the utterance of this compound noun. (JOY:136)

(34b) Not until *The Book of Splendor* (the Zohar) appeared in Spain in the thirteenth century did a formidable metaphysical text on cabalism appear. (JOY:61)

(34c) 'Rarely do I put up with it.' (W:617 C.M., hospital aide)

(34d) 'Only of late, because I'm getting more secure and I'm valued by the agency, am I able to get mad at men and say, "Fuck off." ' (W:107 B.H., producer)

Between fifteen and thirty percent of my examples of these types are from transcribed or attributed speech (most of them involve first person subjects). They do not sound (to me) particularly pretentious, but they do sound rather bookish. A possible explanation for this will be discussed in Section 7.

Another literary inversion that is not uncommon in speech is the inverted conditional, as in (35).

(35a) 'Should I leave this job to go to the bathroom I risk being fired.' (W:222 P.S., spotwelder)

(35b) And could there be an excuse for displayed impatience it was right there before them. (DP:449 play review)

(35c) 'Were I to live another thirty years—that would make me ninety-five—why not try to play?' (W:600 B.F., jazz musician)

(35d) Were he to carry out his threat of telling all to Tipton Plimsoll, disaster must ensue. (PGW:211)

But inverted conditionals, and inversions after *nor* and negative adverbs, while not uncommon in speech, are not found in casual conversation or small talk, as the style clash in (fabricated) examples like (36) attests.

(36a) Gee, dinner Thursday? Could I get a babysitter, I'd love to go.

(36b) Oh, good. We didn't get a parking ticket. Nor did we leave the windows open, so the upholstery is still dry.

(36c) No, I haven't seen the 1981 cars at Market Place. Rarely do I go to large enclosed shopping centers.

The preceding three inversion types are all mainly characteristic of expository prose—explanation, analysis, or description of behavior. This is not to say that they do not occur in narrative prose[10]—examples (33a) and (35d) are from a novel—but when they do, it is in the course of an expository digression.

One final inversion which is basically literary, but also finds its way into speech in certain contexts, is the one after preposed adjective phrases, as in (37).

(37a) 'Important here is the fact that misleading can also be intentional or unintentional.' (overheard, 1979)

---

[10]By NARRATIVE PROSE I mean accounts of events with a plot, i.e. with conflict, suspense, resolution, etc. (cf. Brewer & Lichtenstein, 1981).

(37b) Whatever the reason, and economics are a factor (though not so important as they would have us believe), rare is the publisher who cares a fig for attractive design, well-defined printing on quality paper, and a lasting binding. (Smithsonian, Aug. 1978, p. 106)

(37c) Equally obvious, as pointed out on occasion by Matijevich, are the potential advantages for an incumbent to be able to send out congratulatory resolutions to their constituents. (CUC)

It seems fairly obvious that this construction is characteristic of fairly formal, considered forms of discourse. That it sounds stiff and stilted in casual, spontaneous discourse, whether spoken or written, should be evident from the examples in (38).

(38a) I know that going to the camp-out is important to you. But more important is not disappointing your grandparents, who have come 1300 miles to see you. (Cf. (. . .) But it's more important to not. . .)

(38b) Just a note to say we all miss you—Rare is the day that someone doesn't sigh, "I wish Florence was here." (Cf. (. . .) It's a rare day that. . .)

(38c) Equally important are the good manners you showed by writing to thank me. (Letter from Abigail Van Buren in 'Dear Abby', CUNG 10-23-80)

Abigail Van Buren might include (38c) in a response published in her column to a letter from a young girl, but it seems less likely that she would use it in a personal letter to a niece or a grandchild.

Two other kinds of inversions that seem to me relatively literary, although they are found in speech, are inversions after locative and directional phrases (39,40).

(39a) '(. . .), and on Mr. Degan's left is Saul Panzer.' (RS:182 Nero Wolfe, introducing principals in a murder investigation to each other)

(39b) Just above him hung a steel-engraving of a chariot-race, the dust flying, the chariots careening wildly, the drivers ferociously lashing their maddened horses, the horses themselves caught by the artist the moment before their hearts burst, and they dropped in their traces. (DP:53)

(39c) Beyond it rose the peopled hills. (RM:47)

(39d) And at the stern, all bound with ropes, sat Princess Tiger Lily, daughter of the Indian chief. (GBPP)

(39e) Under his belt, did they but know it, lay the Ruby Eye. (SJP:23)

(40a) 'I'm always afraid that out of the blue is gonna come a bolt of lightning, and (. . .)' (Rhoda, on 'Rhoda')

(40b) The trouble here is that when the needles are withdrawn, the holes are still there, and through them quickly drain the flavor-giving juices of the meat. (PAT, feature article by Bill Collins)

(40c) Into the office of a Dr. Nelson, shouting, 'Oh, Doctor! My feet!' bursts Mrs. Roberts, an attractive young matron. (SJP:156)

(40d) It burst open, and from it rolled a shining golden egg. (JW)

(40e) Last year we were at London Mills and all of a sudden down the road come a bunch of fellows with bagpipes. . .and kilts and all that. (overheard)

With a few exceptions like (40a,b), most examples of these types are found in narrative or descriptive prose, where they may serve a variety of purposes (Green, 1980), including introducing background and principals (39a, 39b, 39c, 40c, 39d), and highlighting the resolution of some narrative tension (39e, 40d, 40e). These constructions appear, from my materials, to be less common in speech than others already discussed in this section, but that may be merely a function of the fact that my corpus of examples does not contain very many extended oral narratives, where they would be likely to appear. The ideal way to investigate their usage in conversation would be to tape-record individuals in a natural situation where they uninhibitedly and spontaneously recount long narratives with a specific point, e.g. a party where everyone gets a little drunk. But ethical considerations and the problem of obtaining properly informed consent would seem to require that this remain a thought-experiment.

The fact is that outside of extended narratives, these constructions sound very odd in speech indeed (unlikely, at the least), as the following found examples indicate.

(41a) 'I braked,' Andrea explained to me later, 'but in the ditch were a smashed Cadillac and a wrecked Comanche with hurt people inside.' (CUC Special report by JoAnne Reiser)

(41b) 'To our right are wide, spreading gardens, rich in every variety of flower; to our left, through the dim mysterious trees, we catch a glimpse of shimmering silver.' (PGW:207-208 Gally, describing a property as he imagines it)

Nonetheless, it seems to me that an association of such constructions as (39, 40) with speech, and especially of (40) with excited speech, [11] must be at least a part of what is behind the fact that these constructions are so much more frequent[12] in children's books than in novels and short stories written for adults.

Two final inversion types, inversion after present and past participial phrases (42, 43), are more characteristic of journalistic prose (42c,d; 43e) than

---

[11]Due, no doubt, to its capacity to serve the resolution function (Green, 1980).

[12]By, I would estimate, at least a factor of 10. Cf. Section 6.2 for more discussion.

Most of my examples of inversion after preposed directional phrases are either from children's books or from S. J. Perelman, whose highly idiosyncratic style is marked by the use of formal literary conventions in the treatment of rather trivial topics, with an incongruous handful of very colloquial expressions thrown in, as in this excerpt.

Should he prove reluctant, simply read him Mr. Gaba's article, and if that fails to stun him, sap him just below the left ear with a blackjack. (SJP:168)

anything else, though they do occur in colloquial speech and writing (42a, 43a) and descriptive prose (42b, 43d).

(42a) And standing at the door is Archie Goodwin, (. . .) (Same as ex. (39a))

(42b) Running along the wall was a narrow ledge. (PGW:190)

(42c) Representing Mayberry in the arguments next week will be Stephen P. Hurley, court-appointed appellate defender. (CUC news story by Carol Alexander)

(42d) Hopping around Robert McKinnel's laboratory is proof that cloning works: a frog. (CUC AP wire story)

(43a) Enclosed is a copy of the graduation program. (personal letter)

(43b) And enclosed with your beautiful prints will be a coupon good for $1 OFF any one of these cereals: Kellogg's Corn Flakes (. . .) (cereal box)

(43c) Diametrically opposed was Pauline Kael of the *New Yorker*. (FM:182)

(43d) The plane circled above the San Francisco area, and spread out under me were the farm where I was born, the little town where my grandparents were buried, the city where I had gone to school, the cemetery where my parents were, the homes of my brothers and sisters, Berkeley, where I had gone to college, and the little house where at that moment, while I hovered high above, my little daughter and my dogs were awaiting my return. (PK:165)

(43e) Reported in satisfactory condition today in the Mercy Hospital intensive care unit were Emery L. Endsley, 46, and Hazel Endsley, 41, both of Mahomet. (CUC news story)

Although (42a) is the only inversion after a participial phrase that I have collected from transcribed or fabricated speech, I would expect to find examples in extended oral narratives or descriptions that serve the same introductory function (Green, 1980) that (42b) and (43d) serve. Nonetheless, occurrences of examples like (43a) in personal letters nothwithstanding, we can see that this construction is definitely on the literary side of the literary-colloquial dichotomy. While someone might write (43a) to her daughter, it seems highly unlikely that she would say it to her, in person or over the telephone, in referring to some package or envelope. Similarly, the inversion after a present participial phrase in (44a) sounds much less likely than even the inversion after locative phrase in (44b), though they both serve the same discourse function.

(44a) A: Where's my $2 bill?
       B: Leaning against my dresser is a linguistic atlas of Oltenia. It's marking the beginning of the index.

(44b) Next to my dresser is a linguistic atlas of Oltenia. It's marking the beginning of the index.

These constructions are a favorite of newswriters, despite not being explicitly taught in journalism textbooks, in part, no doubt, because of their conciseness in relating new information in a story to information previously presented (a connective function; Green, 1980). Perhaps this fact of its distribution contributes to its relative absence in casual speech, by stigmatizing it as journalistic.

Colloquial writing

In addition to finding literary inversions in a variety of kinds of speech, depending on the kind of inversion, and knowledge of the conventions of its use, we also find colloquial inversions in written language.

Let me take up the most provocative case first—two more negative inversion types. Inversion after negated NPs (45), and the temporal construction in (46), of which the only spoken example I have collected is (45a), are both basically colloquial constructions.

(45a) 'You took the words out of my mouth,' I said. 'I hammered on the door for over half an hour, but not a tumble did I get.' (BICI:101 first person narrator of 'Be a Cat's Paw; Lose Big Money')

(45b) No trace of his whereabouts could we elicit until our zigzag course led us to Mme. Embonpoint, *patronne* of the town's leading restaurant, Le Poulet en Empois (The Chicken in Starch). (BICI:251)

(46a) No sooner have I turned my back, a laborious and rather painful procedure these days, than some bright-eyed woman or other rises briskly from her escritoire with a brand-new list of nine or ten ways of preventing something or bringing something to pass. (MW:196)

(46b) Hardly am I back in the Taj Mahal, surrounded by Madeleine Carroll and five hundred million billion trillion dollars, when the masons, carpenters, and assorted technicians arrive, minus tools, but with plenty of noisemakers and confetti. (SJP:244)

(46c) No sooner had the publishers sprinkled their books with blacks in middle-class pursuits, no sooner had they pictured 50 percent females throughout (one publisher carefully drew a skirt on half of the decorative stick figures in a math book) and removed mothers from the kitchen, than there was a cry to portray handicapped persons in normal activities (in effect, to 'mainstream' the handicapped through instructional materials).
(MB:42)

While it is true that only one of these examples is from speech (and that from dialogue fabricated by S. J. Perelman), it is also the case that almost all of the examples I have collected are from narratives written in the first person, and these tend to be more colloquial and personal, imitative of conversation, than more impersonal narratives. Of course this is only suggestive of a colloquial status for these constructions. The proof of the pudding is whether such constructions would sound natural in more formal literary prose. I think not. Imagine (47) or (48) occurring in a scholarly journal or a grant proposal.

(47a) Not a bit of feedback did subjects in this group receive.

(47b) Not a response from a second grader did the researchers include in the ANOVAs.

(48a) Hardly had we administered the materials with the revised distractors in Set 1 when we discovered that the new distractors suffered from the same defects as the old.

(48b) No sooner did we administer the materials with the revised distractors in Set 1 than we discovered that the new distractors suffered from the same defects as the old.

Inversions like those in (45) and (47) sound very emotional to me; sentences like (47) might occur in an informal criticism of some experiment, but it would be considered inappropriate in a (false third person) report of the experiment, and quite possibly in a published criticism. Inversions like (46) and (48) do not strike me as being as highly charged emotionally as inversions after negative noun phrases, but they do strike me as being particularly dramatic, and thus suitable for certain kinds of narrative, whether spoken or merely as if spoken (as in (46a,b)), but not for the kind of dispassionate reportage that is required by the editorial traditions of more formal discourse, e.g. scholarly journals. Example (46c) is from a narrative passage in *Learning,* a popular journal for teachers, on the ins and outs of publishing reading textbooks.

A third inversion type which is characteristic of very colloquial writing and elaborate oral narrative is inversion after temporal phrases, as in (49).

(49a) In '70 came the Vega. (W:260 G.B., UAW officer)

(49b) No—after Sydney came Fred, then Billy. (DP:200 style indirect libre narration in 'Big Blonde')

(49c) When they have passed, comes the last figure of all, a gigantic crocodile. (PP:73)

(49d) Now came the final test. (SJP:23)

No doubt related is a type of inversion with an implied temporal phrase, as in (50), both examples from anecdotes in Leo Rosten's *Joys of Yiddish.*

(50a) Came a terrific flash of lightning and clap of thunder. Finkelstein looked up to the heavens, protesting, 'I was only asking!' (JOY:194)

(50b) 'Comes the revolution,' said Misha, 'we'll all eat strawberries and cream.' (JOY:112)

At least the former construction appears in expository prose as well as narratives, as in (51), taken from book reviews.

(51a) Now appears *The Common Press*. (Smithsonian, Aug. 1978,)

(51b.) Next comes 'The Sleeper', which begins, ominously, with 'What is the matter?' and ends with 'May I open the window?' (MW:302 review of a bilingual phrase-book)

(51c) Next comes an effective little interlude about an airplane trip, which is one of my favorite passages in the swift and sorrowful tragedy: (. . .) (MW:303)

But it still seems to me to have a rather chatty tone, inappropriate (52a, b) to formal kinds of discourse, or at least awkward (52c).

(52a) The instructions were read aloud as the subjects read to themselves, directing them to read each story silently as it was shown on the screen. Next came the presentation of the stories, via overhead projector.

(52b) All of Europe was poised and ready for war. Comes the 14th of August, 1914.

(52c) First would apply a fronting rule, perhaps Topicalization, that would apply to (15) *An elegant fountain stands in the Italian garden* to yield (16) *In the Italian garden stands an elegant fountain.*[13] (DTL:31)

Let us turn, finally, to one of more the stereotypic of colloquial inversions, inversion after directional adverbs, as in (53).

(53a) 'I'm laying around my room, reading a trashy Greek novel, when in comes the head chamberlain of the court, begging me to have dinner with the Empress Livia in her private apartments.' (PHC: xii) Perelman's home companion.

(53b) 'Out come two aldermen, Tom Keane and Paul Wigoda, and they yell at the people, "You should be home with your kids." ' (W:725 L.D., priest)

(53c) In comes the head of the French department, who says in greeting, 'Gentlemen.' (personal letter).

(53d) You put the stick in here, and put in the cranker and turn the banker, and out slides a popsicle. (overheard, from a 3-year-old)

(53e) Up leaped the haggard husband. (JOY:134)

It is similar to inversion after directional phrases (40), but even more colloquial—somewhere in between inversion after directional phrases and the

---

[13]Notice how much more awkward the simple present *applies* (more usual for this construction) would be, and how much substituting *comes the application of* for *would apply* would contribute to an inappropriate and pointless switch of styles.

here comes construction (18). Like inversion after directional phrases, it is found primarily in narrative discourse, although it does not seem to serve all of the same functions. All of the examples in (53) serve in their contexts to introduce new individuals into the discourse, except (53e), which is the least conversational, and thus, if this is truly a colloquial construction, the least natural. The example in (53e) merely describes an action.

But that use is extroadinarily common in picture books for young children, as in the examples in (54).

(54a)   Then off marched the little tailor, cocky as could be, with his thumbs thrust through his boasting belt. (BLT)

(54b.) So back he came, looking for his lost shadow and hoping for a story about himself. (GBPP)

It has apparently become part of the conventions of writing such books that this inversion (along with inversions after locative phrases and directional phrases) may be used very frequently, although I have never seen it mentioned in works about writing for children. In the Golden Press version of *Peter Pan* cited in (54b), there are thirteen instances of inversion constructions—approximately one for every 167 words; in the Barrie original, there are probably no more than thirty inversions of all kinds (I counted nine after locative and directional phrases), about one for every 1770 words. It may be that the extraordinary frequency in picture books is attributable to an effort to make the text sound exciting, an effort based on the (mostly mistaken) assumption that the construction is emphatic or 'excited-sounding'. This is not so implausible when it is recalled that these books are for children who will ask readers to read them over and over; since many readers-aloud lose interest after the first reading, such a text would have the advantage of a built-in counterbalance to the monotonous intonation that might result from being read by a bored adult.

This speculation is to some degree borne out by a comparison of two passages from a book about forest animals, disguised as a story (Dorothy Lathrop's *Who Goes There?*). The first passage, (55), is patently not a story, yet ends with an inversion, presumably to make it sound like it is exciting action that is being narrated. The second passage, (56), which is much closer to being a real story embedded in the text, doesn't need an inversion to sound exciting. In (55), the sequence of events related is not a story (Brewer & Lichtenstein, 1981): there is no expectation regarding the first squirrel as protagonist, no suspense. But the inversion at the end of the second paragraph is story language—to make it SOUND like it was a story.

(55)   Shiny and red, the apples hung over their heads. One squirrel stood on his hind legs. He stretched up until he was as thin as a weasel, but still the biggest apple hung out of his reach.

Another squirrel leaped to the branch above it. He knew a better way than stretching! His sharp teeth gnawed the string that held it. Down plopped the apple on the first squirrel's head. (WGT:[8])

In (56), on the other hand, we have at least the skeleton of a plot: the squirrels are angry at the crow, but afraid (or too smart) to take direct action. Nonetheless they do act, and their action has an immediate, though indirect, effect consistent with their hopes. But between the description of their action (jumping) and the description of the relevant effects (the crow abandoning the corn), there are five sentences which serve to build suspense about the outcome—will the squirrels get to finish the corn?

(56)   'Caw!'
        The crow was coming to the picnic. No one wanted him.
        'Caw!'
        His black wings spread over a dozen backs, and so close that the wind from their flapping ruffled the fur of the other creatures. It blew the chipmunks' stripes crooked.
        Did he like mice or corn best? The mice didn't stay to see. They didn't want to be eaten. They flattened their ears and fled across the white snow like shadows.
        The chipmunk dropped his nut in alarm and darted up a tree trunk with a shrill, sweet chittering. The squirrels, their toenails scratching noisily against the bark, scrambled to the very top.
        Below them, all alone at the picnic, the crow was gobbling corn.
        He would gobble everything else!
        The squirrels leaned over the branches and shouted at him things they would never have dared to say on the ground. Their tails flicked angrily, and they jumped with rage until the branches shook under them.
        Suddenly all the snow with which these were piled toppled and fell. With a soft thud, it landed right on the astonished crow's back. It almost buried him! He squawked. And the squirrels shrieked with delight.
        The crow forgot about corn and forgot about mice. He shook off the snow and sullenly flapped up through the tree tops. (WGT:[16—18])

And significantly, there is no inversion here. There could have been. The relevant paragraph could have read:

Suddenly down plopped all the snow with which these were piled on the astonished crow's back. It almost buried him! He squawked. And the squirrels shrieked with delight.

But the anecdote is exciting by itself; because it builds and resolves suspense, it doesn't need special constructions to make it sound like it HAD BEEN suspenseful.

On the other hand, the extraordinary frequency of inversion after preposed directional adverbs in children's books might be attributable to an attempt to make the prose sound as if it were a story being TOLD, based on the assumption (again largely mistaken) that this construction is especially characteristic of natural speech, for there is an old tradition of writing children's books with references to the reader and the 'narrator' (and sometimes even to the book itself), which seem clearly to have been intended to make the story when read aloud to a child seem as if the reader-aloud were actually TELLING IT. Some examples:

> Lucie opened the door: and what do you think there was inside the hill?—a nice clean kitchen with a flagged floor and wooden beams—just like any other farm kitchen. (TW:21)

> And instead of a nice dish of minnows—they had a roasted grasshopper with lady-bird sauce; which frogs consider a beautiful treat; but *I* think it must have been nasty! (JF:59)

> Once upon a time, there was a little girl called Alice: and she had a very curious dream. Would you like to hear what it was that she dreamed about? (NA:1)

> (. . .) And *then* what do you think happened to her? No, you'll never guess! I shall have to tell you again. (NA:7)

> Just look at the picture and you'll *see* how tall she got! (NA:8)

> I suppose she must have looked rather delightful, for Mrs. Darling put her hand to her heart and cried, 'Oh, why can't you remain like this for ever?' (PP:1)

> (. . .) 'There are such a lot of them,' he said. 'I expect she is no more.'
> I expect he was right, for fairies don't live long, but they are so little that a short time seems like a good while to them. (PP:232)

The Winnie-the-Pooh stories are written as stories TOLD by the author TO Winnie-the-Pooh, at Christopher Robin's request (WTP:4); as such, they are embedded in a skeleton story about Christopher Robin and the narrator, addressed to the reader:

> Winnie-the-Pooh. When I first heard his name, I said, just as you are going to say, 'But I thought he was a boy?'
> 'So did I,' said Christopher Robin.

I say that the assumption that inversions make text sound like speech is largely mistaken, despite calling this construction basically colloquial, because it is in fact only the inversions with *In come* and *Out come* that abound in conversational discourse (at least in my collection); inversions with other prepositions and more specific main verbs have a decidedly literary flavor. In any case, at least in the instance of the Big Golden Books *Peter Pan,* it seems clear that the high proportion of inversions and other dramatic, emphatic language (exclamations and interjections) is the result of a concerted effort to make what is essentially a story SUMMARY sound like a real story. Its total length is about 2200 words. Peter loses his shadow, finds it, and gets it sewn back on in 81 words. You can see that there is no space for building suspense.

So, inversion after a directional adverb is sometimes a colloquial construction (with *come* after *in, out*), sometimes (with other prepositions and verbs) a fairly literary one, restricted pretty much to narratives. Part of this restriction may be due to content—directional adverbs may not figure too often in expository discourses, and even when they might, in formal prose they are likely to be replaced with Latinate verbs that incorporate the verbal and prepositional meanings in a single word (as in (57a)). But some of the restriction is surely a matter of style or register. Examples like those in (57) seem unlikely to occur in either the scholarly or semi-scholarly press.

(57a)   Thirty-six Candida alba seeds were planted in each of the soil conditions just described. Up came 32 to 35 in each condition within five months.
(Cf. Thirty-two to 35 germinated in each condition within five months.)

(57b)   For the first twenty years or so of the history of transformational grammar, proponents were involved in lively discussion of the properties of transformational rules, of which it appeared there were a large number in English—at least thirty or forty. But in 1976, around turned Chomsky and proposed that there are only two transformational rules.
(Cf. But in 1976, Chomsky turned around and proposed (. . .))

An example like (57a) might conceivably appear in a publication like *Organic Gardening* (though not in *Scientific American* or a scholarly journal), although the passive in the first sentence would probably be changed to an active, but (57b) would sound odd in even a popular history of modern linguistics.

VII. EXPLANATIONS FOR THE COLLOQUIAL AND LITERARY CHARACTER OF INVERSIONS

Why is it, we must finally ask, that some inversions are literary, and some are colloquial, and some are sort of one, and some are sort of the other? With such diverse kinds of language, it is not surprising that the answer is not simple or uniform. A few inversions seem to be literary or colloquial for functional or 'organic' reasons connected to their construction. And a few more seem to be the way they are because of facts about their components. But regardless of the historical origins of particular inversions, it may be that now many are the way they are just by convention: you have to learn, as you become enculturated, which constructions belong to which register.

Functional Explanations

Certain inversions, namely inversions after preposed participial phrases (42, 43), are predominantly literary, in fact predominantly journalistic, because their constructional function, that of connecting the old information repeated in the phrasal connective to the new information expressed in the postposed subject (Green, 1980) in a manner sparing of words and space, represents a value esteemed more by the profession of journalism than by the speaking or the writing public generally.

Other inversions, inversions after *nor* and after preposed adjectives in particular, appear to be basically literary because the construction seems to imply deliberation on the part of the user, more deliberation than is likely to be possible under the social pressures of spontaneous conversation to 'keep the conversation going' (cf. Tannen, 1979). It is hard to imagine a heated argument, for example, that could contain (58a) or (58b).

(58a) But I didn't take the car without asking! Nor did I total it at a drive-in!
       (Cf. (. . .) And I didn't total it at a drive-in (either)!)

(58b) Yes, I KNOW I'm supposed to be in by midnight. But important to me is getting in with the right people, and I can't do that if I have to leave just when we're getting ready to do something good. 'Excuse me, I have to go. My dad says I have to be home at midnight.'
       (Cf. (. . .) But it's important to me to get in (. . .))

Some inversions seem to be basically colloquial in character because the functions that they TYPICALLY serve are functions of colloquial speech, for example, the expression of the utterer's affective state. In particular, exclamations and the inversions after negative NPs (25, 45) belie a highly charged affective state (surprise, concern), and presumably are intended to indicate that state. This is the sort of thing that can happen in interpersonal communication (which is a jargonistic way of saying col-loquial), but trafficking in emotions is generally impossible or taboo in written materials that are intended to aid in the transfer of 'information' in an objective and impersonal manner. (Literary prose that seeks to imitate speech, for whatever reason, is generally free to employ colloquial constructions.) Books and faceless authors who avoid self-mention are not in the business of having feelings that they could want to display. Similarly, the *no sooner. . .than/hardly. . .when* construction (46) seems intended to indicate that the event of the second clause was a surprise given the event of the first; cf. the oddness of (59a) to the naturalness of (59b).

(59a) Hardly had he put the Crest on his toothpaste when he began to brush his teeth.

(59b) (= 46b) Hardly am I back in the Taj Mahal, surrounded by Madeleine Carroll and five hundred million billion trillion dollars, when the masons, carpenters, and assorted technicians arrive, minus tools but with plenty of noisemakers and confetti. (SJP:244)

Again, 'objective' writers and books, and omniscient, 'invisible' authors do not belong to a category of which surprise is credible.

Another inversion that is restricted to colloquial contexts for functional reasons is the *Here comes* construction (18). It seems to be restricted to present tense, speaker-oriented deixis *(Here comes/goes, There comes/goes)* because it is basically a description of action occurring simultaneously with the act of utterance, in the presence of the addressee. It follows that it will not be usable in normal written contexts (excluding, for instance, stream-of-consciousness writing, and style indirect libre), since the use of written language usually presupposes that the addressee is remote in both time and place from the source. Ordinarily what is referred to when this inversion is appropriately used is the physical motion of some physical object to the locus of the speaker. *Here* and *come* are generally not used with abstract senses *(*Here comes Spring,* but cf. (18b)). This would contribute as a circumstantial factor to the absence of this inversion from formal literary contexts to the extent that they tend not to be concerned with physical motion.

Circumstantial explanations

The distribution of other inversions is perhaps better explained by facts about the distribution of crucial components than by facts about the nature of the construction as a whole. This is not a particularly interesting kind of explanation, although it is perhaps the most common kind of explanation for distributions in analyses of syntax, for in this case it merely reduces the problem to a previously unsolved problem.

For example, the reason that inversion after preposed quotations (2a) and in *as-* pronominalizations (23) are exclusively literary is probably that the preposed quotations and the conjunction *as* are themselves pretty exclusively literary. Thus, the uninverted (60) is no more likely in conversation than the inverted (7), and the inverted *as-* pronominalization in (24) is as unconversational as it is in straight order, as in (61a), and as unconversational as the conjunction *as* in (61b), though the comparative *as* in (61c) is not particularly unconversational.

(60)   'Sugar is recommended in this cereal,' Robin announced/remarked/said.

(7)   (. . .)'Sugar is recommended in this cereal,' announced/remarked/said Robin.

(61a)   Winston tastes good, as a cigarette should.

(61b)   I didn't pick up any peanut butter at the store as I didn't have any money or checks with me.

(61c)   Jonah is just as aggressive as Sarah is.

Of course, it remains to be explained why preposed quotations and the conjunction *as* are literary.

Similarly, the colloquial character of inversion after directional adverbs (53, 54) is surely attributable to either of two facts about the verb-adverb combinations which are invertable (e.g. *come/fly/run out, come/fall down, go/run/crawl away, come/fly/rush. . . in, fly/dash over, come/turn around, come/rise up,* but not, e.g. *move away, wither away, enter in, burn out, wear down, break up, etc.).* Either 1) the invertable Anglo-Saxon phrasal verbs are decidedly colloquial in nature, so that in more literary discourse they are likely to be replaced by single Latinate words, removing even the possibility of preposing the adverb to trigger inversion; or 2) the invertable constructions are descriptive of actions (manners of locomotion, to be precise) that are ordinarily irrelevant to the purposes of uncolloquial literary prose. Under what circumstances would it be appropriate in a discourse that was not attempting to imitate conversational narrative to say that an individual crawled, crept, flew, or swam, rather than that he, she, or it merely moved, came or went, entered or departed, rose or sank? In any case, again we have still to explain why some verb-adverb collocations are 'decidedly colloquial' and others are not. Here, we have at least a glimmer of an explanation for this fact. They are colloquial because 1) they are Anglo-Saxon in origin, and 2) all other things being equal, Anglo-Saxon expressions are more colloquial than roughly synonymous forms of Classical derivation (cf. *take in:collect, bring around:resuscitate, breathe in:inhale, want:desire, baby:infant, talk:converse, chew:masticate,* etc.).

This explanation is of the sort proposed by J. McCawley (1978): a form with apparently general usability may be in use basically limited to contexts where no special form is available for the relevant subpart of its domain. McCawley argues that we don't say *light red* for the hues that *pink* refers to, even though we say *light blue, light green,* for analogous hues, because we have the term *pink* available; if we used *light red,* we would imply reference to some hue that *pink* didn't refer to. Similarly, if general forms are used in a domain where conventionally literary forms are available, the implicature is that the form of the discourse is purposely informal and colloquial. If this implicature is not apt, the discourse is bizarre.

But in most of the other cases, there appears to be no real synchronic explanation; it is simply conventional that quotations are not preposed in conversational discourse, simply conventional that the conjunction *as* is part of the literary dialect.

Conventional Explanations

Likewise, it seems to be simply conventional that inversion after locative (39) and directional (40) phrases, after negative adverbs (34), in conditionals (35), and in the *so/such* (. . .*that*) constructions (5, 6), is essentially limited to literary usage. In claiming that this restriction is conventional, I am claiming that it does not follow from any principle of universal grammar, any innate mechanism, or (at least directly) from any functional principle, but rather that it is an aspect of the CULTURE which, like the conventions of politeness, is learned largely by observation and imitation. And there is evidence, I should point out, both that the literary constructions are learned, and that the distinction between literary constructions and ordinary ways of speaking is learned at an early age.

To begin with, it not uncommon for young children who have been read to extensively to fail to notice that some constructions are used only in books, and begin, around age four, to use 'bookish' constructions in their own natural speech. Nor is it unusual to find such children, later on, while still far from literate, picking up their books and inventing stories, replete with literary constructions which they never use in their speech (anymore), and 'reading' them aloud with the intonational inflections used by adults reading aloud. The literary inversions they use most often are inversions after directional adverbs and locative phrases. This is hardly surprising, since the inversions in the children's books that might be read to them are primarily of these two types.

Similarly, there are some inversions which appear to be conventionally colloquial (inversion after negated verbs (15), and implied temporal expressions (50)), although it is probably more correct to say that they are conventionally non-literary: one doesn't learn to use them only in conversational discourse; one learns (generally via explicit instruction) not to use them in formal literary discourse. Strictly speaking, the inversion after *so* and *neither,* with identity-of-sense verb-phrase deletion, is probably not conventionally anything in particular. Although it alternates with an uninverted construction with final *too/either,* as in (62, 63), there doesn't seem to be any colloquial-literary or spoken-written difference between the two constructions, although there is a greater possibility of not deleting with *too/either* in literary discourse, than with initial *So/Neither.*

(62a) (= 21a) It'll get your clothes pretty clean, but so will the others.

(62b) It'll get your clothes pretty clean, but the others will (get them pretty clean) too.

(63a) (= 22b) None of the examples in (13) are contrastive, as noted above, and neither are many of the other tokens in the corpus.

(63b) None of the examples in (13) are contrastive, as noted above, and many of the other tokens in the corpus aren't (contrastive) either.

Still, the inversion is perfectly unremarkable in both conversational and literary discourse.

It does not appear to be possible, then, to give a uniform explanation for the distribution of colloquial or literary inversions, or even for inversions characteristic of narrative: two are conventionally literary (apparently)—inversion after directional and locative phrases, one conventionally non-literary (after temporal phrases), and one both circumstantially and conventionally colloquial (after directional adverbs). The overall distribution of these inversions seems hardly likely to be a simple function of their use in narrative discourses.

Proportions

Is it possible to explain why the literary inversion types outnumber the colloquial inversion types, by about two to one? It has been suggested that to the extent that inversions are optional and 'stylistic' variations, it is natural that they belong to the written-literary register, where production of utterances involving deviations from 'canonical' forms can be done at a leisurely, considered, deliberate pace; and that to the extent that inversions are obligatory, ARE the canonical forms, it is natural that they occur freely in spontaneous speech. Suppose that we ignore the problems in distinguishing obligatory forms of expression from optimal 'stylistic' variants, so that we can say, for instance, that the difference between *Is John here?* and *John's here?* is qualitatively different from the difference between *Standing in the corner was a Tiffany lamp* and *A Tiffany lamp was standing in the corner.* Still, there are problems in supporting this explanation. First of all, almost all inversions after a preposed element are obligatory, given the preposing of that element. This holds for both literary inversions like those after negative adverbs, participles, adjectives, and locative and directional phrases, and colloquial inversions like those after negative NPs, *no sooner, so/neither, here/there.*[14] (The sole exception is after directional adverbs, the most conversational of literary inversions.) And if we say that we are talking about the construction, not just the inversion, all of the preposings turn out to be optional, so that will not distinguish the colloquial from the literary inversions either. Second, both of the colloquial inversions that don't involve preposing are also syntactically optional, as shown by the uninverted exclamations and negated verbs in (64).

(64a) He was mad!

(64b) Nobody don't break up no/a fight. (after Labov, 1972)

It will not help to try to save some instances from being classified as optional by saying that the two variants have different meaning, connotations, implications,

---

[14]Of course, inversions that invert over main verbs are blocked if the subject is pronominal:

*Onto the field ran he.
Onto the field he ran.

But if the subject is non-pronominal, these are just as obligatory as the auxiliary inversions:

*Never I had been so relieved.
Never had I been so relieved.

or uses; almost all syntactic variants differ in this way [15]—A-Raising, Passive, Extraposition, Neg-Raising, etc. This list is large and the literature burgeoning (Borkin, 1974; Prince, 1978, 1980; Davison, 1980; Horn, ms., etc.).

VIII. CONCLUSION

While inversions of one sort or another are distributed ove the whole range of spoken and written language, it is not along the spoken-written dimension, but along (and thirty miles either side of, as they say in the tornado warnings) a colloquial-literary dimension, which cuts across the spoken-written classification.

Some of these inversions are colloquial or literary for functional reasons, some for reasons having to do with properties of their component parts, and some are just conventionally colloquial or literary and must be learned as a person becomes literate, along with the conventions about capital letters and periods, and writing from left to right or vice versa.

Regardless of whether inversions are base-generated, or generated by transformations, about which I have made no claims or assumptions, the analysis presented here has implications for a general theory of linguistic competence, encompassing not only the knowledge of grammar that tells which forms are 'in the language', and which are not, but also knowledge of language use, or discourse competence, which, given a semantics, tells when certain forms are appropriate and what they're appropriate for (cf. Green, in press). For it seems from this investigation of English usage that speakers distinguish not only a literary register and a colloquial register, but also distinct styles of literary speech, and perhaps, if they are writers, styles or levels or registers of colloquial writing. If so, then their knowledge of the use of their language is perhaps more sophisticated than might be supposed by someone who assumed that only writers know the literary 'dialect'. I am not claiming that all speakers can do this equally well (cf. (41)), or even that all can do it.[16] This is one of the crucial differences between knowledge of language, which all speakers have, by definition, and knowledge about the language (or knowledge of language use), which is a kind of knowledge of culture, and may be acquired much more slowly than knowledge of the language, continuing no doubt past middle age. Some people are more sensitive to it than others, and it is a good part of what makes some people more articulate than others.

This knowledge is not a kind of grammar, not even 'discourse grammar', but knowledge about how to exploit 'sentence grammar' for rhetorical purposes. I

---

[15]The strongest cases for equivalence that I know of are Dative Movement and Particle Movement cases, and even these are probably not water-tight.

[16]Although I would suspect that even illiterate adults have a pretty fair conception of what is 'bookish' language and what is not.

have sketched elsewhere (Green, in press) how this might work, but the bulk of the descriptive and developmental corroboration remains to be fleshed out.

REFERENCES

AISSEN, JUDITH. 1975. Presentational There-insertion; a cyclic root transformation. Papers from the 11th Regional Meeting, Chicago, Linguistic Society, ed. by R. E. Grossman, L. J. San, and T. J. Vance. 1–14.

BANFIELD, ANN. 1973. Narrative style and the grammar of direct and indirect speech. Foundations of language. 10:1–39.

BOLINGER, DWIGHT. 1977. There. Meaning and form, 90–123. London: Longmans.

BORKIN, ANN. 1974. Raising to object position. University of Michigan Ph.D. dissertation. Unpublished.

BREWER, WILLIAM, AND EDWARD LICHTENSTEIN. 1981. Event schemas, story schemas, and story grammars. Attention and performance IX, ed. by John Long and Alan Baddeley. Hillsdale, N.J.: Erlbaum.

DAVISON, ALICE. 1980. Peculiar passives. Language 56:42–66.

EMONDS, JOSEPH. 1971. Root and structure-preserving transformations. M.I.T. Ph.D. dissertation. Unpublished. (Indiana University Linguistics Club).

――――. 1976. A transformational approach to English syntax. New York: Academic Press.

FOWLER, H. W. 1923. On grammatical inversion. Society for Pure English, Tract 10, 9–25.

GARY, NORMAN. 1975. Discourse functions of some root transformations. Indiana University Linguistics Club.

GREEN, GEORGIA M. 1976. Main clause phenomena in subordinate clauses. Language 52:382—397.

――――. 1977. Do inversions in English change grammatical relations. Studies in the linguistic sciences 7:1 157—181. (University of Illinois, Department of Linguistics).

――――. 1978. Remarks on a proposal presented by Thomas Dieterich and Guy Carden at the NWAVE-VII Colloquium on the validation of introspective judgements. In manuscript.

――――. 1980. Some wherefores of English inversions. Language 56:582—601.

――――. 1982. Linguistics and the pragmatics of language use. Poetics,:1.

HARTVIGSON, HANS H., AND LEIF KVISTGAARD JAKOBSEN. 1974. Inversion in present-day English. Odense: Odense University Press.

HERMON, GABRIELLA. 1979. On the discourse structure of direct quotation. Technical Report 143, Center for the Study of Reading. University of Illinois, Champaign, Ill.

HORN, LAURENCE. In manuscript. Presupposition; variations on a theme.

HORN, LAURENCE, GEORGIA GREEN, AND JERRY MORGAN. In manuscript. Here comes the bus.

JACOBSSON, BENGT. 1951. Inversion in English, with special reference to the early modern English period. Uppsala: Almqvist and Wiksells.

LABOV, WILLIAM. 1972. Negative attraction and negative concord in English grammar. Language 48:773–818.

LAKOFF, ROBIN, AND DEBORAH TANNEN. 1979. Communicative strategies in conversation; the case of *Scenes from a marriage*. Proceedings of the 5th annual meeting, Berkeley Linguistics Society, 581–192. Berkeley: Dept. of Linguistics, University of California.

LAWLER, JOHN. 1977. A agrees with B in Achenese; A problem for relational grammar. Syntax and semantics 8: Grammatical relations, ed. by P. Cole and J. Sadock, 219–248. New York: Academic Press.

McCAWLEY, JAMES D. 1978. Conversational implicature and the lexicon. Syntax and semantics 9: Pragmatics, ed. by P. Cole, 245–260. New York: Academic Press.

McCAWLEY, NORIKO. 1973. Boy! Is syntax easy! Papers from the ninth regional meeting, Chicago Linguistic Society, ed. by C. Corum, T. C. Smith-Stark, and A. Weiser, 369–377.

OCHS, ELINOR. 1979. Planned and unplanned discourse. Syntax and semantics 12: Discourse and syntax, ed. by T. Givon, 51–80. New York: Academic Press.

PRINCE, ELLEN. 1978. A comparison of *It*-clefts and *WH*-clefts in discourse. Language 54:883–906.

———. 1980. A comparison of left-dislocation and topicalization in discourse. In manuscript.

TANNEN, DEBORAH. 1979. Processes and Consequences of Conversational Style. University of California, Berkeley, Ph.D. dissertation.

TERKEL, STUDS. 1974. Working. New York: Avon Books.

VISSER, F. 1963. An historical syntax of the English language. Leiden: Brill.

SOURCES

APN "Sexism in English: A Feminist View," by Alleen Pace Nilsen. In E&R, 134–143.

BICI *Baby, It's Cold Inside*, by S. J. Perelman. New York: Simon and Schuster, 1970.

BLT *The Brave Little Tailor*. Racine, Wis.: Golden Press.

CUC Champaign-Urbana Courier, a fine, lamentably defunct newspaper.

CUNG Champaign-Urbana News-Gazette

DP *The Portable Dorothy Parker*. New York: Penguin Books, 1976. (copyright 1930)

DTL "The problem of grammatical relations in surface structure," by D. T. Langendoen. In Proceedings of the Georgetown University Roundtable, ed. by Kurt Jankowsky. Washington: Georgetown University Press, 1973. Pp. 27–37.

EP = Prince 1980

E&R = Eschholz, Paul, and Alfred Rosa, eds. *Subject and strategy; a rhetoric reader*. New York: St. Martin's Press. 1978.

FM "King Kong: Remaking a Classic," by Frank Manchel. In E&R, 180–192.

GBPP *Peter Pan, a Big Golden Book*. Racine, Wis.: Golden Press.

JB "Stranger in the Village," by James Baldwin. In E&R, 349–361.

JF *The Tale of Mr. Jeremy Fisher*, by Beatrix Potter. New York: Frederick Warne, 1906.

JOY *The Joys of Yiddish*, by Leo Rosten. New York: McGraw-Hill, 1968.

JT *The Beast in Me, and Other Animals*, by James Thurber. New York: Harcourt and Brace, 1948.

JW *The King with Six Friends*, by Jay Williams. New York: Parents' Magazine Press, 1968.

MB "The Making of a Textbook", by Mike Bowler. In *Learning*, March 1978, 38–43.

MW *My World and Welcome to It, by James Thurber*. New York: Harcourt 1942.

NA *The Nursery "Alice,"* by Lewis Carroll. London: Macmillan. 1890.

PAT Palo Alto Times

PGW *Full Moon*, by P. G. Wodehouse. Garden City, N.J.: Doubleday. 1947.

PHC *Perelman's Home Companion*, by S. J. Perelman. New York: Simon and Schuster. 1955.

PK "Movies on Television," by Pauline Kael. In E&R, 175–177.

PP *Peter Pan*, by James M. Barrie. New York: Charles Scribner's Sons, n.d.

PW *Pudd'nhead Wilson*, by Mark Twain. New York: New American Library, Signet. 1964.

RM *The Wycherly Woman*, by Ross MacDonald. New York: Bantam Books, 1963.

RS *Might as Well Be Dead*, by Rex Stout. New York: Viking Press, 1956.

SFC The San Francisco Chronicle

SJP The best of S. J. Perelman. New York: Random House, 1947.

TLCC *The Little Colonel's Chum: Mary Ware*, by Annie Fellows Johnston. Boston: The Page Co., 1908.

TW *The Tale of Mrs. Tiggy-Winkle*, by Beatrix Potter. London: Frederick Warne, n.d.

W = Terkel 1974

WGT *Who Goes There?* by Dorothy P. Lathrop. New York: Macmillan, 1953.

WTP *Winnie-the-Pooh*, by A. A. Milne. New York: E. P. Dutton, 1926.

8 Literary Complexity in Everyday Storytelling

Livia Polanyi
University of Amsterdam

ORAL STORYTELLING AND VERBAL ART

Everyday stories told in conversations are overwhelmingly of a throwaway variety, with the teller quickly recounting some incident which took place, usually in his or her own life, in order to make a point relevant to the embedding conversation. These stories, nonetheless, present much of the complexity and ambiguity to the analyst which is often associated with verbal art—particularly with written narrative prose. In this paper, some small excerpts taken from stories told in ordinary spoken interactions will be submitted to a close analytic reading of the sort normally accorded only to literary texts by critics and theorists. Through this analysis, it will become clear that far from conveying only one level of meaning and being uniformly easy to interpret, everyday oral stories demonstrate the same complexities in manipulating point of view, identity of reference, and multiplicity of meaning which have hitherto been treated as special qualities of literary language.[1]

Specifically, we shall be dealing with the function in everyday texts of the indeterminancy and polysemy which result from the point of view and narrative voice of the storyteller merging with that of one of the characters in the story (sometimes called indirect free style narration). My claim in this chapter is that these mergers of perspective, both in oral stories and literary texts, are sympto-

---

[1]See Pratt (1977), Chapter 1, for an extensive discussion of the issue of 'literary language'. All of the discussion of 'free indirect style' which I have come across, with the exception of Eisner (1975), have used exclusively literary (or made-up) examples and discourse, from an assured stance of dealing with phenomena local to 'verbal art'.

matic of the difficulties narrators face in encoding several levels of information simultaneously and should thus properly be seen as solutions of problems of reporting encountered by storytellers, regardless of medium or artistic intent. Thus, the device of indirect free speech should not be thought a diagnostic for distinguishing the 'literary' from the 'prosaic'.[2]

These complex merged forms do not necessarily fulfill the same functions in oral, interactive storytelling and written (literary) narrative. However, I will not be dealing with the functioning of these forms in written texts, but I will confine myself to pointing out how speakers manipulate the ambiguity inherent in many aspects of the linguistic system to accomplish tasks in the storytelling situation which grow out of social constraints to behave properly as a storyteller and story recipient. Therefore, while much attention will be paid to identifying and describing special properties of everyday talk which distinguish it from literary discourse, the aim of the arguments presented here will be to dispute the notion that literariness can be located in the use of specific sorts of encoding devices in literary texts: differentiating the literary from the non-literary must therefore be made on other grounds entirely.

AMBIGUITY AND INDETERMINACY RESULTING FROM UNEXPECTED SHIFTERS

When a story is told, either in conversation, through letters, or in any sort of literary work, a storyworld is created with its own spatial and temporal reference points. The characters who people the world operate in the timeframe of the story and move about their world from place to place. Likewise, the events and situations which occur are located in time and space within the confines of the created worlds. Tellers, as they recount their tales of other worlds, necessarily must assume a vantage point from which to describe what went on. Normally, narrators speak from one vantage point at a time, describing the goings on sometimes as an omniscient narrator who knows everything, who can see everywhere; sometimes as an external narrator who reports only what a more or less invisible and uninvolved character present on the scene might reasonably notice; and sometimes as one or another character involved in the action at the time it occurred. They are not wedded to one viewpoint, but can switch from one of these vantage points to another as they see fit. Usually such shifts are obvious and unremarkable, but on occasion a narrator does something unexpected, shifting from one viewpoint to another when we would not expect it, and the end result is a text which is indeterminate or ambiguous at a certain point, and it may not be possible to determine where the narrator is 'standing' to report the goings on in the story.

---

[2]I have taken these terms from Pratt (1977).

Very often these complexities result from difficulty in assigning a unique meaning to 'discourse shifters', the category of linguistic forms including deictics, demonstratives, and pronouns, whose meaning is not fixed but is determined at any moment in a discourse by reference to context, either internal or external to the text.

Normally, speakers refer to where they are as 'here'; to themselves individually as 'I' or as part of a group as 'we'; and to things close to them as 'this'. In contrast, places where they are not located are 'there'; other people are 'you' or 'he' or 'they'; and things remote from them are 'that'. In telling stories, however, speakers construct alternative storyworlds, people them with characters not present in the situation of telling, and tell about situations and events which do not obtain at the moment the story is being told. The 'here' and 'I' and 'this' of the characters in the story are thus different from the 'here' and 'I' and 'this' of the narrator. When a speaker switches from the perspective of external narrator to speak as a character in the story, the 'here' and 'I' and 'this' of the speaker shift and must be indexed relative to the character in the story. Story recipients, those listening to the story, then realize that the speaker is no longer speaking 'normally' but is taking the point of view of someone in the story world.

This is all straightforward. There are times, however, when a speaker will be talking either as a narrator located in the conversation, or as a character in a story, and will switch too suddenly to the other viewpoint—speaking as someone or from someplace other than the context of the discourse has so far suggested. As we shall see below, such shifts are often signalled in the surface structure of sentences by unexpected pronomial or deictic forms which frustrate expectations built up from relevant previous context about the speaker's identity or location. Because as story recipients and story analysts we do not discard our expectations immediately, we end up interpreting the sentence or text containing the unexpected form as presenting a combination of expected and unexpected viewpoints, as may become clear with the first example. This example, which is taken from a story told by a husband and wife about the wife's experiences giving birth, illustrates a simple collapse of viewpoints. The speaker effectively collapses the moment of telling with the events in the storyworld by shaking her arm in the air and using *this* instead of the expected *the* or *that* as she says:

(1)   and I shook *this* I-V and said I'm on an I-V and I can't eat.

By shaking her arm as if it were still connected to the long gone I-V bottle and shouting *I can't eat* precisely as she had at the time, she brings the delivery room to life around the dinnertable where the telling took place. The deictic *this* locates the speaker in the storyworld relative to the I-V, while *said* clearly places the time of the events past relative to the time of reporting. The screaming recreates the moment of original screaming. Thus the speaker talks from two worlds at once—a very common device in oral storytelling which is used most often, as is the case here, to highlight the climatic moment in the story.

A more complex situation obtains in the second example, when the speaker, explaining why her (absent) niece will move to a new apartment, comments approvingly:

(2)   The new apartment'll be better for her since it costs $300. *Here* she pays 450.

In (2), the use of the deictic *here* to refer to a place other than where the speaker herself was located during the storytelling unites the teller and her niece. Since it is not a fictitious story and the two women were both alive when the story was told, the *here* which joins them in space in the telling, making them co-present with each other—sharing the *here*—actually acts as well to join them in time, collapsing the temporal reference points of the storyworld with those of the world of the telling, the 'now' in which they both live. The historical present of *pays* is thus not only a narrative tense which must be interpreted relative to the storyworld but is also a normal present tense which is properly interpreted as the 'now of time of speaking'.[3]

Just as an unexpected shifter can redefine the distinction between 'here and there' and 'then and now', the pronominal 'your' used unexpectedly in example (3) collapses seemingly inviolate distinction between 'I and other', as the narrator finishes up a trivial but frightening story about a light going out automatically when she was watching television by saying:

(3)   I try to keep things like that out of *your* head.

(Taken from Eisner, 1975)

After having told a story designed apparently to get frightening things *like that* into her listeners' heads (this story was told during an adolescent round of 'scary-things-which-happen-when-you're babysitting' stories) the *your* seems curiously inappropriate, especially since the story to this point has concerned only the narrator's own feelings and reactions. But by using *your* instead of the expected *my*, clumsy as this may look on the printed page, the speaker has managed to solve one of the problems which she must deal with before finishing her story—she has managed to bring the events and situations out of the storyworld and effected a merger of the storyworld with the conversation in which it was embedded, thereby demonstrating the relevance of the story to the circumstances obtaining in the moment of telling.

With *your*, the story recipients are brought into the storyworld, and 'exiting' from the story back into the conversation is begun.[4] Although the speaker can not

---

[3]The relationship between time and temporal expressions in stories embedded in conversation is much too complex and off the point to be dealt with here. These details are dealt with in detail elsewhere (Polanyi, 1980b; Polanyi & Scha, forthcoming.)

[4]The management of storytelling in conversation, and especially the details of the sequential aspects of entrance, exit, and acceptance talk, has been dealt with elsewhere (See Sacks, 1970–1971; Jefferson, 1978; and Polanyi, 1978, 1980a.)

be *you* to herself, she is properly one of the general 'you' familiar from expressions such as 'you gotta watch out'. Therefore, by using *your* instead of *my,* the speaker has switched from the egostistical perspective focussed upon herself which she had maintained throughout the storytelling, to one in which she was no longer the focus of attention, being only one of the general 'you'. Her reaction to the light going out is thus neatly ascribed to the listeners as well as to herself, and she can no longer be seen as having had an idiosyncratic over-reaction to a commonplace event: everyone would be frightened and needs to have *things like that kept out of your heads.*

Exactly what, one might ask, must be kept out of exactly whose head? This sort of disquieting merger of points of view is called 'free indirect style' when encountered in literary texts. In our example taken from everyday storytelling, the device which allows the 'I' of the teller to remain peeping out from behind the 'you' of *your heads,* in addition to creating an ambiguity for the listener to resolve in trying to decide where the speaker stands in relation to her discourse, also accomplishes a number of interactional tasks, relating the speaker and hearer to the storytelling. Tasks unique to the interactive oral storytelling situation.

FREE INDIRECT SPEECH IN ORAL STORYTELLING

When found in literary texts, free indirect style most characteristically involves reported speech or thought in which the third person perspective of the narrator is represented along with a first person perspective of a speaker, as found in examples (4) and (5), which were both taken from reports of movie plots collected by Eisner (1975). Though not uncommon in modern stream-of-consciousness novels, these two examples below are the only two illustrations of 'classic' indirect free speech which I have come across in examining a fairly large corpus of recorded strokes.

(4)   And he was telling Dolly, I don't want *Dolly.*

(5)   And he goes to her, he goes, I don't think *she's* gonna die anymore. *She's* gonna live.

In both cases there is a mixture of speech forms. If the speakers of the quoted material are, as they appear to be, the two 'he' characters, then they should use some sort of 'you' to address their interlocutors in the storyworlds instead of the third person forms which we have here (*Dolly* in the one case and *she* in the other). On the other hand, if the narrator is not quoting exactly what the character said, but is only reporting approximately what was said from the removed distance of an observer, then the 'I' forms are inappropriate to refer to the speakers, who should be referred to instead with third person forms as in (4a) and (5a):

(4a)   And he was telling Dolly, *he* don't want Dolly.

(5a)   And he goes to her, he goes, *he* don't think she's gonna die. She's gonna live.

We may ask the question, why is this classic free indirect speech, common in novels, found so rarely in oral storytelling and then, our evidence suggests, most commonly in reporting stories which the narrator did not participate in, but only heard or experienced via another teller? My theory is, and I consider it still an open question certainly, that this style may be used principally when there are three levels of individuals involved in a reporting: the character in the storyworld, the narrator who observed goings on in the storyworld via an original telling, and the speaker who must report both the embedded story (what was said in the movies in our examples) and the embedding story (that the speaker heard it said). This complex form, then, would allow the speaker to tell the story more or less directly, speaking much of the time as a character in the embedded storyworld, and yet continue to fulfill the constraint to report what was actually experienced directly—in these cases, watching the movies. Thus the free indirect style for reported speech permits the teller to limit responsiblity to what could reasonably be expected of someone to remember of a situation in which the speaker never was a participant.

OTHER FORMS OF REPORTED SPEECH

Along with the unusual forms of indirect free speech which have been discussed above, we also find a number of other forms of ways to report the thoughts and remarks of characters in oral storytelling. A very common device certainly is normal direct discourse, in which the characters' exact words are quoted with a full tag identifying who was speaking. Indirect discourse is even more common, with the words paraphrased or loosely reported by the teller. Still another familiar device which is frequently found is 'free direct discourse', in which a character's exact words are quoted but without an identifying 'I said' or 'John said' specifying exactly who the speaker is.[5]

In addition to these well documented ways of dealing with quoted material, we also find types of reported speech in conversational storytelling which has not been reported in literature and which may well be unique to oral storytelling, since they exploit resources particular to casual spoken delivery, as is the case in 'double direct discourse' found in example (6), in which exactly what the character, the speaker's grandfather, said to his son, the speaker's father, while killing a rat,

---

[5]In oral storytelling, speakers do make comments on the manner of speaking, such as 'he was talking softly when he said it', but we do not seem to get the unmarked adverbial lexical or phrasal tags so familiar from written prose (i.e. "he said softly"). Since the narration is oral in any case, the most relevant expressive qualities will often be acted out and, should it seem particularly important, discussed at some length.

is said twice, once with the grandfather's diction and once again with the character's:

(6)   And my grandfather says
       Now I'm going to stick the broom under the couch.
       I'm going to pull it out and you start hitting—
       He's telling my father
       Youse start hitting the rat with the hammer
       You squash him, right?

(Taken from Schiffrin, 1981)

Here we do not have mixed speech in the classic sense which we had above. Here there is no confusion about who is talking—the character in the story is speaking, and the grandfather said only *one* sentence which was repeated twice. Grandfather's first command is in the voice and manner of the narrator speaking through the character in his story, or, put more felicitously perhaps, it is the character speaking with the diction of the narrator (*I'm going to pull it out and you start hitting.*) The repetition of exactly what grandfather said, which follows immediately after, is in a conventionalized form of common man speech, with the word choice reflecting a lively dialectal style (*Youse start hitting the rat with the hammer. You squash him, right?*) Due to the de facto repetition of what grandfather said, we get two views of the same event, one distanced somewhat (in the narrator's diction) and one much more intimate (in the grandfather's voice and thus from within his world). The two manners of speaking reflect the upward mobility experienced by this family in just two generations, since the grandson carefully demonstrates his own mastery over the standard language before launching into a quotation with a richer and somewhat stigmatized mode of expression. A novel which employed such techniques might well be considered quite bold, since it would explicitly demonstrate an aspect of social use of narration, yet in oral storytelling such a complex encoding goes by without attracting attention. The entire repetition is over so quickly that there are only the impression of two voices, the identification with the character felt by the narrator and, simultaneously, his distance from him. The double viewpoint, fast cut in speaking, has none of the awkwardness it has when met on a printed page.

In examples (4) and (5) we dealt briefly with what I was calling 'classic free indirect speech' and in example (6) we have looked at 'double direct discourse', which may be unknown in literature. Now we will be looking at some ambiguity-inducing 'mixed' forms which are sometimes lumped in with 'indirect free style', but since they are not directly concerned with reported speech I am discussing them here.

Example (7) is taken from a story about the narrator's experiences while a counselor in a summercamp. She is in the middle of telling about the time she was very late in returning to camp because she was out joyriding with some young boys, along with another counselor:

(7)   We borrowed someone's car
       and we got blown out
       and w- so the car stalled
       but we didn't ca—couldn't call
       because we were supposed to be out t ' lunch
       and why were we *here?*
       Cause we had moved. . .off the road to party

                                                        (Taken from Schiffrin, 1981)

Although the overall tone of this piece is that of a narrator removed in time and space from the storyworld, there is a shadow of one (or more?) conversations taking place, either among the tardy girls struggling to come up with an excuse to explain why they were late when they finally made it back to camp, or between the girls and their angry boss back at camp later. Perhaps we hear several voices from several different conversations jumbled together. Certainly the narrator is explaining, justifying why they could not call. The very tone of justification raises the question of who the real recipient of *Why were we here?* might have been: one of the delinquent girls? The angry boss? The people listening to the story being told? If this last is the case, then the speaker is a somewhat distanced narrator explaining what went on, with the *here* acting to introduce her into her own story—presenting this part of the story from the perspective of someone physically present in the storyworld where the stalled car and its passengers were *off the road to party*.

This is one of the few examples in this paper which I have never heard but know only from reading the transcript. Often the point of view or voice represented in a piece of oral storytelling which may be ambiguous or confusing in print may be easily understood with access to the tape of the storytelling, since narrators often assign distinctive accents, speech rhythms, and pitches to different characters, and reserve a neutral delivery for statements made from the vantage point of narrator in the conversation. Untagged free direct speech is thus often fairly easily ascribed to the proper character, and those listening to the story are informed through how the different speeches sound who is, in fact, making them.

Thus in example (8), which is taken from the same childbirth story as example (1), the narrator signals to the listeners that the character *coming up into obstetrics* and not knowing what is going on is Meyers, the 'bowelman', by the tone of voice which is assigned to this new person on the scene, a loud aggressive manner of speaking quite different from the tonal quality assigned to other characters:

(8)   but this Meyers guy, the bowelman, was really freaked out by it. He's coming
       up into obstetrics. What's going on here? What are you doing?

What's going on here? What are you doing? were said by the 'bowel man', and, as a storytelling competent, I had no difficulty assigning mental quotation marks to these two questions. The bowel man, in the storyworld, asked those two questions, and the storyteller was, in fact, mimicking his voice—or, more accurately, making it clear that the rough loud voice should be taken for mimicry.

On the other hand, I found what happened next more problematic. One of the story recipients, who had never heard the story before, 'entered' the storyworld momentarily and became, very briefly, a co-teller of the story, putting a third question into the bowel man's mouth. Example (9) should make clearer what went on (unlike other examples, who was speaking is indicated, since there is a change of speakers. Kate is one speaker, Susan the other.)

(9)   KATE: but this Meyers guy, the bowelman, was really freaked out by it. He's coming up into obstetrics. What's going on here? What are you doing?

SUSAN: Oh no, Kate! What baby?

The question arises, what to do with *What baby?* should it be considered a direct quotation or not? Indeed, in written stories and in most oral ones as well we take for granted that the words which are put in the form of direct speech are to be taken as reporting exactly what the speaker said in the storyworld at the time the saying took place. However, in this case, there is no possible way for the speaker to know what was said in the delivery room by the bowel man since Susan was not present in the delivery room and had never heard the story told before. *What baby?* is not really put forward as a report of what the doctor did say, but only as an indication of what he might have said. Do we have here a form intermediate between direct and indirect discourse?

What baby? was said in a tone of voice which mimicked exactly the tone of voice assigned to him by Kate in *What's going on here? What are you doing?* and the form of the sentence *What baby?* is also grammatically correct for direct discourse, but the claim of veracity for Kate's questions and Susan's question is necessarily different. Kate is, supposedly, telling a story from her own personal experience, and she is allowed to claim an 'expert status' in relation to the happenings at which she was present. Susan, however, has no such privileged status relative to Kate's childbirth. Does her *What baby?* have the status of a fictional utterance, while *What's going on here? What are you doing?* have the status of non-fictional statements?

In fact, fictionality or non-fictionality are not the important issues for participants in oral storytelling when faced with this sort of chiming in by a story recipient. Competents understand that Susan's mimicry fulfills a function in the storytelling interaction—it signals that the story is being well received. By entering the storyworld and sharing the burden of storytelling, Susan unambiguously makes clear that she finds the story convincing and well worth listening to. Thus

What baby? to those present in the storytelling was a piece of acceptance talk—an appreciative remark made during storytelling which assures the storyteller that the story is being understood and enjoyed.

Acceptance talk is clearly a non-written concept, since the written text is not interactive. Joint responsiblity for a verbal production is ruled out in general for written works—except perhaps for marginal cases such as exchanges of notes during classes at school, or texts composed by several persons over an interactive computer net—and is most unusual in our traditions of verbal art as well. Contemporary theater and performance artists experiment with joint responsibility for how a piece of art, verbal or otherwise, 'works out'—encouraging or even requiring the participation of the audience for a piece to succeed or even to take place at all (i.e. many 'happenings' in the 1960's involved such cooperation between 'artist-producers' and 'audience-performers').

MANIPULATING THE CONVENTIONS OF ORAL STORYTELLING

We have briefly touched upon some of the constraints on story tellers and story recipients in the course of this chapter, and an extensive review of the behavior appropriate to those involved in a storytelling situation goes beyond its scope. However, this final example of reported speech involves the skillful manipulation of the notion of 'exit talk' which was mentioned in relation to example (3) above. Tellers must smooth the way as it were from the storyworld they have created back into the embedding conversation. They normally accomplish this by demonstrating the relevance of what has gone on in the storyworld to concerns outside of the storyworld—making the general message of the story clear so that those who have had to sit more or less quietly by and listen to the story (except for the odd bit of acceptance talk) are convinced that the teller has not taken up their attention with a recital of events and situations with no possible import for their own life or experience of the world. Normally, exit talk is fairly easy to spot, since the events of the storyworld are ended and the teller has begun to elicit responses and remarks from the listeners, giving them the chance to demonstrate their understanding and appreciation of the story ('exit talk' on the part of the speaker elicits 'acceptance talk' on the part of the listeners). As we shall see, the resources of the turn-taking system of conversation allow a storyteller who wishes to continue with telling a story which seems ended to return to the storyworld from the embedding conversation. In Example (10), which we will be looking at in detail, N and S have been jointly telling a long story of having been robbed at gunpoint, when N uses one of the 'discourse shifters' discussed earlier to switch the talk back into the story, in a way which surprised both the story recipients at the time and those analysts who have studied the story since.

In order to facilitate understanding of the point I am making, I will give a rather extensive piece of text as context, beginning with a short discussion of exactly what the robber was wearing (lines 1–13), continuing through a justification of N's inability to see what was going on (lines 17–19), and some strong acceptance moves on the part of the story recipients B and L (lines 20–21). We will focus most attention on lines 23–24 *If it ever happens to you, that cop said, that's a very common reaction.* Spoken by N immediately following L's *God,* (line 22, realized in the talk as a long drawn out moan).

(10) S: You see, I tended to identify him basically on   1
          his clothes. He was wearing sort of this, uh,
          this jersey type . . . what do you call that
          material?
     N: No, I don't think it was jersey, wasn't it   5
          just a sweater?
     S: Yeah. It was a knit but it came long and I
          said even to her *"It's green"* and it was green
     N: Yes, she did. I said
     S: she said   **Z1**   10
     N: *I said "I don't know.* Maybe he was wearing
          a leather jacket." I had no idea. (laughter)
          I didn't notice anything
     B: Well with one auditory person and one visual
          person you ought to be able to get a pretty
          good description there
     N: Well, my eyes were focussed on the gun which was
          only a foot from my head
     S: He was holding it like a cop, you know, like
          that with both his hands (unintelligible)   20
     B: Oh, Jesus
     L: God   **Z2**
     N: **If it ever happens to you**, that cop said that's
          a very common reaction, you know, he said after
          you've been trained you can take your eyes   25
          off the gun cause you know it's there and you
          don't have to keep staring at it.

Without exception, people hearing the tape of this story or reading it for the first time interpret the phrase *If it ever happens to you* as a continuation of the exit talk from the story—N's making it clear that her inability to remember what her assailant was wearing should be thought of as a normal reaction, one which could happen to them as well if they were in a similar situation, and was not an unusual (and thus culpable) failure on her part. The *you* seems clearly to be referring to the story recipients, those present in the room during the storytelling. When N continues with *that cop said*, however, the *you* must be reinterpreted as a 'general you' in the STORYTELLING WORLD and then it becomes clear that *If it ever happens to you* is part of the longer quotation set in the timeframe of the story. Thus, N. very successfully uses what appeared at first to be a general comment directed at those present in the telling to effect a re-entry into the storyworld from the conversation, which was beginning to function as more open and general talk, and furthermore she has managed to do this without disturbing the local coherence of the talk, which would normally have precluded moving back into the story from the exit talk without some sort of explicit apology ('I forgot to tell you', or something similar), which would have had the effect of disturbing the telling and making the strong point about the danger of the gun into an afterthought instead of a naturally uttered comment from the policeman, the expert on guns.

In this case, the 'swing phrase' which effects the movement between worlds is finally assigned a unique interpretation in the storyworld, but there are cases, such as (11) below, in which no final assignment can be made, and the problematic sentence might arguably be interpreted relative to the storyworld, the embedding conversation, or even to a sort of sub-world embedded in the conversation (see note 3).

The following example (11) is part of a very short throwaway story told during a conversation about movies on television. It is a very 'lightweight' story, and therefore is even more representative of conversational storytelling than some of the stories we have studied excerpts from earlier in this paper. However, despite its insubstantial nature, it does present substantial problems for the analyst who might want to 'understand' (assign a semantic representation) to every sentence in the story, which would capture adequately the relationships among the sentences both to each other and to the world which they are describing.

(11)   Well, I mean, when I saw it. . .I mean I thought Oh well, it's really quite a good movie I mean it even has Fred Astaire in it but. . .uh (Yeah) I mean *Fred Astaire's so obviously senile* I mean cause he carries on

The sentence which causes the difficulties is *Fred Astaire's so obviously senile*, and what is difficult (if not impossible) to resolve is how to interpret the scope of this sentence. Is the narrator commenting from the embedding conversation about what he thinks in general about Fred Astaire, a person who lives in the same world as he does at the time of speaking? Is he reporting what he thought at the time about Fred Astaire, a person who was living at the time he saw the movie and is also living at the time he utters this sentence? Or was he claiming at the time he saw the movie that the movie was not very good because Fred Astaire was acting the part of a senile person in the movie? What is being said, about whom, and from what sort of vantage point?

Ambiguity of exactly this sort is not possible in literary texts, or in any sort of written text for that manner, because only non-literary oral texts actually occur in the moment of speaking. Written texts never share the moment of speaking, and, while literary texts often model the moment of speaking and an embedding context, no part of a literary text can actually take place in the real world because the world in which the encoding (and decoding) takes place is never the same as the world in which the situations in the text actually obtain. In a literary text, in other words, there can never be a real 'now', this moment, right now, nor a real 'here'. Clearly, too, the 'I' in a storyworld is never a real 'I' but a persona operating as 'I' in the world of the story. In oral storytelling, on the other hand, all of these modelled discourse shifters also are used, but, in addition, there is the real 'now' (in which both encoding and decoding are taking place), a real 'here' in which the telling takes place, and a real 'I' who is speaking and 'you' to whom the 'I' speaks. Therefore, since an oral story can model all of the contexts which are modelled in a literary text and is, in addition, itself unfolding in the real world, oral stories are theoretically more complex than literary narratives and will always present more ambiguity to the analyst who would want to assign semantic interpretations to every sentence in every text. The literary narrative, on the other hand, often considered 'more complex' and, therefore, more 'artistic' than an everyday text because literary texts are assumed to be more 'ambiguous', are actually less ambiguous than everyday story texts. I am not arguing that this little story about Fred Astaire is greater 'art' than Virginia Woolf's stream of consciousness novels (that would be absurd), but merely that 'ambiguity' is not necessarily the hook on which to hang a differentiation between supposedly 'artistic' and 'mundane' texts.

AMBIGUITY AND VERBAL ART IN ORAL STORYTELLING

In this last section, then, I want to follow up the arguments which I have been making above and to look particularly at polysemy and multi-functionality in non-literary texts. The following excerpt from Nowottony, quoted (unsympathetically) by Pratt (1977, p. 22) is typical of the sorts of confusions which literary theorists often have about 'literariness' and 'ambiguity':

> A verbal structure is literary if it presents its topic on more than one level of presentation at the same time, or, alternatively, if one and the same utterance has more than one function in the structure of meaning in which it occurs.

A close reading of the following short text, part of a very long story collected by Mike Agar from a drug addict as part of a series of interviews dealing with 'the life career of a junkie', provides us with a clear, but by no means untypical, example of multi-level and multi-functional semantic structuring in oral storytelling.

(12)   I had been sort of deserted by everybody and I was making the streets, I used to. . .*if you shoot down underneath* the subway at 41st street and 6th avenue there's an underpassage that will take you all the way down to the Penn station, you can walk through the Pennsylvania station and hit the 8th avenue. . .well my route was usually a couple of hours in the Grand Central, then I'd put my coat around me and try to *hustle over* to 41st street and *shoot down there* and it was warm you know, and *I'd make it down there* and I'd get as far as the Penn station, and I'd sit there for a couple of hours until, you know, I *began to get uncomfortable* and I didn't want to get stopped by the law.

As we shall see, this text works simultaneously on two levels, being at the same time a description of the narrator's usual route and a poignant prosepoem of junk, the preoccupation and ruling passion of a junkie. These two levels come together in the homophonous expression *shoot down* in lines 2 and 9. *'Shoot down'* in the sentences in which it occurs here, can be parsed in one of two ways: [*shoot down*], in which case it would mean dart quickly down into the ground and travel underground quickly, a reasonable gloss for this phrase since the speaker is describing his usual route, which involves darting into the subway and going along the subterranean passageways around Times Square; or [*shoot*] *down* in the sense of shoot up on drugs (i.e. inject oneself with drugs).

At the first mention of *'shoot down'* (line 2), the 'darting ' reading feels most probable, with the echo of 'inject drugs' present subliminally under the text. That faint echo is strengthened somewhat by the phrase *to hustle over* (line 8) used in the sense 'to hurry towards', but carrying along the strong street connotation of 'get what you need no matter how'. The second mention of *shoot down* (line 9), *I'd shoot down there and it was warm down there you know, and I'd make it down there* forces a reappraisal of our original interpretation of *shoot down* in line 2, and also poses its own problems. Are these lines (9–10) three sentences consisting of an event (*I'd shoot down there*); a comment (*it was warm down there you know*); and a second event (*and I'd make it down there*)? Or should they be read as event (*I'd shoot down there*); comment (*it was warm down there, you know*) and RESTATEMENT of the first event (*I'd make it down there*). In the first case, *I'd shoot down there* would have the meaning of 'dart', while in the second case, it would have the meaning of *I'd make it down there* which in this case would unambiguously mean 'I'd inject heroin down there'.

We have no clear way to decide. However, the text is open as a literary text is, with information which comes later in the text unsettling earlier interpretations and the entire text demanding to be read on more than one level. In addition, this text is constructed around codes which need to be mastered if one is to understand the text at all. *I began to get uncomfortable* (line 13) for most of us is unproblematical: sitting in a railroad station for a couple of hours with nothing to do in the middle of the winter seems enough to make anyone uncomfortable. But, as Mike Agar has pointed out, this phrase has a special meaning for junkies. Drug addicts have a special relationship to time, and to a junkie a couple of hours since he has last shot heroin is exactly when he would begin to need another dose of the drug, because as the effects wear off a junkie begins to FEEL UNCOMFORTABLE, begins to experience the first warning signals of withdrawal. Alternatively, he may FEEL UNCOMFORTABLE because he thinks he should get moving, so that he does not begin to look ill and attract attention which he does not need or want.[6]

---

[6]I would like to thank Mike Agar very much for sharing both his data and some of his observations with me. I only hope that I have not in any way, misrepresented the glimpses into the junkie's world which this text offers us. (See Agar & Hobbs, 1980), for a discussion of 'junkie time' and an in depth analysis of part of the transcript from which this excerpt was taken.)

This is in many respects a deeply moving and complex text, but many very 'ordinary' everyday texts display similar linguistic ambiguities and poly semantic properties. And they are not 'literature', whatever that may be.

CONCLUSION

In this chapter, I have presented examples and arguments which suggest that literary texts do not have a monopoly on phenomena such as indirect free style, and complexities of point of view, and ambiguity, such as many literary theorists appear to believe. Thus, for some texts, uncertainty and ambiguity arise from a combination of several points of view peeking through in one utterance while, in others, the possibility exists to interpret one and the same sentence in more than one way, with resulting implications for the semantic representation of the entire discourse. These are the sorts of problems which have long concerned literary theorists and the sorts of problems which pose the greatest challenges for the interpretation of prose narrative texts.

My argument in this paper, then, is that the presence of floating points of view and various other types of indeterminacy in a text do not render a text 'literary'. Rather, both for literary artists and everyday tellers, the problem of finding a place to stand in order to report the goings on in another world while carrying out one's role as a competent and trustworthy member of society (who can not know what he or she could not know, for example) is a problem of telling and not the locus of 'verbal art'. The devices which tellers employ to meet the often conflicting constraints under which we all must operate may be complex, amusing, or enlightening as to the structure of narrative language, but they are not, per se, what makes a text 'literature'. Literary theorists, then, would do well to examine the devices and problems which they see as defining 'literariness' to make sure that mundane, everyday texts do not exhibit exactly the same features which they would argue separate the literary sheep from the down to earth, everyday goats.

REFERENCES

AGAR, MICHAEL AND JERRY HOBBS. 1980. Interpreting discourse: Coherence and the analysis of ethnographic interviews. SRI International Tech Note 225.

EISNER, JANET. 1975. A grammar of oral narrative. Unpublished Ph.D. dissertation, University of Michigan.

JEFFERSON, GAIL. Sequential aspects of stories in conversation. Studies in the organization of conversational interaction, ed. by J. Schenkein. New York: Academic Press, 1978.

POLANYI, LIVIA. 1978. The American story. Unpublished Ph.D. dissertation, University of Michigan.

———. 1980. Time and tense in stories and conversation. Talk delivered at the 1980 Annual Winter Meeting of the Linguistic Society of America, San Antonio, Texas.

———. 1981. On telling the same story twice. TEXT, 1 (4) 315–336.

POLANYI, LIVIA AND R. J. H. SCHA. Forthcoming. Temporal semantics of stories in conversation.

PRATT, MARY LOUISE. 1977. Toward a speech act theory of discourse. Bloomington, Indiana: Indiana University Press.

SACKS, HARVEY. 1970–1971. Unpublished lecture notes.

SCHIFFRIN, DEBORAH. Tense variation in narrative. Language 1981, 57:1, 45–62.

9 Poetic Structure in Oral Narrative

William Bright
University of California, Los Angeles

INTRODUCTION

What is the position of literary art with respect to the difference between speech and writing? I take the term 'literature' or 'literary' here to refer, roughly, to that body of discourses or texts which, within any society, are considered worthy of dissemination, transmission, and preservation in essentially constant form. We typically associate such literature with the written medium; however, works originally composed in writing can also be performed in the oral medium. In our society, this occurs, for example, when parents read aloud to children, or when poets give public 'readings'. Furthermore, the established term 'oral literature' reminds us that literature may also be composed orally, and regularly performed in that same medium. Some examples are (a) the oral composition and performance of epics such as the *Iliad* or the *Odyssey* in ancient Greece, or a whole host of poetic and learned works from ancient India; (b) the whole body of myths and legends existing in preliterate societies such as those of the American Indian; and (c) the large number of jokes, riddles, song texts, etc. which exist in the oral traditions of literate societies such as our own. The term 'folklore' is, of course, often used for much of this material. And it is clear that texts which were originally oral may be transcribed and transmitted in the written medium; examples would include printed versions of the *Odyssey* as well as much of the contents of the *Journal of American Folklore*. Finally, if I read a printed folktale aloud to a child or a friend, the text passes back into the oral medium. It must be recognized, then, that the difference between speech and writing is not necessarily basic to a definition of literature.

Among literary texts, the distinction between prose and poetry also seems independent of the difference between speech and writing. But here the definition of 'poetry' can become a problem. A concept of poetry which is traditional in our society, and is still held by many individuals, is that it refers exclusively to texts organized in regular phonological patterns such as those which we designate as meter, and often rhyme as well. By this definition, it is clear that many oral texts have been composed in well-defined meters, and are thus good examples of poetry; examples include the *Odyssey,* as originally composed in Ancient Greek, or Anglo-American folksong texts of recent centuries. But among the literary texts of our society, at least since the time of Walt Whitman, there has been increasing recognition of 'free verse', or poetry without well-defined metrical structure.

At the present time, most new poetry published in English lacks any recognizable meter. The question then arises of how it can be distinguished from prose—along with the subsidiary problem of defining the so-called 'prose poem'. Poets don't seem to worry much about how to define poetry; they simply know a poem when they meet one. However, a rough definition that appeals to me is this: a poem is a text in which linguistic form—phonological, syntactic, and lexical—is organized in such a way as to carry an aesthetic content which is at least as important, as regards the response of the receiver, as is the cognitive content carried by the same text. In traditional English poetry, both oral and written, a large part of the aesthetic content was carried by well-known phonological patterns of meter and rhyme. In more modern English poetry, phonology still plays an important part, insofar as the sounds of words are still used for aesthetic effect; but grammatical and lexical structures are also exploited extensively for poetic ends.

NON-METRICAL POETRY IN TRADITIONAL CULTURES

Given this recognition of non-metrical poetry in our own modern society, can we recognize similar poetry in older or more traditional cultures? In fact, it has long been realized that parts of the Hebrew Bible—the so-called 'poetic' books, such as the Psalms—are examples of non-metrical poetry, presumably of oral composition; linguistic features other than meter—e.g. syntactic parallelism, as discussed by Jakobson (1966)—carry much of the aesthetic content of these texts. By contrast, the historical books of the Bible lack these special linguistic features, for the most part, and are thus identified as prose.[1] But what about the works of oral literature which have been transcribed in preliterate societies of our own century, by linguists and anthropologists? Can a distinction between prose and poetry be recognized in, for instance, American Indian materials?

---

[1]For a general discussion of poetry in non-literate societies, especially in the old world, see Finnegan (1977).

In many older writings on American Indian literature (e.g. Day, 1951), we find the implicit viewpoint that song texts are poetry—but that everything else, such as myths, are prose. This view perhaps derived from the traditional notion, in English literature, that poetry must be metrical; and a musical performance would, of course, associate a song text with a particular meter. By contrast, since American Indian myth texts were normally not sung, they were classified as prose. More recently, this view has been eclipsed, and modern collections of American Indian literature translated into English (e.g. Rothenberg, 1972) contain numerous examples of myths which are presented typographically as poems. We need to ask, however, whether the poetic structure exists in the original Indian-language text, or whether it has been imposed by the English translator. In fact, although the translators have often been skilled poets, they have just as often been totally ignorant of the Indian languages concerned; their procedure has simply been to take literal English translations published by linguists and anthropologists, and to rewrite them in more poetic form. In such cases, we have no assurance that the Indian-language texts are in any way recognizable as poetry rather than prose.

However, the recent writings of two scholars, Dennis Tedlock and Dell Hymes, have done much to demonstrate the existence of poetic form in American Indian narratives. One might say that a first step was taken by Tedlock (1972) in his translations from Zuni. Here we have a translator who knows the original language. He has scrupulously recorded the expressive features of pitch, loudness, rhythm, timbre, and silence as used in the oral performances of Zuni storytellers. Thus, although Tedlock does not explictly point out many linguistic features which would define Zuni narratives as poetry, his poetic renderings into English strongly point to a poetic structure in the Zuni originals. By contrast, Hymes (1976, 1977, 1980) has focused not on features of live performances, but rather on patterns that can be observed in published texts—namely, the ways in which vocabulary, word-formation, syntax, and semantics are used to create literary structures. Thus Hymes has shown that Chinookan texts can be divided into VERSES—not on the basis of meter or rhyme, but on the basis of features such as SENTENCE-INITIAL PARTICLES, translatable into English as 'and', 'so', 'then', etc. With this concept of the verse as our basis, it is possible to recognize other structurally defined units, both larger and smaller.

Building on the work of Tedlock and Hymes, I have attempted in earlier publications (Bright, 1979, 1980) to identify units of poetic structure in the myths of the Karok tribe of California, and to produce English translations in a corresponding poetic form. Studying a tape-recorded text both with the approach of Tedlock—focusing on the expressive features of performance—and with the approach of Hymes—identifying verses etc. in terms of linguistic structure—I find that the two approaches coincide 90 percent of the time in their identification of basic units. This gives me confidence that occasional ambiguities of one approach can be resolved by reference to the other. For example, linguistic sequences which have two possible grammatical interpretations can be disambiguated by reference to phenomena of pitch and pause; conversely, accidental hesitations which create 'false' pauses in performance can be recognized by considering features of sentence structure.

In the remainder of this chapter, I wish to offer a more detailed demonstration of the 'ethnopoetic' analysis of a Karok myth which I transcribed from dictation in 1951. My method is that of Hymes rather than Tedlock, since the myth in question—like, perhaps, most of the native North American myth literature available to us—was not tape-recorded from actual performance, but rather transcribed from dictation.

POETIC STRUCTURE IN A KAROK MYTH

The Karok are a Hokan tribe living along the middle course of the Klamath River in northwestern California (Humboldt and Siskiyou counties). Their aboriginal culture, which was very similar to that of the neighboring Yurok, has been sketched in Bright (1978). A grammar of their language, with dictionary and texts, is published as Bright (1957). A large and important collection of previously unpublished Karok texts in English translation is now also available (Kroeber & Gifford, 1980).

The present text is one of those Karok stories in which Coyote, as a member of the pre-human race of *ikxaré·yavs* or 'spirits', acts as something much more than a trickster: through his tricks, he provides humans with their basic foods for all subsequent time. This text (published previously in Bright, 1957:204–7) was dictated to me by Mrs. Mamie Offield, at her isolated home on the slopes of sacred Offield Mountain (called *ʔikxariyá-ttu·yšip*, lit. 'spirit-mountain', in Karok). Mrs. Offield had worked with Gifford, both as a source of data and as a translator for older Karok. A photograph of her appears in the Kroeber-Gifford volume.

The identification of poetic structures in Karok narrative—first of all, the recognition of VERSES—can be readily carried out by following Hymes' method of looking for sentence-initial particles. In Karok, the first verse of a myth begins either with *ʔuknî·* 'Once upon a time . . .', or simply without a particle; thereafter, verses normally begin with such particles or particle-combinations as *kári xás* (the commonest of all) 'and then', *víri* 'so', *taʔíttam* (with Anterior-tense verbs) 'so', or *yakún* 'you see'. Sometimes we even find sequences of these particles, e.g., *kári xás taʔíttam* 'and so then'.

This concept of the verse enables us to recognize other units, both smaller and larger. Within the verse, we can identify LINES, such that each line corresponds to a possible predication. (Lines are indicated here by successive indentations within the numbered verses.) One type of example simply has two or more independent verbs, as in the following verse from our text:

(9) *kári xás va· ká·n ?u?u·m,*
   and then that there he arrived

     And then he got there,

    yô·ram ?ukrî·š.
    corner   he sat down

     he sat down in the corner.

Or there may be one or more subordinate clauses:

(43) *víri po·pkíya·vrin*
   so   when she turned

     So when she turned,

    sâ·m   tó·ppárihfak.
    downhill she started down

     she started downhill.

Or a quotation may constitute one or more lines within a verse:

(12) *kári xás ?uppi·p,*
   and then he said

     And then he said,

    "tánaxxúriha,
    I'm hungry

     "I'm hungry,

    tî·matê·   ?á·ma   kan?am."
    let a bit   salmon   I eat

     I think I'll have a bite of salmon."

Or, finally, word order may signal line structure. The normal order for Karok is Subject-Object-Verb; when Noun Phrases occur AFTER the verb, they may be regarded as independent predications. (Any Noun Phrase can act as such a predication in Karok: *tú·yšip* '[It's a] mountain.') I then consider them separate lines:

(27) *ta?ittam kun?íffikahe·n*
   so   they'd gathered them

     So they'd gathered them,

    paxuntáppan,
    the acorns,

     [it was] those acorns,

    pa?asiktávaansa.
    the women.

     the women [did].

On levels above that of the verse, we can first identify SCENES, marked in the text by capital letters A, B, C etc. In Karok, these seem to be definable most consistently in terms of the participants involved. Thus, in the present text, the participants in Scene A are the two sisters who are hoarding salmon and acorns; in Scene B, only Coyote speaks and acts; in Scene C, there is conversation between the sisters and Coyote; and so on. (Thinking operatically, as I like to do, we might say that Scene A is a duet; B is Coyote's solo; and C is a trio.) In addition, some scenes—but not all—are introduced by the particle *ta?ittam* 'so' with a verb bearing the suffix *-he·n* 'Anterior tense'. This sequence typically indicates a lapse of time after the action previously described:

(26) *kári xás   ká·n   kunívyi·hma*   And then they went there.
    and then there   they went to

[End of scene.]

(27) *taˀíttam   kunˀíffikahe·n*   So they had gathered them,
    so   they had gathered them

    paxuntáppan . . .   those acorns . . .
    the acorns

A final level to be distinguished here is that of ACTS, which seem to correspond to major changes in the locale of action. Verbs of motion act as formal markers, either at the end of one act or the beginning of the next; thus, in the present text, Verse 26 (quoted just above) ends Act I. The following verse opens the first scene of Act III:

(40) *taˀíttam   kunpiyâ·ramahe·n*   So they had gone off again.
    so   they had gone again

For me, the discovery of measured verse in Karok myths is exciting both because it helps me understand, for the first time, the distinctive functions of the sentence-initial particles, and because of the insights it gives into these texts as literary creations. In my free translation, I have attempted to convey the poetic values which I feel in the Karok original, and yet to use language as it might be used in original English verse of the 1980's.

[Coyote Gives Salmon And Acorns to Humans]
[Act I: Amekyaram Village.]
[Scene A: The Two Sisters.]

(1) *ˀáxxak   ˀasiktâ·n   kunˀí·nanik*   Two women used to live,
   two   women   they used to live

    kustá·ras   sisters,
    sisters

      ˀame·kyá·ra·m.   at Amekyaram.[2]
      at Amekyaram

(2) *kári xás   kunpi·p,*   And then they said,
   and then   they said

    '*púra kára   vúra   ˀá·ma   ˀa·mtíhe·šara.*   'NOBODY's going to eat salmon.
    nobody   just   salmon   won't eat

---

[2] *ˀame·kyá·ra·m*, literally 'salmon-making place', is at Ike's Falls, on the west side of the Klamath River, not far below the confluence with the Salmon River. As the concluding verses of this text indicate, it was the site of the Jump Dance, one of the sacred ceremonies of Karok world-renewal.

(3) *yukún tánupíššunva,*
    see   we've hidden it

    pa?á·ma.'
    the salmon

You see, we've hidden it,

that salmon.'

[Scene B: Coyote.]

(4) *kári xás pihnê·fič ?uxxus,*
    and then coyote   he thought

    'púxay vúra va· kupitíhe·šara.'
    not   just   that they won't do

And then the Coyote thought,

'They're NOT going to do that.'

(5) *kári xás ?uxxus,*
    and then he thought

    'čími   kanimússan.'
    FUT   let me go look

And then he thought,

'Let me go take a look.'

(6) *kári xás muvíkkapu ?uppê·čip.*
    and then his quiver   he picked it up

And then he picked up his quiver.

(7) *kári xás ?é·pa·x   ?úkruh.*
    and then alder bark   he peeled it

And then he peeled bark from an alder.

(8) *kári xás víkkapuhak ?uθθa·námnih.*
    and then in quiver   he put it in

And then he put it in the quiver.

(9) *kári xás va· ká·n ?u?u·m,*
    and then that there he arrived

    yô·ram   ?ukrî·š.
    corner   he sat down.

And then he got there,

he sat down in the corner.

[Scene C: The Sisters and Coyote.]

(10) *kári xás kunpatánviš,*
    and then they asked him

    'fâ·t   kumá?i·   ?ivúrayvutih.'
    what   for   you're roaming

And then they asked him.

'Why are you roaming around?'

(11) *kári xás ?uppi·p,*
    and then he said

    'káruk ?iθ ivθane·n?ıppan nivâ·ramutih,'
    upriver world-end   I'm going to

    xás vúra ká·n ?úkri·.
    and just there he sat

And then he said,

'I'm going to the upriver end of the
                   world,'

and he just sat there.

(12) *kári xás ?uppi·p,*
    and then he said

    'tánaxxúriha,
    I'm hungry

And then he said,

'I'm hungry,

tî matê· ?á·ma kan?am.'   I think I'll have a bite of salmon.'
let a bit salmon I eat

(13) kári xás ?u?ê·θrišuk,   And then he took it out,
and then he took it out

    pa?é·pa·x.   that alder bark.[3]
    the alder bark.

[Scene D: The Sisters.]

(14) kári xás ta?íttam ?u?uávahe·n.   And so then he'd eaten it.
and then so   he'd eaten it

(15) kári xás kunxus   And then they thought,
and then they thought

    pa?asiktáva·nsas,   those women did,
    the women

    'hô·y ?u·m po·?aramsî·privtihirak,   'Where is it he comes from?
    where he   where he comes from

        ká·n hínupa ?á·ma kun?á·mtih.'   It looks like they're eating
        there look   salmon they're eating it   salmon there!'

(16) kári xás ?uppê·r   And the she told her,
and then she told her

    pamukústa·n yíθθa,   one told her sister,
    her sister   one

    'čími numnî·ši.'   'Let's cook.'
    FUT   let's cook

(17) ta?íttam yíθθa mušvírik   mû·k   So one struck with her elbow
so   one   her elbow with   uphill   uphillward,
                   mâ·ka ?u?i·k,
                   she struck

    θivrihvassúruk.   under a wall-plank.
    wall-plank under.

(18) kári xás ?íššaha ?uvuníššuk.   And then water flooded out.
and then water   it flooded out

(19) kári xás ?á·ma ?úkyi·mnišuk.   And then salmon fell out.
and then salmon it fell out

[Scene E: The Sisters and Coyote.]

(20) kári xás ta?íttam kunimníššahe·n. And so then they had cooked it.
and then so   they had cooked it.

---

[3]Alder bark is red, the same color as salmon flesh.

(21) *kári xás tákunʔav,*   And then they ate it—
    and then they ate it

    pihnê·fič   vúra va·   ʔúmmu·stih.   Coyote was just watching.
    coyote   just that he's watching

(22) *kári xás kunpi·p,*   And then they said,
    and then they said

    'čími ʔíppaho·.   'Go on your way!'
    FUT go again

(23) *yakún nu· tánuʔíffikar,*   You see, we're going to gather them,
    see we we go gather them

    xuntáppan.'   acorns.'
    acorns

(24) *kári xás ʔuppi·p,*   And then he said,
    and then he said

    pihnê·fič,   Coyote did,
    coyote

    'xâ·tik niθívke·.'   'Let me go too!'
    let I go along

(25) *kári xás kunpi·p,   'pû·hara'*—   And then they said, 'No'—
    and then they said no

    'vúra xâ·tik niθívke·,   'Just let me go too!'
    just let   I go along

    miník niθθâ·viš'—   I'll knock down the nuts'—
    there I'll knock them

    xás kunpi·p, 'čímmi   man.'   and they said, 'All right.'
    and they said all right then

(26) *kári xás ka·n kunívyi·hma.*   And then they went there.
    and then there they went to

[Act II: In the Mountains.]
[Scene A: The Sisters and Coyote.]

(27) *taʔíttam kunʔíffikahe·n*   So they had gathered them,
    so   they'd gathered them

    paxuntáppan   the acorns,
    the acorns

    paʔasiktáva·nsa.   the women did.
    the women

(28) *kári xás   pihnê·fič ʔuʔíffik.*   And then Coyote picked up a stick.
    and then coyote he picked it up

(29) *kári xás kô·kaninay vúra ʔúktir*
and then everywhere just he beat them

    paxunyê·p,
    the tan-oaks

        máruk, sáruk, yúruk, káruk.
        uphill downhill downriver upriver,

And then he beat them just everywhere,

    those tan-oaks,

    uphill, downhill, downriver, upriver,

(30) *kári xás ʔuθáha·sha*
and then he scattered them

    paxuntáppan.
    the acorns.

And then he scattered them,

    those acorns.

(31) *víri va· kúθ payê·m*
so that for now

    paxuntáppan kô·kaninay vúra
    the acorns everywhere just
        ʔuʔí·ftih.
        they're growing

So that's why it is now,

    the acorns grow just everywhere.

[Scene B: Coyote.]

(32) *kári xás ʔupíkvip,*
and then he ran back

    sáruk,
    downhill

    ká·n paʔasiktáva·nsa kunʔí·nirak.
    there the women where they lived

And then he ran back,

    downhill,

    to where the women used to live

(33) *kári xás ʔusxáxxaripa·*
and then he ripped them out

    paθivrî·hvar.
    the wall-planks.

And then he ripped them out,

    those wall-planks.

(34) *kári xás paʔíššaha ʔuvuníššuk,*
and then the water it flooded out

    xás ko·vúra paʔá·ma kunívyi·hrišuk.
    and all the salmon they came out

And then the water flooded out,

    and all the salmon came out.

(35) *víri va· kúθ sâ·m*
so that for downriver
        ʔussa·mnúputih,
        it flows down

    káru va· kúθ 'á·ma ʔukvíripra·tih.
    and that for salmon it runs upriver

So that's why water flows downhill,

    and that's why salmon run upriver

[Scene C: The Sisters.]

(36) *kári xás kunpirúvi·š*
and then they came back down

And then they came back down,

pa?asiktáva·nsa.   the women did.
the women

(37) kári xás kunpi·p,   And then they said,
and then they said

'tá hínupa ?utá·yvar   "Look, he's spoiled it,
PF look   he spoiled it

papihnê·fič.   that Coyote has.
the coyote

(38) víri čô·ra,   čémmi,   So all right, let's go,
so   let's go   all right

xâ·tik nupkê·viš.   let's be transformed.
let we be transformed.

(39) yakún   yíθ   ?ára·r   ?u?i·níšrihe·š.'   You see, a different race is coming into
see   other person will come to exist   being.'

[Act III: On the Ridge.]
[Scene A: The Sisters.]

(40) ta?íttam   kunpiyâ·ramahen.   So they had gone off again.
so   they had gone again

(41) kári xás kun?íffukra·   And then they climbed uphill,
and then they climbed uphill

?asanamkarayúrukam.   downriver from Stony Flat.
Stony Flat-downriver

(42) kári xás yíθθa ?uppi·p,   And then one of them said,
and then one   she said

'tánapipšítta·ni   'I forgot it,
I forgot it

nanisímsi·m   my knife—
my knife

čími kanpávan,   let me go back for it,
FUT I go back for it

čími ?i·m ?ô·k ne·krû·ntih.'   you wait for me here.'
FUT   you   here   be awaiting me

(43) víri   po·pkíya·vrin   So when she turned,
so   when she turned

sâ·m   to·ppárihfak.   she started downhill.
downhill   she started dow

(44) víri   po·píttiθun   So when she looked around,
so   when she looked around

yánava pamukústa·n   there was her sister,
behold her sister

ʔasaxyíppit   tó·ppárihiš—   she'd turned into quartz—
quartz   she'd turned into

  xás   sâ·mvanihič   and a little downhill was their dog
  and   little downhill

                pamukunčíšši·
                their dog

  va· káru ʔasaxyíppit   he too had turned into quartz.
  that too   quartz

                to·ppárihiš.
                he'd turned into

(45) yakún yíθ ʔára   tuʔí·niš—   You see, a different race had come into
     see   other person had come to exist   being—[4]

  ʔiθyáruk   po·tkáratih   when she looked acrossriver,
  acrossriver   when she looked over

  yánava   pavuhvúha   there was the Jump Dance lined up,
  behold   the Jump Dance

                tuʔíššipva,
                it extended

  ʔuθítti·mti   pakuníhyi·vtih.   she could hear them shouting.
  she's hearing that they're shouting

(46) kári xás va· ka·n   ʔasaxyíppit   And then SHE turned into quartz
     and then that there   quartz   there.[5]

                ʔuppárihiš.
                she turned into

[Scene B: Epilogue.]

(47) víri hû·tva   kó·   ʔiθívθa·ne·n   So as long as the world exists,
     so   however   much world

                ʔuʔi·náha·k,
                when it exists

  va· vúra ko· kuníhru·vtihe·š   that's how long they'll be using it,
  that just much they'll be using it

  pasímsi·m.   that knife.
  the knife

(48) va· kummû·k kuníhvi·θtihe·š   That's what they'll clean it with,
     that with it they'll clean it

  pe·šyâ·t,   the spring salmon,
  the spring salmon

---

[4] I.e. the human race.

[5] Three quartz rocks can still be seen on the ridge: two large ones are the sisters, and a smaller one is their dog.

pe·θívθa·ne·n   tákunpikyâ·ha·k.
the world   when they make   when they make the world new.
               it again

CONCLUSION

The preceding definitions offered for Karok verses and lines differ in a number of specific ways from those proposed for Chnookan by Hymes. Of course, there is no reason to think that all American Indian narratives must be analysable in exactly the same way. Nevertheless, it seems clear that Karok narrative has a detailed structure which can be expressed in terms of verses and lines, and which can appropriately be called poetic. However, a question arises in any such study: if this is Karok poetry, what are the characteristics of Karok prose? Does a distinction in fact exist, in the literature of the Karok or the Chinook, between prose and poetry? Or should we say that, as was perhaps the case in Homeric Greece, that ALL literature was poetic, and that prose was used only for non-literary discourse?

The data on Karok discourse are, unfortunately, inadequate to answer these questions. During my major period of field work on Karok, in 1949 and 1950, the texts which I transcribed were mainly limited to narratives—because I was interested in the myth literature, because 'stories' were an easy type of text to elicit, and because, except for a few days at the end of my work, I had no tape-recorder. So I never obtained any conversational texts. I did transcribe some non-narrative, ethnographic texts (Bright, 1957:282–301), and they show a structure of sentence-initial particles similar to that found in narratives. Does this mean that I was actually getting ethnographic poetry? Probably not; the situation in which a Karok speaker dictated texts to me, word by word, was analogous to the native situation in which stories were told to children for piece-by-piece repetition, and so the style of narrative may have artificially been extended to descriptions of salmon-fishing and sweathouses. To be sure, elderly speakers of Karok are still living, and it may still be possible to tape-record more natural samples of Karok discourse. However, no functioning Karok speech-community exists now, and so conditions are not ideal for resolving these matters.

Elsewhere, of course, many American Indian speech communities do continue in full function, and deserve study in terms of all aspects of Hymes' 'ethnography of communication'. Specifically, it is time that living traditions of American Indian oral literature are taken seriously AS literature. We should learn, for a broad range of native American societies, how to differentiate prose and poetry—and possibly other genres; we should learn the defining characteristics of each genre; we should learn the social function of each; and we should attempt to understand the nature of written literature as it develops in American Indian languages. Students of these topics have much to gain, not only in increased appreciation of the richness of literary traditions in Native America, but also in improved comprehension of the nature of literary discourse among human societies in general.

REFERENCES

BRIGHT, WILLIAM. 1957. The Karok language. (University of California publications in linguistics, 13.) Berkeley and Los Angeles.

――――. 1978. Karok. Handbook of North American Indians, vol. 8: California, ed. by Robert F. Heizer, 180–189. Washington, DC: Smithsonian Institution.

――――. 1979. A Karok myth in 'measured verse': The translation of a performance. Journal of California and Great Basin Anthropology 1.117–23.

――――. 1980. Coyote's Journey. American Indian Culture and Research Journal (UCLA) 4.21–48.

DAY, A. GROVE (ED.) 1951. The sky clears. New York: Macmillan.

FINNEGAN, RUTH. 1977. Oral poetry: Its nature, significance, and social context. Cambridge: University Press.

HYMES, DELL. 1976. Louis Simpson's 'The deserted boy'. Poetics 5.119–55.

――――. 1977. Discovering oral performance and measured verse in American Indian narrative. New Literary History 8.431–57.

JAKOBSON, ROMAN. 1966. Grammatical parallelism and its Russian facet. Language 42.399–429.

KROEBER, ALFRED L., AND EDWARD W. GIFFORD. 1980. Karok myths. Berkeley & Los Angeles: University of California Press.

ROTHENBERG, JEROME (ED.) 1972. Shaking the pumpkin: Traditional poetry of the Indian North Americans. Garden City, NY: Doubleday.

TEDLOCK, DENNIS. 1972. Finding the center: Narrative poetry of the Zuni Indians. New York: Dial. [2nd ed., Lincoln: University of Nebraska Press, 1978.]

10 Context in Written Language: The Case of Imaginative Fiction

Margaret Rader
University of California, Berkeley

TOWARD A NOTION OF CONTEXT
FOR WRITTEN LANGUAGE

Recently the idea seems to be gaining ground that written language should be considered decontextualized language. In this chapter I'd like to quarrel a bit with the idea that written language is bereft of context and, using written fiction as my example, suggest some of the kinds of things we should consider when we look for the context of writing.

In an article which is representative of the kind of thinking that sees written language inevitably tending toward decontextualized language, Paul Kay has suggested that when writing developed, language became free to evolve toward autonomy. Kay defines autonomous language as language 'minimally dependent on simultaneous transmission over other channels, such as the paralinguistic, postural, and gestural, and. . .minimally dependent on the contribution of background information on the part of the hearer' (1977:21–22). People who learn to write must learn to use the verbal channel alone since they cannot depend on prosody and gesture to carry any information. They also learn to initiate, sustain, and develop a written 'utterance' without depending on signals of agreement, disagreement, or confusion from an addressee. And, since they cannot see the addressee to judge if they share a common background, in writing (if they are wise) they try to make the premises of their reasoning and the logical connections explicit so they can communicate with those who do not share their basic assumptions. This same desire to be understood by anyone who might pick up the text leads one to look for words with fixed and unambiguous denotations and no connotations at all, so that unwanted associations can be avoided; whenever possible,

the meanings of terms are stipulated. Writing, together with the complex civilization it makes possible, puts certain pressures on language, pressures which may,
Kay suggests, cause language to evolve in the direction of 'the precise and explicit
speech of the analytic philosopher, the scientist, and the bureaucrat' (30).

In order to be a vehicle for autonomous communication in speech or in writing, a language must develop the resources to mark subtly different logical relationships. These include syntactic resources such as relative clauses and other
kinds of subordinate structures, and lexical resources, especially subordinating
conjunctions. Besides logical and subordinating connectors, the language needs a
rich vocabulary which makes available a wide choice of terms, allowing the
speaker to focus on the same object or event at any desired level of concreteness or
abstraction or from a number of different perspectives. Autonomous language
aims at ruling out the possibility of misunderstanding in the transference of information between two communicators, who, it is presumed, share only a grammar
and a dictionary. As such, it is especially suited for international or cross-cultural
communication. It follows that, in the effort to make misinterpretation impossible, the addressor of this kind of communication will try not to leave any interpretive work for the addressee to do, so that the role of the addressee is limited to that
of a passive registerer and storer of information.

Perhaps autonomous language is not so much a reality as it is a goal or a felt
need on the part of those who must communicate with people from a wide variety
of cultural backgrounds. If it is true that language is an instrument of infinite flexi-
bility which shapes itself to the communicative needs of those who use it—hence
the proverbial twenty-seven terms for snow among the Eskimo—then the need for
a language which cannot be misunderstood and which is maximally precise may
exert pressure on languages to develop more resources for explicitness. Whether
the language of the bureaucrat has, as Kay suggests, actually become precise and
explicit is another question. A goal may be impossible to attain and still exercise a
teleological effect, as, for instance, the goal of Christian perfection exercised on
another age than ours.

At first glance, it is natural to assume that the distinction between autonomous and context-dependent language corresponds to the distinction between
written and spoken language. When one looks at transcripts of spoken language,
there seem to be many more coordinating markers than subordinating—one is immediately struck by all the *and*s scattered throughout transcripts. In contrast, even
when researchers control for subject matter, more complicated structures appear
in an individual's writing than in his or her speech (Kroll, 1977:98; O'Donnell,
1974). Some structures—complicated passives, long strings of what Francis
Christensen (1967) calls 'free modifiers', some inverted structures studied by
Georgia Green (1976, this volume)—are virtually impossible to find in transcripts
of spoken language. Examples of these:

(1)   . . .features introduced by transformation into lexical formatives are not to be
       considered in determining when deletion is permitted (Chomsky, 1965:181).

(2)   It is with the coming of man that a vast hole seems to open in nature, a vast black whirlpool spinning faster and faster, consuming flesh, stones, soil, minerals, sucking down the lightning, wrenching power from the atom, until the ancient sounds of nature are drowned out in the cacophony of something which is no longer nature, something instead which is loose and knocking at the world's heart, something demonic and no longer planned—escaped, it may be—spewed out of nature, contending in a final giant's game against its master. (Loren Eiseley, quoted in Christensen, 1967:20).

(3)   Very important to the Japanese is the amount of mercury being pumped into their bays (Green, 1976).

In fact, written language as we practice it today is so formally and functionally different from most spoken language that some people have suggested that it is a distinct dialect (or rather 'grapholect') of English (Hirsch, 1977). This lends credence to the idea that it is in the medium of writing that the tendency toward autonomous communication is carried the furthest.

The idea that the medium of writing has allowed language to develop in directions closed off to speech has been a significant insight of researchers into oral and written language. I challenge the idea, however, that this development is always in the direction of autonomy, i.e. greater and greater context-independence. Recall that Kay's definition of 'autonomous' had two parts: autonomous language is language that is 1) minimally dependent on information from other channels; and 2) minimally dependent on the contribution of background information by the hearer. Of necessity, any writing depends on the verbal channel alone. However, nothing intrinsic to the medium of writing dictates that no contribution should come from the reader. This requirement is dictated instead by the communicative purpose: the most efficient transfer of information to those who may not share one's background and assumptions. Writing is quite well suited for this purpose, but we should not then assume that this is the only or optimal use for writing.

I suggest that writing, because of its well-known characteristic of being removed from an immediate conversational situation, is particularly well suited for a kind of language use which maximally depends on the contribution of background information on the part of the reader, even as it minimally depends on paralinguistic, postural, or gestural channels. This kind of language use tends toward syntactic complexity and lexical elaboration, not to serve the function of making explicit logical relationships, as in autonomous communication, but to control and make possible the development of a complex image in the mind of the reader. The kind of writing I am speaking of is, of course, imaginative fiction. This kind of language use deserves to be placed along side of what David Olson has called 'the essayist technique' or scientific prose as one of the ways gifted language users have explored the potential of language in its written form during the last two hundred years of Western culture (Olson, 1977).

At the same time that the essayist technique, that apotheosis of logical thought, was developing, the modern novel took on its characteristic form. Olson points to John Locke (1632–1704) as one of the first thinkers to exploit the essayist technique, the technique of stating premises as clearly as possible and then making explicit their implications, subjecting the validity of the reasoning to close scrutiny. In part in reaction to Locke and his doctrine of empiricism, Laurence Sterne in *Tristram Shandy* played games with the developing conventions for the novel (Iser, 1978:74–75). Sterne's characters and narrator may display illogical thought processes, but it would be a mistake to think of the author himself as displaying the illogical, unsystematic thinking characteristic of an earlier age. Instead, Sterne saw and played with the possibilities of the printed book, throwing into relief those conventions of reading which disguise the artificiality of the novel and make it possible for the reader to build a world from a few shreds of language. It may be that no one between Sterne and James Joyce saw so clearly the nature of the novel as written artifice.

> Dr. Slop drew up his mouth, and was just beginning to return my uncle Toby the compliment of his Whu-u-u or interjectional whistle,—when the door hastily opening in the next chapter but one—put an end to the affair. (*Tristram Shandy* III, 161)

The novel, although it can be a long, complex, and elaborated form, does not aim at putting all the meaning into the text and reducing the role of the reader to passive registering of information, as the explicit prose of the logical philosopher seems to do. In a frequently quoted passage, Sterne wrote:

> . . .no author, who understands the just boundaries of decorum and good-breeding, would presume to think all: The truest respect which you can pay to the reader's understanding, is to halve this matter amicably, and leave him something to imagine, in his turn, as well as yourself. For my own part, I am eternally paying him compliments of this kind, and do all that lies in my power to keep his imagination as busy as my own. (*Tristram Shandy* II)

In this view, a novel is not a collection of information but an experience. In a novel, the meaning is not 'in the text' as David Olson suggests that it is for the essayist technique. Instead, meaning is, as Iser puts it, 'something that happens' to the reader; as such it can never be reduced to a set of propositions or semantic representations (1978:22). But the dichotomy here is not between oral and written language but between two different uses of written language. Neither of these language styles, I suggest, is closer than the other to the essential character of the medium of writing (whatever that may be); both depend on writing for their full development. The scientific essay is maximally explicit prose in which the role of the reader is reduced to that of checking the reasoning for validity, matching the conclusions with what he knows of the way things are, and remembering the information. Imaginative fiction, at its best, is never vague but neither is it explicit, since it implies more than it states, demanding an active reader who brings to the text an understanding of narrative conventions and who is willing to do the work, basing himself on the language representations of the text, of imagining a world in which people move and act.

Let me illustrate what I think the active reader adds to the text of a piece of fiction by reproducing a very short story and then an expanded version of that story which is maximally explicit. The story was written by a fifteen year old girl.[1]

Almost Home

by Micah Perks

(1) The little boy walked along the street, his breath coming out in big gusts. (2) He pretended to himself that he was smoking a cigar like some of the Christian men did. (3) He sang under his breath. (4) He recounted his Hebrew lesson again. (5) Still he could not forget the cold. It seeped into his mind and engulfed his body. (6) 'If I wasn't five, I would cry,' he thought. (7) 'Almost home, almost home, almost home. . .' (8) He made it into a chant and walked in rhythm to it. 'Almost home, almost home.' (9) Finally he saw his house. He quickened his pace. Running up the steps, he slammed the door.

'Eli!' Mama exclaimed. 'You're blue with cold.' Her eyes looked red and tired. 'Mama,' he asked uneasily, 'what's wrong?' What's wrong, what's wrong. . .The old man awoke with a start. He had dreamt again of his youth. 'A sign of getting old,' he thought.

He got up and put on the old gray suit. After his breakfast of bagel and juice, he put on his brown overcoat and he closed the door. The subway seemed further away each day. 'Almost there, almost there,' he thought, and he made it like a chant.

EXPANSION OF "ALMOST HOME"

Title   This text is a fictional story entitled 'Almost Home.' The author is named Micah Perks. The story is probably about a character who leaves someplace and reaches home. The setting is the path along which the character travels. Possibly reaching home will be the problem and arriving home will be the solution.

(1)   The main character is a little boy. The setting is a street, possibly in a city. When the story opens, the boy is walking, probably toward his home, which may be close by.

---

[1]Perhaps a word is in order here about why I have chosen to study fiction written by young peole. By showing that skills specific to written language have been mastered by young people, I can demonstrate that the language competence involved is not just the possession of a small group of highly skilled adult professional writers. I hope to substantiate my belief that this competency is not the result of a long apprenticeship or of explicit teaching but rather that children who are immersed in written language learn the conventions of written language in a way that most resembles natural language learning.

At the same time that he walks, his breath is coming out in big gusts, possibly because he is breathing heavily. Maybe he has walked a long way, which has made him tired.

(2)   At the same time that he walks and breathes, the boy pretends to himself that he is smoking a cigar. He is walking alone. Probably he does not mimic a cigar smoker by pantomiming raising and lowering a cigar but by pretending to blow out puffs of smoke. It must be that the boy is pretending that his breath, which is visible as steam, is cigar smoke. If this is so, he may not be breathing heavily after all, and 'big gusts' may refer simply to his visible breath. The weather is probably cold, and possibly the boy is cold. He may be pretending to smoke a cigar to get his mind off the cold.
He pretends to smoke the way the Christian men do. Probably the boy is not Christian. Possibly the Christian men are the prosperous men of the community and the boy's family are poor.

(3)   After the boy pretends, he sings under his breath while walking. Possibly he sings because he wants to get his mind off the cold. Possibly he sings UNDER HIS BREATH and earlier pretended TO HIMSELF because he does not want to draw attention to himself.

(4)   After he sings, he recounts his Hebrew lesson while walking. Possibly he re-counts it because he wants to get his mind off the cold. Before the events of the story began, he had recounted his Hebrew lesson. Possibly he said it at Hebrew School, which may be where he is walking home from. Probably the boy is Jewish.

(5)   Even though he pretended, sang, and recounted while walking, he could not forget the cold as he did those things. I am now sure he did those things to forget the cold. He is uncomfortably cold. He can think of nothing but how cold he is.

(6)   Then he thinks, 'If I wasn't five, I would cry.' The boy is five years old. Al-though he feels like crying, he does not cry. He feels like crying because he is very cold. He does not cry because he thinks only babies cry and he is too old at age five to cry. He is a brave little lad.

(7)   Then the boy says 'Almost home' an indefinite number of times. Since the boy has done a number of things while walking continuously since the story began and he has not yet reached his home, it could be that the boy was not close to his home when the story began. Perhaps he is not close to home now but is trying to keep his mind off the cold and is encouraging himself by pretending he is al-most home. He wishes to get home so he can get warm.

(8)   Then the little boy makes the words 'almost home' into a chant by repeating them rhythmically as he walks in rhythm to it. He continues to repeat it.

(9)   Then he sees his house. He is close to his home. Then he quickens his pace because he is hurrying to get home. Then he runs up the steps of his house. As I expected, he has arrived home. After opening the door of his house and en-tering, he slams the door of his house because he doesn't want any cold air to get into the warm house, and because he is relieved to be home. [Only the first paragraph of the story has been expanded.]

The idea of making an expansion of a text owes a great deal to the work of Labov and Fanshel (1977). In their analysis of an interview between a young woman whom they call Rhoda and her psychotherapist, they provide an expansion of the transcript. Their method is to make explicit the meaning of paralinguistic cues and to fill in the meaning of vague terms such as 'thing' and of deictic expressions. In order to do this, they must reconstruct the shared background information of the participants from information they glean by inspecting the entire text of the conversation and from discussing the tape with the therapist. Labov and Fanshel speak of the 'mode of expression', i.e. the relation of text to expansion (120). When there is a low T/E ratio—a lot of expansion and only a little text—this would be an example of what Kay would term non-autonomous language, language which depends on paralinguistic cues and shared background knowledge. In contrast, autonomous language would have a high T/E ratio, and a principled expansion would not be able to add a great deal to the text itself.

As Olson (1977) maintains, oral language is usually characterized by an indirect mode of expression with its meanings determined by context and shared understandings. But on inspecting 'Almost Home', we realize that written language as well as oral language can use the indirect mode of expression. Although both are indirect, 'Almost Home' bears little resemblance to any story that might be told in conversation. The difference between 'Almost Home' and, for example, one of Rhoda's stories in *Therapeutic Discourse* arises from the different kinds of shared understandings which underlie the two stories.

In order to expand 'Almost Home' as I did,[2] I had to assume a rich system of knowledge on the part of the reader about what one does with a written text such as this. Jonathan Culler, speaking of poetry, says:

> . . .anyone. . .unfamiliar with the conventions by which fictions are read, would, for example, be quite baffled if presented with a poem. His knowledge of the language would enable him to understand phrases and sentences, but he would not know, quite literally, what to *make* of this strange concatenation of phrases. (1975:114)

This is true, I believe, not only for poetry but for imaginative fiction of all kinds: sketches such as 'Almost Home', short stories, novels. Readers know ahead of time what they are likely to find in some piece of discourse they identify as a story, and they know what, as dictated by the conventions of this kind of language use, their own contribution to the story should be. For instance, if one were listening to an oral story, a definite article occurring at the beginning of a story ('*The* little boy. . .') would signal that the speaker believed the addressee could

---

[2]A detailed account of the principles by which this expansion was made may be found in my forthcoming University of California dissertation, *Implication and Convention in Children's Self-Generated Writing*.

identify who the speaker was referring to (Chafe, 1976:39). Searching one's memory in order to make this identification, then, is part of the work that the addressee does in conversation. But readers of fictional stories know they are freed from the task of trying to figure out which little boy is being referred to. The author and his or her readers share a universe of discourse which includes the conventions for narrative fiction. Readers then simply identify the boy as a character in the story. They know there is no real little boy which the narrator is inviting them to recall. But if readers need not identify a referent, this kind of story invites them to imagine, according to the instructions given by the text, a little boy and a world in which he moves and acts.

I would suggest that the definite article at the beginning of a written story does not serve the function suggested by Clark and Haviland of inviting the reader to pretend '. . .the story [is] being told to someone else and the reader [is] merely an uninvolved onlooker' (1977:37). Readers do not pretend to break in on a story-telling event already underway. Instead, they realize that the narrator (if any sense of a narrator remains) has chosen to present the events which are part of the story structure as already underway when the reader begins to observe them. In this story the boy is not presented statically but walking.

The constitutive rules of the game which the author and readers play dictate that readers, from the beginning, bring to bear all their reasoning abilities, making solidly- or shakily-based inferences about what is going on in the story. These inferences form hypotheses which are confirmed, rejected, or modified by later sentences in the story. Readers actively look for 1) the temporal ordering of events in the story; and 2) the causes and consequences of these events, and especially the reasons, motives, and intentions behind the actions of the characters. The author plays his part in the game by doling out the information on which the reader makes these judgments. Just as Sterne said, the author does not 'tell all', but enlists the readers as collaborators so they can 'share the game of the imagination' (Iser, 1978:108). If the reader can be counted on to figure out, for example, how events in the story are related temporally, the author is spared the necessity of always explicitly indicating which events are sequential and which concurrent. Notice that the temporal relations of the boy's first actions in 'Almost Home' are underdetermined by the text. Readers use their notion of likely cause or temporal sequence both to infer how one statement relates to the next and to posit explaining generalizations on which to base their inferences about cause or reason.

The author may first suggest and then confirm the suggestion. In 'Almost Home', we suspect that the boy is cold by line three; the author confirms our suspicion in line four. The author may also make us doubt a previous conclusion: at first we think that the boy is actually near his home, but later we wonder if he is not simply encouraging himself by telling himself that he is almost home. In this story, the most dramatic reorganization of initial understandings comes when we discover that the main character is not a little boy at all but an old man, and the events related have been a dream of his past. According to Iser's phenomenological theory of reading, it is not the information in the text per se which causes a world, a gestalt, to take shape in readers' minds; rather it is the activity of the readers as they use the information in the text as raw material for their sense-making faculties that allows a whole to arise from fragments. Texts, says Iser, are 'instructions for the production of the signified' (65).

The object of the game of imaginative fiction, for both writer and reader, is the creation of a world. The more active the readers are—the more they are engaged in processes similar to those by which they give shape to the world of experience—the more the world they imagine 'comes alive', becomes an experience taking place for them at the moment of reading. And according to Iser, the more the image built up by the readers is shaped, modified, shattered, and rebuilt, the more the readers are led into an experience not of their own making, an experience which they could not have imagined without the text to direct them. Merleau-Ponty put it this way:

> . . .the book would not interest me so much if it only told me about things I already know. It makes use of everything I have contributed in order to carry me beyond it. With the aid of the signs agreed upon by the author and myself because we speak the same language, the book makes me believe that we had already shared a common stock of well-worn and readily available significations. The author has come to dwell in my world. Then, imperceptibly, he varies the ordinary meaning of the signs, and like a whirlwind they sweep me along toward the other meaning with which I am going to connect. (1973:11–12)

Iser and Merleau-Ponty are primarily speaking of 'reconstructions of past syntheses' (Iser, 111) which take place on the higher levels of one's understanding of theme or character; however, I believe that written fiction uses these same kinds of processes for the construction of its simplest and most mundane images. The story 'Almost Home' is exemplary in this respect. It is just a sketch, and yet our image of what is going on is underdefined at the beginning and takes shape slowly, something like the way a Polaroid picture develops over time. Causes– –for example, why the boy's breath is coming out in *big gusts*—and reasons—for example, why the boy performs the seemingly unconnected actions of pretending, singing, and recounting his lessons—are left for the reader to figure out. We infer that the boy is Jewish from his recounting a Hebrew lesson. The author does not tell us why the mother's eyes are red or why the boy cries *'What's wrong?'* but we try to figure it out, and at least two readers suspected that his father had died. What we thought was the meaning of the first part has to be restructured when we learn it was a dream. Narrative conventions suggest to us that we see parallels between what happens in the first part of the story and in the second, and since we know parallels ought to be significant, we are led to look for the thematic significance of the story at this level.

For the author to depend on the reader to do all this work, she must assume she shares with her audience a great deal of general knowledge as well as the knowledge of specific narrative conventions. The story will give a concrete detail, but the reader must draw on a general premise in order to infer something further from that detail. One can infer that the boy is Jewish from the information that the boy recounts a Hebrew lesson only if one draws on general knowledge that usually only Jewish children study Hebrew. The kinds of knowledge readers must draw on in 'Almost Home' range from propositions like 'When the weather is cold, one's expelled breath is visible as steam and resembles smoke', to 'There is a stereotype that men who smoke cigars are prosperous', to 'Big boys don't cry'. Without depending on 'shared background information' (recall Kay's definition of autonomous language), the writer cannot invite inferences and instigate other complex processes in the reader. And unless these processes occur, readers will not have the experience that fiction is designed to give them—the creation of a world which they would not have otherwise imagined.

I have explained in what sense I believe written fiction to be maximally dependent on shared background information. It remains for me to describe why I think this kind of language use depends on writing for its effects. It has been argued (by Goody & Watt, 1963; Havelock, 1963; Olson, 1977; and others) that only when statements could be written down was it possible to notice whether they were contradictory or if their implications were out of line with experience. In these writers' views, logic depends on writing, at least for its codification and systematization. Alone at a desk, pondering the wording of every phrase, the essayist[3] could frame a general statement and then make explicit its entailments, subjecting the reasoning by which these entailments were drawn to rigorous constraints in order to insure valid deductions. If the implications were nonsensical or counter-intuitive, or were shown to be false by empirical testing, the general statements could then be reformulated or rejected in favor of principles which, perhaps, were not so common-sensical but whose implications could be shown to be true. Writing freezes language so that these operations can be made. In this technique, the essayist is the active reasoner whose activity depends on the planning and reworking which can go into a written utterance. The essayist makes explicit the results of this activity, so the reader remains relatively passive.

The activity of the novelist is just as dependent on isolation, planning, scrutiny, and reworking as that of the essayist. When stories are fixed in writing, contradictions, for example behavior of a character which is inconsistent with what has been established about the character, become as obvious as contradictory statements are in essays. Novelists do not formulate general principles of human behavior, yet they must describe characters whose actions are comprehensible to us because they conform to our understandings of how people behave. Novelists reason as actively as essayists, but since their goal is to make available to the

---

[3]I will accept (with several grains of salt) Olson's characterization of what the seventeenth-century essayists were up to.

reader an experience of a world rather than a line of reasoning, they must make their readers be active as well. The reader of an essay simply follows a line of reasoning; the reader of a novel creates a world according to the instructions given.

Novelists, just like essayists, push language toward precision, grammatical and lexical complexity, and even explicitness, but for a different purpose. Essayists are explicit in order to signal logical relationships; Novelists leave the relationships between statements implicit, letting their readers do this work, but they must fulfill their contract with readers to take them beyond what they could imagine on their own. To do this, the novelist constrains the imaging of the reader. Novelists work for explicit images, vivid details, well-chosen words whose connotations deepen and enrich their denotations, setting in motion in the readers imaginative processes of the novelists' choice. A novelist may direct the readers' imaging by beginning with a nondetailed generalized image which develops gradually, detail by detail, causing the readers to continually modify the first image.

Frequently this kind of gradually developed image is a moving one, as in the following excerpt from a story written by a twelve year old boy:

> [Adam] checked his luggage, keeping the travel bag with him. Out of it he pulled a small bag of fur that began to rumble, and unfolded itself into the unlikely shape of a blue-furred kitten with one eye planted squarely in the middle of its forehead.

Compare this compression of information units into one sentence with what frequently occurs in spoken language. According to the 'one clause at a time' hypothesis of Syder and Pawley (to appear), in speaking, people can only encode ahead of time one clause of about seven to ten words. Rather than go out on a syntactic limb, not knowing exactly how they will finish a complex sentence, speakers generally choose a 'coordinating strategy' which allows them to string clauses together with *and*s. In writing, one has the leisure to compress information units into one sentence in order to control the flow of information and the development of the image and also to signal what is foregrounded and what is backgrounded. This method of development of the image has consequences for syntactic complexity. The kind of structure in which strings of 'free modifiers'—participle phrases, absolutes, appositives—follow a main clause, is particularly well-suited to this kind of image development. Christensen (1967:34) points out that Hemingway, who has a reputation for short, simple sentences, can write something like this:

> Manuel swung with the charge,
>
> sweeping the muleta ahead of the bull,
>
> his feet firm,
>
> the sword following the curve,
>
> a point of light under the arcs.

Compare this image, which takes shape over time, with a motion picture image in which everything comes at once, so that one notices the firm feet (if at all) at the instant Manuel swings.

I suggested earlier that because readers know what is expected of them according to the conventions for written narrative, they come to the story eager to try to figure out what is happening in the story. They are willing to build images which will be shaped, broken, and reshaped. They work to make sense out of the story, using the same general principles by which they make sense out of the behavior of people they meet in 'real life'—rough and ready theories about what motivates people and how the world is. Because authors can count on readers to work to find out what is going on, they don't have to spell everything out. Readers do some of the work, and their thought processes create the illusion that they are on-the-spot observers of the events of the story. This is why we approach a novel asking ourselves what WILL happen, not what happenED.

This effect depends crucially on the writtenness of the story. For any speech event, the primary situation for the addressee remains the communicative situation. Addressees understand their main work to be figuring out what is happening NOW at the time of speaking, not what happened in the story being told. If they do not understand what happened in the story, they ask for clarification rather than puzzle it out. They have a social role to fulfill as listeners, and they must continuously judge how well the other participants are fulfilling their social roles. The energy which the reader puts into text-reasoning, the speaker/listener puts into what Gumperz (1977) calls conversational inference. We invite a speaker to tell a story by asking 'what happened?' not 'what will happen?' If a story comes alive for us in the telling, it is because the teller brings the events of the story into the present by acting them out, by 'replaying' them, to use Goffman's (1974:504) term. The listener wants to know what happened, but the storyteller's personal presence, vocal quality, facial expressions, intonation, and gesture remain the primary experience. Along these channels, cues are received which tell us how the story-teller wants us to take the story. As Goffman (1974:503) says, speakers are providing 'grounds for sympathy, approval, exoneration, understanding, or amusement'. Listeners have a responsibility to demonstrate immediately that they are competent members of the society by providing the right kind of 'audience appreciation'.

Of course all language users imply more than they say. I am simply suggesting that in fiction this process conventionally is hypertrophied, even as the inference-suggesting stimuli are restricted to the verbal channel alone. The information on which readers base their acts of text-reasoning are carefully controlled by the author so that the readers can build up a world they would not have otherwise imagined. Readers proceed on the faith that the author has provided just the information needed—no more, no less—in order for the imagined world to be a coherent and satisfying whole. In this view, fiction serves the purpose of being an arena in which we rehearse sense-making, using stimuli carefully selected to ensure success. Only in writing can the inference-suggesting information be so carefully controlled and restricted even as inferring and imaging are given full rein.

Throughout this chapter I have taken for granted the assumption that there is such a thing as autonomous language and that it can be found where Kay and Olson say it resides, in the scientific essay or the speech of the bureaucrat and analytic philosopher. I have demonstrated that another style of language, imaginative fiction, is dependent on writing and yet not autonomous in Kay's sense. But as I work with children's written fiction, trying to discover the tradition in which they work which allows them to be fluent users of written language, I wonder if it would not be possible to describe such conventions of reading for any kind of written discourse. What could we do with an article in a scientific journal if we had only a grammar and a lexicon of the language? Moreover, is it ever true that there is no nuance to the language, no signs of personal involvement? Would we know enough not to bring in extraneous information from our personal experience in evaluating the argument? Would we be aware that our response should be skeptical, and that our reader's work includes trying to tear each argument apart? Dictionary meanings for the terms used might not be informative if we did not have members' knowledge of the meanings as well, built up through our experience of other such texts and our socialization into the scientific professions. These conventions for reading and our experiences of many other written texts form the CONTEXT for written utterances, a context which is different from the context for spoken utterances and yet is as crucial in determining meaning.

Perhaps the idea of decontextualized or autonomous language is not just a goal: perhaps it is a dream. If it is a dream, then we do not need to be afraid (as Olson and Kay seem to be) that literacy in itself will propel its users inevitably into the land of banal, colorless, one-dimensional prose. Instead we can count on human beings' propensity for exploiting the potentials of language in every direction that promises to yield some use or some delight.

REFERENCES

CHAFE, WALLACE L. 1976. Givenness, Contrastiveness, Definiteness. Subject and Topic, ed. by Charles N. Li, 25–56. New York: Academic Press.

CHRISTENSEN, FRANCIS. 1967. Notes Toward a New Rhetoric: Six Essays for Teachers. New York: Harper & Row.

CLARK, HERBERT H. AND SUSAN E. HAVILAND. 1977. Comprehension and the Given-New Contract. Discourse Production and Comprehension, ed. by Roy O. Freedle. Norwood, NJ: Ablex.

CULLER, JONATHAN. 1975. Structuralist Poetics: Structuralism, Linguistics, and the Study of Literature. Ithaca: Cornell University Press.

DRIEMAN, G. H. J. 1962. Differences Between Written and Spoken Language: an Exploratory Study. Acta Psychologia 20: 36–57, 78–100.

GIBSON, J. W., C. R. GRUNER, R. J. KIBLER, AND F. KELLY. 1966. A Quantitative Examination of Differences and Similarities in Written and Spoken Messages. Speech Monographs 33: 444–451.

GOFFMAN, ERVING. 1974. Frame Analysis: An Essay on the Organization of Experience. New York: Harper.

GOODY, JACK AND IAN WATT. 1963. The Consequences of Literacy. Comparative Studies in Society and History 5:304–345.

GREEN, GEORGIA M. 1976. Main Clause Phenomena in Subordinate Clauses. Language 52.

GUMPERZ, JOHN J. 1977. Sociocultural Knowledge in Conversational Inference. Georgetown University Round Table on Languages and Linguistics 1977. Linguistics and Anthropology, ed. by Muriel Saville-Troike. Washington, D.C.: Georgetown University Press.

HAVELOCK, ERIC A. 1963. Preface to Plato. Cambridge: Harvard University Press.

HIRSCH, E. D., JR. 1977. The Philosophy of Composition. Chicago: Chicago University Press.

ISER, WOLFGANG. 1978. The Act of Reading: A Theory of Aesthetic Response. Baltimore: Johns Hopkins University Press.

KAY, PAUL. 1977. Language Evolution and Speech Style. Sociocultural Dimensions of Language Change, ed. by Ben G. Blount and Mary Sanches, 21–33. New York: Academic Press.

KROLL, BARBARA. 1977. Combining Ideas in Written and Spoken English: a Look at Subordination and Coordination. Discourse Across Time and Space, ed. by Elinor O. Keenan and Tina L. Bennett. Los Angeles: Department of Linguistics, University of Southern California.

LABOV, WILLIAM AND DAVID FANSHEL. 1977. Therapeutic Discourse: Psychotherapy as Conversation. New York: Academic Press.

MERLEAU PONTY, MAURICE. 1973. The Prose of the World. Evanston, Il: Northwestern University Press.

O'DONNELL, ROY C. 1974. Syntactic Differences Between Speech and Writing. American Speech 49, 102–110.

OLSON, DAVID R. 1977. From Utterance to Text: the Bias of Language in Speech and Writing. Harvard Educational Review 47, 257–281.

STERNE, LAURENCE. 1970. Sterne: Selected Works, ed. by Douglas Grant. Cambridge: Harvard University Press.

SYDER, FRANCES AND ANDREW PAWLEY. To appear. English Conversational Structure.

III EXPERIENCING CHANGE IN TRADITIONS

11 Alternative Paths to Knowledge in Oral and Literate Cultures*

Jack Goody
Department of Social Anthropology
University of Cambridge

I have one continuing thread in this offering. It is a thread that I unravel from research and writing that I have been doing over the years. In this work I have been trying to specify certain differences between oral and literate cultures, or, more precisely, to outline certain implications of the introduction of the written register. But I have also seen, I might almost say lived through, an African society acquiring writing over the last thirty years; have watched the internal differentiation that emerges; have reflected more generally about what is happening and going to happen about schools and schooling in Africa; and have been led by these concerns to think about what we have been doing in our own society over the last hundred years since the moment when, for the first time ever, a society, Western society, systematically tried to turn all its citizens into members of the species homo legens, reading man.

Let me leave all that in the background, except to add that what most worries me about the expanding system of education in Africa and about the compulsory situation in Europe is the over-valuation of literate tasks, or, if you prefer, the continuing undervaluation of essential work in a society holding what it claims are egalitarian values. For there is evidence that, when the written mode achieves a dominant cultural position, the result is a systematic devaluation of, not so much the oral register itself (we understand that we have to speak to each other, and that we have to speak well to influence others), but of those tasks and experiences that do not require an advanced level of literate skill and, more relevant to my present argument, of forms of knowledge that are not acquired through books, or anyhow

---

*The last half of this paper appears in French translation as "Les Chemins du Savoir Oral" in *Critiques*, Dec.-Jan. 1979–80.

not from specialists in book learning (teachers, professors, etc.), or not at least in those places uniquely devoted to book learning (whether we are in the arts, sciences, or social sciences), that is, the schools and universities.

The situation is far worse in developing societies in Africa. There, some 80% of households are engaged in small-scale agriculture on their own account, the produce being used for subsistence, for exchange and for sale. Education, that is, school education, is oriented toward quite different sorts of activity, and it substitutes a universalized scribal curriculum for a particularistic oral one. To educate 20% of the people in such a way may be possible. Universal education, universal training in a scribal tradition, is bound to create social problems of a very serious kind, at least in the short and middle terms.

But let me turn more specifically to the task of discussing paths of knowledge in oral cultures, compared to literate ones. While I shall touch briefly on other forms of knowledge, my main emphasis will be on knowledge acquired through the use of language. This approach is adopted not only for simplicity's sake but because the LoDagaa, a group in Northern Ghana among whom I worked, themselves make this connection.

TRADITIONAL KNOWLEDGE AMONG THE LODAGAA

For the LoDagaa, traditional knowledge (TENKOURI YIL) is speech (YILI), because all knowledge in this sense is acquired not necessarily by means of speech (much ritual, much dance, is acquired by action, imitative action), but with the accompaniment or intervention of speech. So that the term *yil* really has a much wider semantic field than simply the flow of words; it can mean practically any 'matter', almost a human action (a 'social act').

On the other hand, it is unlikely that certain forms of knowledge would be classified by the LoDagaa as TENKOURI YIL. Though it is the basic form of acquired knowledge, language would not be so described, though the meanings of particular words, 'deep' ones, 'secret' ones, might be, for example, some special words that are used in the Bagre, an 'association' with restricted entry and an elaborate myth. In the version of this myth, of which I call the First Bagre, language is the one cultural instrument the beings of the wild, those intermediaries between men and gods, the 'fairies' or 'dwarfs' of West African English, did not teach mankind; it is assumed to be part of his natural make-up. Again, farming would not usually be so described, but the myth tells us this was taught to man by beings of the wild, and it is more clearly an activity in which an element of instruction is explicit; there is an obvious handing down, whereas with speech, as with motor development, there appears to be simply an unfolding. Tenkouri yil is then an explicitly mediated knowledge, although not a category in which the LoDagaa would normally (if I may be so bold as to speak on their behalf on such a topic) include the practice of farming or that of cooking.

Tenkouri yil may be literally translated as 'the speech (or matter) of the old country', 'the matter of old times', more idiomatically 'traditional knowledge'. Continuity is emphasized, for such knowledge is acquired from one's elders, and in general the older a man is, the more knowledge he is assumed to have—indeed the more knowledge he does have, since he remembers incidents, practices, and people of earlier times. In an oral society, one can neglect the words of the elders only to one's detriment, not simply because of a general idea of respect, but also because those words constitute the major sources of information. The only way of finding about the past, about interpretations of the world, is from them. Clearly, there are other ways of knowing, of knowing that someone has just died because one has heard a certain phrase on the xylophone, that it is time to plant the maize because of the appearance of some insect. This is basic primary knowledge, knowledge through experience, that makes the wheels of society turn. But an interpretation of, a gloss on, this primary knowledge is often provided by the elders in the form of a history or genealogy (a 'historical explanation'), or by placing a particular incident in a wider frame ('generalization').

The idea of tenkouri yil is related to that of TENKOURI SOR—'le chemin des origines' or 'way of the past' as Erbs (1975) translates it. This is both a concrete and a metaphorical expression. The road exists. It is the path leading to the old country, the place from which the particular clan section has come in the past, the route of migration. The path is recognized not only in speech but in sacrifice too, and it is there that one sacrifices, for example during the traditional oral recitation called the Bagre, on the side of the path leading to the 'old country.' But 'path' also means 'way' in the metaphorical sense. In the First Bagre, man is led astray by the beings of the wild, and loses the path to God (Goody, 1972: 275). In the Lawra Bagre, a new unpublished version of which includes a long recitation on the migration of the particular clan (the Kusiele), not only is there a description of the path, indeed of the whole movement, but this account is associated with a description of how the clan rediscovered the ceremony of the Bagre which they had lost. In other words, they rediscovered the 'path' of the ancestors in the course of their movement along the path their ancestors had followed.

I believe the LoDagaa would regard 'traditional knowledge' as most critically imparted in ceremonies (rituals if you like) and possibly most critically of all in the course of the Bagre ceremony, when the neophytes are shut in for many hours in the long-room of the house where it is being performed while their elders (the "Bagre elders") recite to them a long 'myth' which is partly about the ceremony itself and partly about the origin of culture and the problems of mankind. My own contrary view is that little is imparted on these occasions that is not already known to the neophytes, having been acquired, less formally, in the give and take of ordinary life. Much of the myth is concerned with the detailed description of well-known technical proceses, and this whole account is repeated many times during the course of the series of ceremonies. In addition, there is also a special recitation, the Funeral Bagre, where little or nothing is imparted on a cognitive level other than a general statement of the joys and dangers of life and death (Goody 1981). This is the most secret of all the performances. When I at last heard it, I was told, 'Now you know all'. In fact I knew little more than when we started. What had been revealed was a 'secret'—emotionally heavily-loaded, as are many funeral chants—but almost nonsense from the semantic point of view. An alleluya, an helas, an amen.

One aspect of this knowledge is a certain similarity, in the setting of its transfer, with the way that written knowledge, and knowledge of writing, is transferred in that central institution of literate culture, the school itself. The neophytes are separated off from society by being enclosed within the walls of the long-room, where they are kept cooped up for several hours at a time. Some of the participants in the ceremony, the Bagre elders, take on quasi-kinship roles; there are the Bagre fathers and the Bagre mothers, who, as is made explicit in the recitation, take over the roles of the domestic father and mother. Seniority of entry supersedes genealogical status. Note that the use of kinship terms was characteristic of early Sumerian schools, where the monitor was known as 'big brother', conjuring up an Orwellian vision of the past.

Not only was there separation and enclosure, and the substitution of metaphoric kinship for kinship authority, but there was also repetition, by the speaker as well as by the neophytes, who repeated his every phrase. Again the LoDagaa often think of this repetition as making for 'perfect' reproduction. In fact there is a good deal of creation, judging by the variants, large and small (Goody, 1977); there is little evidence of exact copying, of verbatim reproduction.

SPIRITUAL KNOWLEDGE

But there is one important source of knowledge which supplements the knowledge coming from the elders (tenkouri yil) and the knowledge coming from our own immediate experience (what I have called 'primary knowledge' but which one could perhaps call 'information' rather than 'knowledge', though the former is interpreted in terms of and transferred into the latter). I refer to the knowledge that comes from beyond the human universe, directly from spiritual agencies, and especially from the beings of the wild (KONTOME), a type of spirit or genius (in the Roman sense of that word) that mediates between God and man.

In appearance, in some of their actions, the beings of the wild are not unlike the dwarfs, fairies, trolls of the European tradition, who were no doubt to be taken more seriously before they were pushed aside by God, as the consequence of the dominant position He played in Christianity. Among the LoDagaa, these beings have to be taken very seriously indeed, because they constitute an important source of knowledge, in the past and in the present, and hence a channel by which culture may extend itself beyond 'traditional knowledge'.

In the First Black Bagre it is the beings of the wild who show man how to cultivate, how to make iron—who show him everything except how to speak and except the act of creation itself. The creation of the first child takes place in front of God; it is creation rather than procreation, for later on procreation (as distinct from creation) is separately shown to woman, who then shows man, being revealed by animals, by the natural, rather than by the supernatural. Apart from accounting for, in the sense of being responsible for, a great deal of traditional knowledge, the beings of the wild have another function, for they continue their revelatory role into the present. Their revelations are partly direct, showing man the secrets of the natural world (e.g. the virtues of plants and the power of the roots of trees) just as they had originally shown him the major features of his cultural order—at least at the technological level. They reveal this knowledge not in an institutional way, but by direct communication to individuals. It is also they who reveal to diviners what offering their clients should take to what agency. Typically, a client consults a diviner after a bad dream, but he also does so when illness strikes. The diviner himself holds in his left hand a small version of a sleeping mat as he calls upon the beings of the wild, shaking his bell and his rattle to put himself in touch with them. Revelation is associated with sleep, trance possession itself playing little or no part in the life of the LoDagaa, although I have come across a case where an epileptic was thought to have been taken over by the beings of the wild. Indeed any form of 'madness' is linked with these spirits and is seen perhaps as a form of unsuccessful communication.

More successful communication is established by those humans who acquire knowledge, about new shrines for example, by journeying to the places of the wild, the hills, the river banks, the woods themselves. These are the dwelling places of the beings of the wild, whose livestock are the animals men hunt. They are the complement to man, the revealers of knowledge, frequently to the more deviant members of the community (if I can use that term for my acquaintances: for Zuko who drank no beer and for Bechaara, who spent much time at the river's edge, moved his house nearby, and was eventually drowned there trying to rescue Nimidem, the Master of the Earth). For there is in fact no direct communication with God, the creator God. One cannot speak to Him, that is, pray to Him. 'Le pot ne connaît pas la femme qui l'a fabriqué. Le champ de mil ne fait pas connaître le semeur. Le tissage oublie son tisserand'* (Erbs 1975: 9).

---

*"The pot doesn't know the woman who made it. The field of millet doesn't know the sower. The cloth forgets its weaver".

TWO PATHS TO KNOWLEDGE

We see that among the LoDagaa, as among other African peoples, there are two recognized paths to knowledge, apart from that by which primary knowledge is acquired, which is practical life itself. One path leads to the relatively codified knowledge passed down by elders, the other to the more individual, creative knowledge derived from other powers, whose acquisition is linked with dissociation, with madness and with inspiration (or possession). At this stage, the terms of the analysis may appear to bear a resemblance to Victor Turner's 'structure' and 'anti-structure' (or 'communitas'); if so, it is simply because the poles of his dichotomy are all inclusive, while my inquiry is more specific, at least from the standpoint of content. We can extend the geographic range of our observations by briefly pointing to the widespread distribution of these two paths of knowledge, and particularly to the important role of the beings of the wild, among other West African cultures. Among the Ashanti certain new medicines are revealed to man by those brave enough to immerse themselves in the woods, whose secrets are disclosed by the MMOATIA, beings described in a very similar way to those of the LoDagaa and equated by Muslims with the *djinn* (the Gonja *alejina*) of the Middle East, where they too were founts of knowledge and power for mankind. Knowledge, therefore, can be acquired in various ways, but there is also some recognition of a growth, or at least change, of knowledge.

Interesting institutional forms of these different ways of acquiring knowledge are found among the Ojibway of North America, where we find two kinds of 'shamanism', shamans being essentially the recognized transmitters of special knowledge. First, associated with the Midéwewin association for 'medicine' or 'curing', there is a type of what has been called 'tutorial shamanism', which used a graphic system (a system of so-called pictographs on birch-bark scrolls) as mnemonics, or rather as 'prompts', for accounts of tribal migrations, of the other world, and so on. At the same time, knowledge of the same general kind could also be acquired directly in the course of the widespread vision quests of the North American Indians; the 'visionary' shamanism, possibly of earlier origin, supplements the tutorial shamanism which depended upon an individual becoming a pupil of a senior member of the society and handing over a large amount of wealth in exchange for instruction by means of the scrolls. Indeed in the 1930's, when the depression made initiation too costly (James Red Sky Senior reckoned he paid $10,000), there was a return to the cheaper and more direct visionary forms; as in Southern Nigeria and Melanesia, a sequence of initiatory rites, involving high contributions by the prospective members, was associated with an acephalous but nonetheless wealthy society. The relative emphasis on tutorial or visionary shamanism responded in some measure to variations in the amount of wealth circulating in the society.

The general situation in 'traditional' societies bears some resemblances to the present situation with regard to the indigenous priesthood among the Agni (or

Aowin) to the west of Ashanti, recently described by Ebin (1978). On the one hand there are the priestesses of the state cult, who proceed through consultation and sacrifice. On the other we have a more marginal set of priestesses who are transported into trance-like states and who reveal the words of those by whom they are possessed. Both of these roles were formerly performed by men, but, given the increasingly peripheral nature of the local cults, they have moved into the arena of medicinal cures, where local practices happily mix with imported drugs. It is an area at once more profitable and more adapted to the new social order. As in many African countries, it is possible to become a registered practitioner of traditional medicine, a possibility not open to the priestesses, who suffer competition from churches, old and new.

THE GROWTH OF KNOWLEDGE

I have spoken of the growth of knowledge by the search, the quest, the journey, the disappearance in the woods, all common themes of oral recitation. I am concerned to stress that oral cultures are not simply incessant reduplications of the same thing, the model of perfect reproduction, a pre-literate photo-copier. There is some growth, or at least change of knowledge, sometimes perceived as growth by the actors.

From one standpoint, the growth of knowledge is clearly limited. Changes come slowly, certainly in the technological field. Indeed, that is one of the major characteristics of pre-modern societies. But there are other areas in which the changes in knowledge, knowledge about the world, come much more rapidly. I refer principally to ideas about the world that we, from our post-modern standpoint, call supernatural beliefs. The evidence of such changes in ideas and cults is of two kinds. First, the pantheon is often in considerable flux, not fixed or unalterable as we wrongly imagine the Greek schema to have been. Of course among the LoDagaa, as elsewhere, there are fixed points, Heaven and Earth, the ancestors and the beings of the wild. But there is also a whole set of deities, gods, shrines, call them what you will, who change in emphasis and in actuality. I have argued that this change is related to the kind of internal contradiction that is generated by much human thought about the universe, whether utopian in a secular sense or millenarian in a religious one. It is the problem of the God who failed, the problem of evil, and on the more specific level of cures, the built-in obsolescence of patent medicines, from whatever source they come. Disappointment generates the search for new shrines, new curing agencies (possibly in an attempt to resolve cognitive dissonance), and these new forms are never simply repetitions of the last. A new cult may, for example, introduce a new prohibition (or taboo) on some food or action, which (if we may refer to the structural analyses of oppositions and analogies) will modify to some degree the classificatory schema of the society, forbidding what was otherwise allowed.

The second type of evidence comes from the Bagre recitation. If one looks at the recordings from different villages, different times, and even the same reciter at different times, it is clear that important variations are arising, variations that elaborate or slim down certain aspects of cultural potential, the ideo-logic, to use Augé's expression. Once again, though this can be seen as a transformation of similar patterns, it is more than a simple transformation, more than bringing a potential into being. A creative act is involved. Something new is born, an idea which may well conflict with other ideas, though I would not claim (for reasons that will become apparent) that there is the same clash, the same contention of ideas in non-literate societies that some have seen as the critical factor in the growth of knowledge in our own. In oral societies such contradictions are more easily swallowed up, as I have elsewhere argued is the case with scepticism. They are not absent certainly, but not transmitted either.

THREE MODES OF ACQUIRING KNOWLEDGE

There are, then, grossly, three modes of acquiring knowledge among the LoDagaa, and these seem widespread in oral societies. There is the basic knowledge that men and women require to carry on their daily round. Although this knowledge is 'traditional' in one sense, and some of it enters into the Bagre recitation, basically it is acquired in interaction, largely within the house and peer group, by participation in the events themselves, by experience. It is in this way that the bulk of LoDagaa culture, the sum total of learned behavior, of communal knowledge, is acquired.

Second, there is the rather specialized forms of knowledge, tenkouri yil, which anglophone West Africans often designate by the word 'deep', and which is transmitted in the partially decontextualized situation of the Bagre (at least so the LoDagaa often think) as well as in the course of other ceremonies, such as funerals, the Night Cow (with the bull-roarer), the Cleansing Ceremony (where the houses are painted white), and so forth. But it comes largely from participation in ceremonies and in discussions with elders. It has to be said that some of this knowledge, certainly about the problems of man's relationship with God and with death, is a knowledge that one has been deceived, a verbal parallel to the revelation that it was not a mysterious monster (the Night Cow) making that bizarre noise, but the bull-roarer, a piece of wood with a hole at the end.

Third, there is the knowledge that is not mediated by humans, either informally or formally, but comes direct from powers, spiritual forces, agencies (I do not know what other expressions to use), who alone seem to have the ability to reveal to man the secrets of his universe. It is in a way extraordinary that man should allocate to the beings of the wild and other agencies all the responsibility, both the glory and the blame, for having introduced into his world not only himself but virtually the whole of his cultural apparatus, old and new. We are a far cry from the 'Man Makes Himself' of the historian and pre-historian. Durkheim would see in this dependence man's dependence on society, which is the kind of truism, at the verbal level, on which the social sciences flourish. Going beyond the mystification of the obvious, the problem is why the recognition of the omnipresent social factor should take this particular form. But this is not the place for a more detailed enquiry into the sociology of fairies, nor that of cosmological structures. It is sufficient to insist upon the external sources of knowledge, even about oneself.

LITERACY

Among the Ancient Greeks, and it is time we turned to literate societies, there was an analogous division, at least as far as the transmission of a certain type of knowledge was concerned. I refer to the distinction between those who recited Homer or other works (the *rhapsodes*) and those who were 'inspired' in the literal sense, received the breath, the anima of another, and created new knowledge (the *aoidoi*). In the spheres of music and in literature the distinction between artist-creator and artist-performer is largely a function of the introduction of writing. It is now that exact repetition, associated with the reproduction not so much of the anonymous, but of the named, personalized contribution to culture, is differentiated from the act of creating, often still conceived, at least in the fields covered by the Muses, as inspired from outside, the signed, attributed work of these creators of culture that weighs down our bookshelves and our gramophone cabinets. It is now creative activity in the field of the arts that continues to come from outside, whereas other forms of knowledge get transmitted, modified, and increased in the context of the school, of book-learning.

Creative knowledge gets written down in books, just as in preliterate cultures it can get incorporated in oral tradition. But books themselves are a double-edged weapon. First they serve as stores of knowledge, to be copied exactly (physically so in the days before printing), as in the splendid versions of the Koran or of the medieval Prayer Books. Later on they are copied mentally as text-books. The whole process of literate education becomes a matter of absorbing abstracted knowledge through mediators, either directly from books or indirectly from teachers; it is as if the initiation of Bagre were prolonged so that it took over virtually the whole instead of only a small part of the life of each new entrant into the culture, teaching him about the world in which he lives by a series of verbatim exercises as a prelude to action and possibly as a prelude to making a creative contribution to knowledge. Knowledge here has been separated off from 'artistic' activity, which continues to be associated more with inspiration, with dissociation, with direct communion with the forces of nature, than with the bookish learning of the schoolroom.

As an example of what now happens as far as the wider acquisition of knowledge is concerned, let me turn to the curriculum of the temple school near the Step Pyramid of the ancient Memphis, dating from the sixth century B.C.

From the crumpled fragments of papyri in rubbish dumps surrounding the temple buildings, it is possible to reconstruct the learning process.

> 'The poor apprentices began with small demotic groups, and graduated to the chore of paradigms such as the "I said to him; he said to me" type. The next stage was perhaps month-names, or artificial sentences. One scribe informs us dutifully that dogs bark and cats miaw, and it must be admitted that there is a "postillion struck by lightning" note to many of his model sentences. Lists of names may be dull, until we recognize that they are arranged according to something very like an alphabetic scheme; the height of this is reached with a remarkable text in which alphabetic birds perch on alphabetical bushes before heading for suitable destinations. It is as if we recited "the crow perched on the chrysanthemum and flew away to Croydon". The scheme is certainly strange: it begins with the letter 'h' but Plutarch tells us that the first letter of the Egyptian alphabet was an ibis. The Egyptian word for this began with 'h' and the ibis was the bird of learning; and Plutarch was a watchful man (*Quaest. conv.* 9, 3.2). Once released from such tasks the scribe was free to copy literary texts (Ray, 1978:155).

Now what is happening here is that in the first instance a great deal of textual material was learnt 'by heart', that curious expression which means verbatim, word for word, and which as I have argued elsewhere is very difficult to accomplish without a written text, a written text that is in itself a formalization of speech,

'the crow perched on the chrysanthemum. . .'

'amo, amas, amat. . .'.

Essentially one is not ingesting or conveying any information about the world outside or the world within; one is 'learning to learn', acquiring the techniques of the written word, of written composition, which are so different from speech. One is learning to order words differently and for different ends.

And after all this has been achieved, the scribe 'was free to copy. . .texts'. Note the use of 'free' in juxtaposition to 'copy'. One was freed from one automatic task so that one could accomplish another, copying, so essential to written culture before the advent of printing, and even now, in the shape of the photocopier, one of the great academic money-spinners of all time.

The modes of acquiring knowledge affect the nature of that knowledge and the way in which knowledge is organized. In Scotland, with the fall of the Dalriadic Kingdom in the 11th century, Norman feudalism played a centralizing and unifying role, partly politically (the organization of sheriffdoms), partly economically (the organization of royal boroughs), but also through the reform of the church, the institution of bishoprics, the plantation of abbeys, the introduction of European 'rule'. 'For the first time there was an organised body of literate intellectuals in the country, men of one common purpose to whom the location of their dwelling place. . .was almost irrelevant' (Smout, 1969:26).

Contrast, perhaps too starkly, the acquisition of sacred knowledge in the earlier period. One old Norse story, represented on stones at Manx and Iona, relates how Sigurd killed a huge dragon, and toasted its heart over a fire. In doing this he touched the hot dragon's heart, and, burning his finger, put it in his mouth, with the result that he immediately became possessed of 'all the knowledge of the two worlds' (Macleod, n.d:7).

With the rise of 'an organised body of intellectuals', we also get its complement, the differentiation of ideas into ideologies, the fragmentation of the world view, the conflict of ideas.

What is the relation of knowledge to ideology? A widely accepted definition of knowledge is 'justified true belief' (Quinton, 1967:iv,345), a definition which presents problems not only for philosophy but for comparison as well. An ideology, according to Gellner (1978:69), is a system of ideas or beliefs, not any system but one that attracts and repels (and hence must surely be 'partial'). From these partial systems, Gellner attempts to distinguish ideology from the social construction of reality, the inclusive 'central belief system of a society', the 'total vision of reality'. Thus it is 'pointless to include pre-literate, tribal religions within the class of ideologies' (p. 81). 'Ideology involves doctrine; ideological conflict arises when doctrines, not men and shrines, are in opposition' (p. 82).

Once again it would be patently untrue to claim that there was NO conflict of doctrines in the pre-literate societies to which Gellner refers, no differentiation, no fragmentation. But the sharpness of the challenge, which is intrinsic to his discussion, does seem to be (like the sharpness of the conflict of ideas in the growth of knowledge) a function of the use of writing.

I want to comment on some aspects of this change that effect the accumulation, transmission, sources, and nature of knowledge. The first has to do with the change in God-man, and hence, man-God communication. The world of Islam is very definite about the nature of God to man communication. Chapter 96, vv. 3–5 of the Koran (the organization is highly literate) runs, 'Read: for your Lord is the Most Generous One, who taught by the pen, taught man what he did not know'.

In oral societies, too, God, or some other category of spiritual being, teaches man what he did not know. For originally he was simply a poor bare forked animal who knew nothing. But when writing appears, God shows the way by means of the book or tablet, the tablets that were shown to Moses, the golden ones revealed to John Smith and other Mormons, and the books which were written under the instructions of God and which then become Holy to man. Ever since man himself became literate he has assumed, as Chadwick said of Crete, that the gods were literate too. Hence the stuffing of written words into the cracks in the Temple wall at Jerusalem, the recourse to written talismen in Ancient Egypt and in contemporary Israel, as well as our own letters to Father Christmas.

Once writing was introduced, the Voice of God was supplemented by His hand; scriptural authority is the authority of the written (scripted) word, not the oral one. Written religion implies stratification. The written word belongs to the priest, the learned man, and is enshrined in ritualistic religion; the oral is the sphere of the prophet, of ecstatic religion, of messianic cults, of innovation. (It is one of the contradictions of the written word that at one level it restricts and at another encourages innovatory action.) The two different paths to knowledge we noted in oral societies become increasingly separate; the conflict between priest and prophet, between church and sect, is the counterpart of the fixed text and the fluid utterance.

TWO PATHS TO KNOWLEDGE AS SOCIAL CONTROL

But the opposition between 'learned', i.e. booklearned, and 'unlearned', i.e. unschooled, is not only a matter of individual roles; it divides the whole society and the whole culture. For most of the history of civilization, by which I mean no more than the history of towns with writing (in one meaningful sense, there cannot be a 'history' of any other towns), people who were taught by literate methods, i.e. in schools that removed individuals from the primary productive processes, formed only a limited percentage of the population. Not that the rest of society was uninfluenced by the presence of this additional means of communication. Far from it, for apart from all else, it encouraged (in places introduced) a radical differentiation within culture, a differentiation between the 'high' culture of the consumers of books and the 'low' culture of those confined to the oral register; between the audience of Chaucer and that of a singer of ballads. The 'two cultures' (to borrow a phrase from the waspish controversy between Snow and Leavis) interacted, and each clearly contributed to the other, but they were also distinct, and defined themselves in opposition to one another. What was high was what was not low; the low set aside the high, at least in the form in which it was offered. The non-literates could of course have the works of Bunyan or the books of the Bible read out to them. They could watch the plays of Shakespeare and listen to the sagas of Icelandic bards. But they had to do so through intermediaries and in this area of culture they were essentially a category of receivers rather than transmitters, let alone creators.

Of course at one level this statement applies with similar force even in societies where literacy is quasi-universal, that is to say in certain industrial societies of the last 100 years. The difference is that, in the earlier situation, the non-literate were unable to contribute to written culture (they were unable by definition to do so) or to communicate (e.g. by letter) as other men did. They were unable to operate one of the major channels of communication, and hence were in that sense 'deprived', though it was perhaps a deprivation that did not make itself really felt until the advent of printing vastly increased the availability of books and reading matter (e.g. the printed almanack).

The differentiation into high (derived from the written) and low (primarily oral) was not simply a division of the kind of cultural activity, it was also a matter of the division of labor. Some jobs (the scribal, bureaucratic, academic jobs) needed literacy; to many productive jobs, especially in the rural areas, it was far from essential. The kinds of knowledge involved in the first set of activities was increasingly valued more highly than the 'practical' knowledge, knowledge by experience, the knowledge of the bricoleur, as well as of the craftsman, which was acquired by some form of participation, apprenticeship, family labor, servanthood. Indeed there is now some tendency, at the popular level, to see proper knowledge as coming from books alone; it is they that tell the truth, not what we obtain from our parents (i.e. the elders) or from our peers, nor directly from nature itself. If I may take refuge in personal experience, in default of more systematic information, in the house where I grew up, there was an encyclopaedia called *The Book of Knowledge,* especially for children wanting to know (or more exactly, for children to answer the questions set by the school and for parents to answer those posed by their children). Knowledge was in a book, or in the head of a bookish person like the teacher (who, though we did not then know, had consulted the book the night before) rather than in the head of mere parents, whose role in 'education', in 'upbringing', did not involve the passing down of anything except fringe subjects.

I now see the other side of this process, my children learning botany from a book and getting to know the flora without knowing the trees and flowers, though admittedly some urban environments take pains to keep nature as far away as possible—flowers are patterns on plates, designs on material, even bunches of blooms collected in a vase.

It is clear that most of our knowledge does not come to us directly from the outside world. It is mediated by books, magazines, and newspapers. The study of botany is carried out by means of textbooks that explain verbally and diagram visually the structure of a flower. In biology the dissection of the dog-fish follows months, perhaps years of learning about the respiration of fishes. The source of knowledge, for both pupil and teacher, is the book, the text-book, whose contents are memorized the night before the lesson, the weeks before the exam. An 'authority' may even be a book, or someone who has read them studiously and can explain their message to others; it is not even necessary for him to make his own contribution to knowledge. He is the acknowledged mediator.

When the bulk of knowledge, true knowledge, is defined as coming from some outside, impersonal source (a book) and acquired largely in the context of some outside, decontextualised institution such as the school, there is bound to be a difference in intra-familial roles, roles with the elders, than in societies where the bulk of knowledge is passed down orally, in face-to-face contact, between members of the same household, kin-group, or village. There the elders are the embodiment of wisdom; they have the largest memory stores and their own experience reaches back to the most distant points. With book cultures, particularly with mass cultures of the printed word, the elders are by-passed; they are those who have not 'kept up'.

Mass literate cultures are the product, even in the developed nations, of the last hundred years. This is the point where attempts were made to generalize school education. The result is a generalization of the devaluation, including the self-devaluation, of knowledge and tasks that are not gained through the book but by experience. It is not my intention to take this analysis into the realm of socio-political action, although the implications are obvious and the possible solutions limited in number and utopian in character. But intrinsic to any effort to change the situation is a revaluation of forms of knowledge that are not derived from books. Not a return to 'savagery', but a modification of one's concessions to the civilisation of the book. ·

CONCLUSIONS

Some of the most significant differences between the societies I have studied in Africa and those I have experienced in Europe relate to the changes (and I put the matter quite deliberately in a developmental framework) that have occurred, and are occurring, in the means, and modes, of communication. But the nature of this change is far from simple, far from unidirectional, as we can see from the stress placed on different pathways of knowledge.

Oral societies such as the LoDagaa conceive of knowledge as of different kinds. Tenkouri yil, traditional knowledge, is explicitly associated with ceremonial contexts but is mainly transmitted in more general ways, in the same general contexts of social life in which 'practical' knowledge is passed along. There is no specific way of designating this knowledge, except that it is usually excluded from the category of 'traditional'. Both are set aside from the kind of knowledge acquired by contact with spiritual agencies, and specifically with the beings of the wild, a form of knowing that allows for innovation in apparently static cultures. Innovation is authorised by outside agencies.

In literate societies, we still emphasize inspirational access in the arts and in one segment of religion, but we no longer deem this knowledge in the usual sense, even though the imperialism of the school tries to transfer its training to the classroom rather than the workshop or the family. Of course, book-learning has its inspirational figures, its gurus, but it is their teaching rather than their 'knowledge' which displays this quality. The paths to knowledge in the more restricted sense become more sharply differentiated into the bookish mode and the practical one of empirical action, largely acquired by oral discourse, even though in many cases an outcome of bookish activities. Indeed 'knowledge', 'science' has become almost synonymous with book-learning, to be distinguished from most productive activities which are largely learned by apprenticeship, by imitation, by participation.

With the establishment of schools among the LoDagaa, as throughout the world, it is this second dichotomy that is imposing itself upon the first, a dichotomy that is value-laden (the high and the low), not only on the general level of the assumed quality of 'knowledge', but also in relation to the nature of the jobs to which such training leads. School-teaching is high, farming is low. Massive world-wide emphasis on literate education, the largest part of the budget of most developing countries, has certain clear concomitants, leading to a devaluation of non-literate skills, even food-getting skills, of learning by experience, as well as of occupations essential to society (though these were in some cases already devalued).

In Africa the result is the emergence of what, in another context, Djilas called the New Class, the class of literate bureaucrats, politicians, school-teachers, etc., with the non-literates filling the lower roles. In Europe, facing the problems arising from universal scholarization, the valued jobs become scarce, the devalued ones unwanted. So that you import gäst-arbeiter, Turks in Germany, Algerians and Portuguese in France, Indians and West Indians in Britain, to do the jobs the indigenes have been educated to regard as unworthy. Having imported them, you attempt to train them for scribal jobs. The reduction of structural unemployment must depend in part upon a revaluation of our paths of knowledge, our ways of knowing. I do not suggest that a consideration of the LoDagaa or other oral societies provides answers. But it does at least bring the problem to the surface.

REFERENCES

DEWDNEY, S., 1975. Scrolls of the southern ojibway. Toronto: University of Toronto Press.

EBIN, V., 1978. "Vessels of the Gods: A Study of Aowin Spirit Mediums". Ph.D. Thesis, University of Cambridge.

ERBS, A., 1975. *Approche de la religion des Birifor*. Paris: Institut d' Ethnologie.

GELLNER, E., 1978. Notes towards a Theory of Ideology. *L'Homme* 18 (3–4): 69–82.

GOODY, J., 1972. *The Myth of the Bagr*. Oxford: Clarendon Press.

————. 1977. Memoire et apprentissage dans les societes arec et sans ecriture: la transmission du Bagré. *L'Homme* 17:29–52.

————. 1981. *Une Recitation du Bagré, Classiques Africaines, Paris*.

MACLEOD, R. C., 1930. *The Island Clans during Six Centuries*. Inverness: R. Carruthers and Sons.

QUINTON, A., 1967. Knowledge and Belief, *The Encyclopedia of Philosophy*, 4:345–352. New York: the Macmillan Company and The Free Press.

RAY, J. D.. 1978. The World of North Saqqara, *World Archaeology* 10: 149–157.

SMOUT, T. C., 1969. *A History of the Scottish People 1560-1830*. London: Collins.

12 The Poetics and Noetics of a Javanese Poem*

Alton Becker
University of Michigan

". . .contextual shaping is only another word for grammar."
--Gregory Bateson (1978)

NOETICS ACROSS CULTURES

A philological journey can happen in space or time, or both, or in the imagination, right at home, though this latter might better be called poetry rather than philology. In this essay, the journey is from an English understanding of a short Javanese poem to a more nearly Javanese one, not in order to criticize the English version (it may be the best of all possible English versions) but to make the reader more responsive to the meanings evoked by the grammar of literary Javanese and the meanings not evoked by literary Javanese although basic to English understanding. The assumption is that poetic interpretation surely rests on the possibilities of grammar, and that across cultures one must be quite conscious of these possibilities in order to unlearn one's own.

Across cultures, what one learns is very rarely the same as what one is taught, since not only the content of learning but also the framework are new—the

*There is a long list of people who have, over the years, taught me what little I know about macapat songs. In chronological order: Soebowo Tjitrowidjojo, Susan Walton, Richard Wallis, Rahman Djoko Pradopo, I Made Gosong, Hidris and Margaret Kartomi, Joseph Errington, Retno Saraswati, Soemandiyo Hadi, and Rama Kuntara Wiryamartana, S. J. In respect to this essay, I must thank Judith Becker and Deborah Tannen for insightful critiques, and Indro Soesilo for a very useful batch of clippings from Indonesian newspapers about the recent renewal of interest in Ranggawarsita's work.

cohesion within and epistemology behind each lesson are inseparable from any possible content. With a new language, particularly a distant one, come eventually and always incompletely a new perspective on what and how a language MEANS: a new set of possibilities for meaning in a text. A useful term for all this, for language considered as the shaping, storage, retrieval, and communication of knowledge, is the term NOETICS, used frequently in recent years by Walter Ong, and known earlier in English mostly in Coleridge's essays.[1] That the entire process is deeply linguistic is what Benjamin Whorf had such trouble telling us: not that the whole process was entirely linguistic—as many have seemed to misread him—but rather that language is deeply involved in the entire process of shaping, storing, retrieving, and communicating what one knows. We may never know how deeply involved, since we cannot yet step outside of language as a mode of knowing language. The closest we can come to plumbing the noetic depths is to learn another language, another noetics—the less related to one's own, the better. Let me illustrate, briefly, what I mean.

A common strategy within the most elaborate and profound non-English noetic that I have studied—the Javanese shadow play—is etymologyzing (Becker 1979a). It happens early in a performance, and it is one of the ways one judges the skill and depth of a puppeteer. One of the descriptive terms for this kind of etymologyzing is JARWA DHOSOK—that is, FORCING (dhosok) old words (jarwa) into present contexts. Etymologyzing as a text strategy makes sense as a way of retrieving and communicatiang knowledge IF one believes that language is not arbitrary but in some sense TRUE or natural. How can a language be true or natural? Part of the LINGUISTIC impact of Sanskritic culture on Southeast Asia must have been the message not only that language itself was divine (not just particular texts), for surely many Southeast Asians already believed some version of that, but also that Sanskirit was MOST divine, most purely divine. The Language, Sanskrit, was the basis and source of knowledge, the true noetic. (The Buddhists appear to differ profoundly on this linguistic issue and tend, it seems to me, to see all language as more or less pathological.) With Sanskritic culture came to the people of Java new modes of shaping the perceived world, new modes of storing knowledge (particularly, writing as such a mode), new modes of retrieval (e.g. new mnemonic strategies as discussed in Yates 1966), and some new language acts (such as mantra, kekawin, stone inscription, etc.). Although Sanskrit was 'correct', other languages could—either naturally or, with great effort, artificially—be closer or further from the true noetics (Sanskrit), and thus be proper vehicles for the knowledge contained in Sanskrit, particularly the sastras.

That this effort to be closer to Sanskrit was really happening in Southeast Asia is clear from several kinds of evidence. The loan words, calques, and rhetorical-grammatical figures (e.g. Sanskritic compounding) are still there in all

---

[1]The word first comes to me from Ong (1975:95). For the Coleridge citations, see the Oxford English Dictionary entry for *noetics*.

those Southeast Asian languages which came to be called by their users BHASA (bahasa, basa, batha, patsa, etc.)—a term which did not and does not mean precisely what we mean by LANGUAGE: it means a Sanskritized, literary language, with a divine core and a large body of prior texts. This same process was happening in more or less the same way in India itself during the same period—the period of greatest Indian intellectual and economic hegemony over Southeast Asia. The period begins obscurely, but culminates in India as in Southeast Asia around the 10th century A.D. with the emergence of written vernaculars, the modern 'bhasas'. Before that, as Madhav Deshpande (1979:65) has recently written,

> The status of Sanskrit in classical and medieval times resembles that of the world of Platonic Ideas. This is clearly reflected in the linguistic speculations of the Sanskrit grammarians, ritualists, and logicians. Therefore, the process of Sanskritization of non-Sanskrit languages continued to dominate the Indian linguistic scene and remained a very significant way of increasing the prestige of those languages. . .In later times, the Persian and English compete with Sanskrit in this regard.

For Southeast Asia, add Arabic, Dutch, French, and Chinese to the list of later competitors.

Another kind of evidence is in the statements that Southeast Asians translated into their new literary languages. As a brief example, the Old Javanese (Kawi) *Tantri Kamandaka* (Hooykaas 1931:12) begins:

> 'Who does not know the acts of syllables and the seven cases of the noun, he, because he wants to know the true way, will stay close to a sage.'

The sage sounds like a linguist.

In such a context (i.e. searching for and creating Sanskrit in one's own language, and finding appropriate translations for Sanskrit grammatical, poetic, and rhetorical strategies) etymologyzing is a way of making/finding sense. Sanskrit (and later Dutch and English) roots are there in Javanese, waiting to be discovered and understood, even today.

My point above was to illustrate how languages AS NOETIC PROCESSES can differ, and also how they can be made to appear similar. The study of grammar is always abductive and comparative, across space and time. Not many languages, I suspect, even have original terms for nouns and verbs—to say nothing of tense and aspect.[2]

For scholars in Southeast Asia, the terminology for what we call grammar seems almost entirely borrowed, as either loanwords or calques. This does not mean, however, that Southeast Asians have not paid close attention to language,

---

[2]Cultures, like people, seem to be self-conscious about language in different ways and to different degrees. One source of self-consciousness appears to be a strong challenge to a culture's noetics, e.g. colonialism, religious conversion, sustained failure, etc.

but rather that they traditionally noticed different things about it; for instance, about the parts of a shadow play, kinds of preserved oral texts and their minute divisions, fine levels of linguistic politeness, kinds of speech acts, etc. In all these areas, local terms dominate. However, a grammatical concept like ASPECT is an imposition—a metaphor (with a strongly visual root) about how one LOOKS AT action. Somehow in examining literary Javanese, we must be ready to transform the metaphor, at the same time we are using it to 'look at' an action as a poet, far off in space and time, froze it into words.

A NOTE ON JAVANESE POETICS

The poetic genre, MACAPAT,[3] has been a viable discourse strategy for over 700 years, and macapat songs/poems are still sung and composed today, still in an archaic language, as if the past were still speaking. Macapat songs first appear to us in written texts toward the end of the great translation period of Javanese literature, the period of the Kakawins. (For details on the history of Javanese literature see Zoetmulder (1974) and Pigeaud 1967:1–42). The Kakawins, for the most part translations/adaptations/imitations of Sanskrit literature, were written in a language (Kawi) which was elegant, learned, elaborate, and somewhat formulaic, like Homeric Greek. It was a language heavy with Sanskrit terms, and heavy is the right word: Sanskrit's power to build and compound terms probably always made the Southeast Asian languages it touched heavier (i.e. longer, more complex bound forms). Compounding became a text strategy throughout Southeast Asia, often compounding across Sanskrit and one of the bhasas.[4] The Javanese poets had learned to write quantitative verse from Sanskrit, and had familiarized Javanese at all levels of the society with Sanskrit words; terms for powerful ideas, terms for language and grammar, names for distant people and places.[5] As power shifted—and perhaps diffused, and Islam and Christianity appeared, a new literary language appeared (evolving probably out of autochthonous oral forms), one that has been shaped and preserved to the present in Java, Bali, and Lombok.

Macapat poems, one of the important genres in this language, are defined by 1) number of syllables in a line, 2) line final vowel quality, and 3) number of lines. The kind I will be translating, SINOM, has nine lines:

1   Eight syllables ending in *a*

2   Eight syllables ending in *i*

---

[3]This genre of sung poetry is described in detail in Kartomi (1973).

[4]See Gonda (1973:456–70) and in many other places in that pioneering compendium.

[5]A similar noetic transition was described by Mary Zurbuchen, who told me that on T.V. in Bali there was an American government film on the space program followed immediately, with no comment, by Star Trek.

3   Eight syllables ending in *a*

4   Eight syllables ending in *i*

5   Seven syllables in *i*

6   Eight syllables ending in *u*

7   Seven syllables in *a*

8   Eight syllables ending in *i*

9   Twelve syllables, a longer line, ending in *a*

There are also constraints on caesura placement, which aids in binding the poem to one of the numerous melodies it can be sung in. It may be sung alone or with a gamelan ensemble, in which case the sinom floats above the gong patterns of the gamelan, the singer just one more instrument, coinciding with the ensemble at certain points in the musical structures of each. When one hears a sinom one hears the vowel patterns (aided by the irregular lines, 5, 7, and 9) very clearly, particularly the long last line that closes the verse. The vowels (a, i, and u) are the most important in the grammatical prosodies of the language, defining a wide prosodic vowel space. Some other forms of macapat have a tighter vowel space, by using final ē and o. Furthermore, the a and i vowels have closer variants in closed syllables, so that the vowel music is more subtle than might appear from the description above. The rhyme vowels are usually elaborated by the singer, with turns and figures described in Javanese with the same word used for the waves of a kris, *eluk*. The line ends are always major breaks in grammatical structure, as will be apparent below, and are further enhanced by gongs, flute elaborations, and calls by the other singers.

When macapat is sung with a gamelan, readers and musicians might assemble in the evening, sitting on the floor around a low wooden table, on which are books of poetry and glasses of sweet tea. There's a lantern on the table, and behind the singers the instruments of the gamelan. Soloists change, verse forms change, and the non-soloists comment on the soloist, in a traditional vocabulary of sung interjections.[6] The two string viol anticipates the melody, the flute embellishes it, and the gamelan fills in pitches and overtones of a particular mode and melody. The texture is very rich, socially, musically, and, as we shall see, grammatically.

Or a macapat may be sung alone, unaccompanied. Someone once used one to wake me from an afternoon nap. (For more details on the uses of macapat, see Kartomi 1973:3–15).

---

[6]These are *senggakan* (see Kartomi 1973:54), meaning various senggakan things like, 'Mango stones, hurrah, hurrah', or 'Oh, forgive me'. They also fill holes in the musical texture.

A GRAMMATICAL TRANSLATION OF A SINOM

We have lived to see a time without order
In which everyone is confused in his mind
One cannot bear to join in the madness
But if he does not do so
He will not share in the spoils
And will starve as a result
It is God's wish
Happy are those who forget
Happier yet are those who remember and who have deep insight.
(Kartomi, No. 70, tr. by Clifford Geertz, 1973)[7]

The translated sinom above is an interpretation of the Javanese original grammatically as well as referentially. The grammar, however, is English, entirely. I must emphasize again that this was the intent of the translator, and his translation was one of the things that first got me interested in macapat. But I would like to go 'deeper', to the grammatical meaning and the linguistic coherencies of the poem. It is a process, for us, of taking out the English coherencies, and putting back the Javanese ones.

To get an idea of the first step, which we can only do very artificially, I will remove all grammatical forms in the English which have no Javanese counterparts IN THIS POEM,[8] while leaving in the lexical translations—although these, too, rarely fit in semantic range the Javanese words they take the place of.

Stage 1 of un-Englishing the poem:

Live-to-see time without order
Confused in mind
Cannot bear to join madness
But if not
Not share spoils
Starve as the result

---

[7]There are several versions of this sinom, which, though originally written (by the great Javanese poet and scholar, Ranggawarsita), passed quickly into the oral tradition, where freedom to reshape it to changing contexts is still quite great. The greatest motivation for change seems to be religious, e.g. 'Allah' becomes 'Dewa' in line 7. I have used here the version given in Kartomi, op. cit. I heard a second version later in a tape recording of sinom lent me by Susan Walton. Later I read the entire *Kalatida* (The Age of Darkness) by Ranggawarsita and saw a third version, which—according to our noetic conventions—is the 'original' version. I am very grateful to Joseph Errington for sending me the text of the *Kalatida*, to Retno Saraswati for helping me read it, and to Rama Kuntara Wiryamartana, S. J., for singing this sinom on tape for me. (see also footnote 14).

[8]Some of these grammatical functions are possible in Javanese, though not obligatory, and not used in this poem.

God's wish
Happy who forget
Happier who remember and deep insight

Even this doesn't clean out all the English cohesion, since these words evoke their normal English grammatical contexts, and the verbs, particularly, carry their UNMARKED functions in English. I have tried to remove tense, aspect, most articles, auxiliary verbs, and, above all, ALL pronominal deixis. There is no first person reference, directly or indirectly in the poem. There is an indirect second person reference (higher statue, respected hearer) in the anaphoric 'article' suffix on the word translated by 'result' (*wekasanipun*). There is no third person reference, except the generic *who* of the last lines, and God.

We are left at this point with a very sparse poetic landscape—not a rare experience when reading very careful translations of literature from languages unrelated to English. OUR grammatical cohesion, our most basic linguistic background, is gone, though we still UNDERSTAND (i.e. interpret the Javanese) as if it were there, unmarked, in the Javanese. And we do not notice what IS there.

The speech situation is of course there in the context, if not in the text. One may 'hear' (interpret) the singer telling of personal experience, or one may 'hear' (interpret) the singer telling about oneself, or someone else, real or imaginary. (The song to wake me from my nap began, 'Young men should not waste the day sleeping. . . .') But this is interpretive. There is more power in the song if it hits someone in the speech situation. That is to say, poems like this are what Kenneth Burke calls 'equipment for living'—just as practical and everyday as mnemonic rhymes, prayers, proverbs, everyday metaphors, and cliches: small (or large) texts widely known and repeated frequently to interpret or evaluate things that happen, locally, nationally, or internationally.[9] They help shape and give coherence to those events.[10] Context, not text, provides the person-number cohesion which English marks heavily in the text.

---

[9]For a discussion of evaluation as a discourse function, see Labov & Waletzky (1967:12–44). The concept is expanded richly into a methodology for cultural description in Polanyi (1978).

[10]Here is an English translation of a macapat about the coming of the white settlers and their new agriculture, from Kartomi (1973:211).

The destruction of the land of Java
Came with the arrival of a white spirit
Her weapon is a violet sugar-cane stalk
The Javanese are scattered and in disorder
Many villagers are sad
Captured under the spell
Pray to God
For a ray of light
A ray from the north-east

A Javanese poet or singer could break the sinom into Adegan Ageng and Adegan Alit; ADEGAN means 'a unit of meaning' (Kartomi [1973:52] calls it 'sense unit')—it also means a scene in a play, while AGENG means 'large'/ALIT 'small'. The whole poem is usually one Adegan Ageng, made up of smaller Adegan Alit. In this poem, according to a Javanese musician I discussed it with, there are three Adegan Alit, the first six lines—a paradoxical dilemma; a one-line evaluation (line 7); and the last two lines, a paradoxical solution. Thus, rhetorically, the poem is dialogic, like riddles, questions-and-answers, Shakespearean sonnets, etc.

At the highest structural level of the text, then, this is a didactic statement, in the form of a sinom. Its overall thematic coherence is paradox, and there are three major parts, a dilemma or problem, an evaluation, and a solution.[11]

Since lines of the macapat are grammatical units, it seems reasonable to examine the three major parts as if they contained six, one and two-line sub-parts, respectively.

I will give a Tagmemic[12] parsing of these lines, and describe them both internally and in relation to one another.

Line 1: A BiIntransitive Clause Root:

(Eight syllables ending in -*a*)

Predicate	BiIntr. Verb		Adjunct	Noun Phrase
Statement	BiIntransitive	+	Scope	
Anglakoni			*jaman edan*	
walk through			period unsteady	

---

[11]There are also specific prior sinoms, of which this is in some sense an imitation, and which are evoked by it. They make up a linguistic context for this sinom, and in that sense are a higher or broader structural level for this text. This dimension of meaning, called by J. Lotman 'literary equivalence' is as yet inaccessible to me in Javanese; that is, I do not have enough knowledge of Javanese to have a sense of prior text, in literature or everyday conversation.

[12]See Pike & Pike for an explanation of the methodology used here.

The basic principles of tagmemic parsing are: 1) that units are related to each other in multiple ways, 2) that these ways are not universal but are to be defined emically for each language and from the perspective of each language, in so far as each language creates a different observer.

Units are related phonologically, semantically, and grammatically—three overlapping but independent hierarchies. In this paper, phonological and semantic relations are described informally, but grammatical relations at the level of 'lines in the sinom' (mostly clauses and sentences) are parsed using names for analogous units in English, reshaped to fit Javanese. As noted earlier, any grammatical parsing is necessarily abductive and comparative.

A few terms may be unclear. Each grammatical tagmeme is within a larger unit, and it is related to other units in four ways: function, role, filler class, and cohesion. Thus a tagmeme is a complex unit which is usually displayed as:

Commentary: The initial predicate will be discussed in a later section. It is the only active, fully inflected predicate in the poem, and the one whose aspect provides a major part of the poem's cohesion. As a word the root (*laku*) has a rich set of derived meanings from a central meaning 'walk': conduct, path, put in motion, act in a play, the word for 'a play' itself, fate, plot, a cycle, to endure—voluntarily or not, and many more. The English version gives 'have lived to see' which adds, besides English tense and aspect, a notion of age (have lived) and detachment (to see, not to experience). I will return to the inflection of this form after looking at the whole poem.

What is being endured is the adjunct of scope: an era, a time of craziness, but crazy in the sense of unsteadiness, a time of change and transition.[13]

	SLOT	FUNCTION
FORM	FUNCTION	CLASS
MEANING	ROLE	COHESION

Although one expects all these four relations to be manifest in any language, particular categories are not assumed a priori to be relevant.

A clause root is a construction whose functions include a predicate and its major adjuncts. The kinds of adjuncts define the kind of clause (e.g. Transitive, stative). The basic adjuncts of a predicate are often subject (with various roles), and the other adjuncts or objects (with various roles). For many languages, there are from one to three adjuncts (or 'terms') related to a predicate, and the basic roles include actor, undergoer, scope, and item.

These doubly defined slots (i.e. specified for function and role) have doubly defined fillers (i.e. specified for class and cohesion). The class terms define the internal structure of each filler unit. Thus subjects might be filled by words, phrases, or units at any level. Cohesion terms define co-referentiality or governance across units in a text. Not all terms have equally complex cohesion, a point illustrated in section IV of this paper.

The Javanese clause types described in this paper have been called, by analogy with English, transitive, intransitive, stative, and equative, depending upon their constituents. Any clause type with *bi-* as part of its name includes a scope tagmeme (i.e. a role which in English includes both indirect objects: I gave the book *to John*, and nuclear locatives: I put the book *on the table*).

In tagmemics, parsing is not automatic (i.e. rule governed) but interpretive (i.e. hermeneutic). Parsings are not unique. As a weakly predictive, very sensitive parsing methodology, tagmemics is designed specifically for approaching TEXTS (oral or written) in DISTANT languages, and has been shaped by several generations of field linguists, primarily missionaries.

[13]The notion of unsteadiness appears in many Javanese proverbs and larger texts. People have refered to the pre-colonial times as 'back when the world was steady'. The *Tantu Panggelaran* contains the lines:

Ya ta matangnyān henggang henggung nikang nusa Jawa,
sadakāla molah marayegan,
hapan tanana sang hyang Mandaraparwata,
nguniweh janma manusa.

(For that reason—i.e. There was no great mountain
to stabilize it—Java was shaking,
incessantly moving and swaying,
because there was no great Mandaraparwata, to say nothing of human beings.)

Line 2: A BiStative Clause Root:

(Eight syllables ending in -*i*)

Predicate	Compound Stative Verb Phrase		Adjunct	Locative Phrase
Statement	BiStative	+	scope	

éwuh aya
Uneasy, not at home, struggling

ing pambudi
in mind-soul-consciousness

Commentary: Lines 1 and 2 are grammatically parallel, though the fillers of the two slots are different and the first is active, the second stative. In function and role they are the same: Predicate: Statement + Adjunct:Scope.

The first word in line 2 is one that might be used if one were staying in a strange house, awkward, reluctant to act—confused in that sense.

The second word, *aya,* might describe a situation in which one was wading upstream, against the odds, increasingly having to make more effort. This word is more active than the first word, but the first is marked as a stative (*a+iwuh* becomes by sandhi *éwuh*; *a−* (or *ma-*) might be called a stative prefix) and this second verb is unmarked, although sense of motion (against resistance) makes the second line more parallel to the marked active of line one.

The locative phrase includes a noun derived from the Sanskrit loan *budi,* which is bigger than 'mind'—'consciousness', perhaps. On this loan is a Javanese prefix, *pam-*, a prefix marking an agent or instrument, somewhat like English *-er*. So it's consciousness seen as active: the 'consciousness-er'.

The first two lines present an external world, which is unsteady, and an internal world in which one is not at home.

Line 3: A Transitive Clause Root with an Embedded Intransitive Clause Root:

(Eight syllables ending in -*a*)

Adjunct	Intransitive C1Rt		Predicate	Neg Verb Phrase
Item		+	Statement	Transitive

melu édan
join-in being crazy/unsteady

ora tahan
not stand

Commentary: It is not until the final verb of this line that the constituent structure becomes clear. The first two words are parallel in sound and structure to the first two words of line two, a compound predicate: join-in + be crazy. But instead of a scope tagmeme, as in lines 1 and 2, there is another predicative of which this compound predicate is the adjunct. Since the final predicate is transitive (can't stand SOMETHING), the hearer-reader reinterprets the first part of the line as an embedded clause. I think this is a matter of reinterpretation, since the strong parallelism of the first half of line 3 with line 2 starts one off on the wrong grammatical track, as it were.

There is no temporal marking here. That is, the line might be read in English, where temporal decisions must be made, as either of the following:

1. X won't/couldn't/can't stand going along with being crazy (and won't do it).
2. X went along with being crazy and X couldn't stand it.

Fortunately, none of the decisions need be made, except by translators.

There is an archaic and frozen aspectual distinction in this line, which I will return to in the next section.

Line 4: A Dependent BiIntransitive Clause Root:

(Eight syllables ending in -i)

Margin	\<lamun\>		Nucleus	BiIntr. Clause Root-Neg
relator		+	related	

Lamun	*datan anglakoni*
But if	not walk through (same as ln 1)

Commentary: A poem like this is said to be CEMPLANG ('not complete') unless a few, well known Kawi (Old Javanese) words are used. (Kartomi 1973:55). This line begins with two of them, *lamun datan* ('but if not. . .') , followed by the initial word of the poem—the only active, inflected verb, here foregrounded by repetition, in clause final position, where the word may be drawn and elaborated by the singer.

Line 5: Scope-focus BiIntransitive Sequential Clause:

(Seven syllables ending in -i)

Predicate	\<nora\>		Subject	Compound BiIntransitive Clause Root
Negation		+	Item	

nora	*keduman*	*melik*
not	get share	have things

Commentary: This clause is the second part of the figure begun in line 4: IF NOT A, NOT B. In both of these the negative is a predicate, at clause level, not part of the verb phrase (as the negative is in sentence 3, for instance). Here it negates two predicates, 'get share', which is marked for a subject with a role of scope (somewhat like our dative), and 'have-' 'things' ', which is marked for a stative actor subject. In neither case is the subject given: the subject of all the lines in the poem is the same unmentioned person. Its role changes (agent in lines 1 and 4, for instance, and scope in line 5), but it is the same referentially in each line, and always in focus, where focus is marked.

So far each line has gotten more complex, syntactically. Here there is not only embedding, but embedding a compound in which each verb has the same unmentioned subject in different roles. The English reader gets a brief vision of the Javanese syntactic landscape here: topic, focus, and role filling in that previously sparse translated world (after its English coherencies had been removed).

Line 6: Irrealis Intransitive Non-Actor Focus Clause

(Eight syllables ending in *-u*)

Nucleus	Intrans. Non-Actor Focus Cl. Rt		Margin	Result Phrase
statement	irrealis	+	result	Cohesion to Script
kaliren			*wekasanipun* (wekas-an-ipun)	
starve, be lacking			result/remainder of	

In this case, it might be better to describe the structure at two more levels:

Intransitive Non-Actor Focus C1 Root—irrealis:

Predicate	Intr. Undergoer Focus Verb Phrase
Statement	irrealis

Intransitive Undergoer Focus Verb Phrase:

Nucleus	Intrans. Verb Root		Margin	Non-Actor suffix
statement		+	focus	irrealis
Kalir			*-én*	
starve, lack			will happen	

Commentary: Here we meet what has been called by Kawi Grammarians a passive irrealis. In the end, the unmentioned subject will (irrealis) be lacking the necessities. All we know of the role of that subject is that it is not, at this point, actor.

The suffix (*-ipun*) on the nominal meaning result/remainder is an anaphoric 'article' (the result of something already mentioned, presupposed) which also marks respect for topic or hearer.

Line 7:

(Seven syllables in *-a*)
There are several ways to parse this line, but the following seems most fitting:

Equative Clause Root:

Topic	Noun	+	Comment	Noun Phrase
Item			Character of Topic	
Dilalah			*kersa*	Allah
Misfortune			intent	God
opposition				

Commentary: The first word might also be interpreted as an exclamation. I have interpreted it as a part of a clause somewhat like an English equative: this misfortune *is* the intent of God. A variant version of the poem has the predicate *awit* in place of *dilalah*. *Awit* means something like 'hampered', 'confronted', 'meet with', 'coincide with'. The version with *awit* also has *dewa* (Sanskrit 'god') in place of *Allah*. (There is nice internal rhyme, called PURWAKANTI SWARA, between *Dilalah* and *Allah*.)

This line stands alone. It is a different speech act from all the lines before it: the unmentioned subject is not one of its constituents. It is, on a more general level, an evaluation of the preceding lines. It seems to say that what one confronts—the paradox itself—is God's intent (kersa). (The conceptual space of KERSA is too vast for me, still.) This line might be considered the end of the first section, or the beginning of the second, or—as here —standing alone.

Lines 8 and 9: Stative Clauses

(Eight syllables ending in -*i*, and 12 syllables, a long line, ending in -a)

Predicate	Adjective Phrase		Subject	Nominal
Statement	Stative	+	Actor	
8 *Beja-bejane*			*sing lali*	
9 *Isih beja*			*sing eling lawan waspada*	
8 Joyous			he who forgets/is absent-minded	
9 More Joyous			he who is mindful and pays deep attention	

Commentary: These two, closely parallel lines both begin with an adjective phrase and end with a nominalized clause as subject. In the first (line 8), the reduplicated adjective (or stative, perhaps) plus article has a meaning somewhat like the English 'happier than happy'.

The adjective phrase in line 9 is comparative: more happy, more joyous (than happier than happy, even).

What does the unmentioned actor forget in line 8 and pay deep attention to in line 9? The embedded transitive clauses in these parallel lines do not mention an adjunct (object). It is clear, however, from the structure of the poem itself, that the thematic nucleus is the very first word *anglakoni:* 'walking', 'playing a part', 'enduring'. Just why that word is the thematic nucleus depends upon understanding of the aspectual system, and the ways it indicates the network of textual relations that word establishes. For the moment, however, I only want to point out how there is something evoked by the grammar but unstated both at the beginning and at the end of the poem: the unmentioned actor evoked by *anglakoni,* and the unstated adjunct: goal of the final predicates, which is that same word, *anglakoni.* Here is a subtle circularity.

By now the structure of the poem should be emerging for the reader: the three parts of the poem (andegan alit) are 1) a paradoxical dilemma, (lines 1–6), 2) a general truth (line 7), and 3) a paradoxical solution (lines 8 and 9). In each of these parts, there is a different subject, evoked by the verb inflexions in lines 1–6 but never mentioned, stated in 7 (perhaps), and generic in lines 8 and 9. Each of these sections is a different language act, too: description (lines 1–6), evaluation (line 7), and advice or admonition (lines 8 and 9).

Having seen something of the inter- and intra-clause level structure of the poem, I would like to go down into (or up out of) the inflected verb, to see how it marks an aspectual relation with an unmentioned subject, a deep, grammatical level of coherence in the poem.

At this point the reader should ALMOST be able to read the Javanese:[14]

Anglakoni jaman edan	1
Ewuh aya ing pambudi	2
Melu edan ora tahan	3
Lamun datan anglakoni	4
Nora keduman melik	5
Kaliren wekasanipun	6
Dilalah kersa Allah	7
Beja-bejane sing lali	8
Isih beja sing eling lawan waspada.	9

THE CONTEXTUALIZING FUNCTIONS OF ASPECT

There is only one definite action in this poem, *anglakoni*. The rest of the poem is an overlay on that action, an evaluation (in Labov's sense) of it, a linguistic elaboration of it. The rest of the poem builds contexts for that action (as in Figure 1).

On the model of the Greek topoi (topics), a text may be viewed as a sequence of rhetorical strategies (definition, comparison, contrast, narrative, etc.)

---

[14]The original text version from Ranggawarsita's *Kalatida* reads as follows, as romanized by G. W. J. Drewes (1974):

Amenangi jaman edan
Ewuh-aya ing pambudi
Milu edan nora tahan
Yen tan milu anglakoni
Mbaya kaduman melik
Kaliren wekasanipun
Ndilalah karsa Allah
Begja-begjane kang lali
Luwih begja kang eling lawan waspada

Drewes translates this as:

Living in a foolish age/ One is too much hampered in one's efforts/ However loath to join in its follies/ by keeping aloof/ One will not share in the gains/ And eventually perish with hunger/ But what can one do? It was ordained by god/ Still, be the heedless ever so lucky/ Luckier by far are those who are heedful and keen-sighted.

This translation, like Geertz's, is a free interpretation—as far as I can see no closer to the original, though Drewes feels Geertz's translation 'leaves much to be desired'. How do we count the steps from English to Javanese, or—a different route—Javanese to English? Or another, Javanese to Dutch to English?
The controversy grows from an unfortunate footnote in Drewes' otherwise very admirable article.

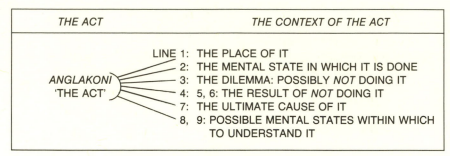

FIGURE 1. Rhetorical Context (Javanese *Topoi*)

built around one or more central word (or 'theme'). The word is CONTEXTUALIZED via these rhetorical strategies. If one assumes that the meaning of something is its relations with its contexts, the scope and density of those relations will make some words more 'meaningful' than others within a text. These prominent words might be called THEMATIC. (For a discussion of theme in tagmemic grammars see Jones 1977). I would like to show now that a thematic word (or larger unit) is not just a rhetorical or referential concept but a grammatical one as well. From the perspective of text function, clause syntax is micro-rhetoric. From the perspective of clause syntax, rhetorical structures are larger, looser analogs of syntax—macro-syntax, perhaps.

The grammatical relations of the thematic word *anglakoni* with the rest of the poem are established by its inflexions. The complex network of these grammatical relations are displayed in Figure 2.

The gramatical relations of a predicate with its contexts might be called its aspection, to revive an earlier, heavier term (see the Oxford English Dictionary)

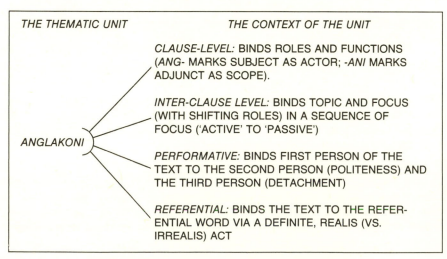

FIGURE 2. Grammatical Context (Javanese Aspection)

which is less tightly bound than the term ASPECT. (It always seems important to loosen and slow down one's metalanguage when one is describing another language in one's own language. It's a kind of AHIMSA for scholars.) In order to explain the aspection of the predicate *anglakoni* (a rich example of the full system of Javanese aspection), I will sort out the kinds of contexts that predicate relates to. These are listed in Figure 2.

Clause Level Contexts

The inflected form here has a prefix *ang-* and a suffix *-ani*. (By vowel sandhi, the final *-u* of the verb root *laku* blends with the *-a* of the suffix *-ani* to produce the *-o-* of *anglakoni*.) These two affixes are not simple from an English perspective, since what they mark is not simply (i.e. monomorphemically) marked in English. Within the clause, the prefix *ang-* marks that the subject (in other terms, the focused argument) is an actor acting intentionally. The prefix *ang-* is one of a set of verb prefixes active in LITERARY (perhaps older oral) Javanese which are mutually exclusive with *ang-*. This set, as Figure 3 illustrates, includes the following:

	ACTOR SUBJECT	SCOPE SUBJECT	UNDERGOER SUBJECT
ACTIVE/ TRANSITIVE	(M) ANG-	-IN-*	-IN-*
STATIVE/ INTRANSITIVE	(M) A-	KA-	--

(*The archaic infix *-in-* gives way in time to the prefix *di-* and a set of pronoun clitics with the same function.)

FIGURE 3. Subject-Role Prefix/Infix

I must emphasize, particularly to those who know literary Javanese (what might be better called the language of the macapats, though this, too, changes over time) that this is not a complete set of all prefixes one might find before a verb: there are derivational prefixes and some, to be mentioned below, which have other functions than clause level cohesion. These affixes under consideration here mark the role of the subject (actor, scope, or undergoer) and the transitivity of the act or state.

Within the clause, the suffix *-ani* marks that the adjunct is in the role of scope (that is, the place—or, by extension, person—to or from or within which an action takes place). This is a secondary focus system: the prefix marks the role of the subject, the suffix marks the role of the adjunct. As we have seen, there are three possible subject roles: actor, scope, or undergoer. (A more neutral subject role, perhaps 'item', is possible with the stative-intransitives, but will not be examined here.) There are also three predicate-marked adjunct roles (Figure 4).

SCOPE ADJUNCT	UNDERGOER ADJUNCT (1)	UNDERGOER ADJUNCT (2)
-(AN)I	0	-AKE

FIGURE 4. Adjunct-Role Suffix

Other adjunct roles (e.g. non-subject actor) are marked by prepositions, not by inflexion. The two undergoers in Figure 4 are 1) a simple 'direct object' and 2) the object of a causative.

To complicate the explanation a bit more, the adjunct-role suffixes mark the role of the subject (in combination with *ka-*, *-in-*, or *di-*) if the subject is not Actor. That is, with Actor subject, there is possible secondary (adjunct) focus. Otherwise not.[15]

At the level of the clause, then, the initial predicate *anglakoni* carries information about the roles of the subject and adjunct. The subject is not, as we have seen, independently mentioned, so the information on the predicate is all we have: an actor acting intentionally. This predicate, *anglakoni,* is mentioned again in line 4, and is implied as the adjunct of lines 8 and 9, since it is rhetorically THEMATIC (Figure 1).

Inter-Clause Level Contexts

Since there are no grammatical signals until line 7 of a change of subject, the subject of *anglakoni* remains in force to that point. The function of the inflexion of the initial predicate, therefore, is to thus establish the topic not just for the initial clause but for a sequence of clauses. The roles change, but the topic in focus remains constant in a sequence of focus (somewhat like the English sequence of tenses), in which a topic begins as an actor, and ends the sequence as scope (the locus of other people's action) in line 5 and undergoer (the victim) in line 6. This movement of roles-in-focus is one of the most important ways of marking a unified sequence of clauses in traditional Javanese literature. When a topic moves out of actor role or moves out of focus, that is an important signal of closure for a sequence of clauses. (For a description of this same phenomenon in Malay see Becker 1979b).

This grammatical movement in the first six lines parallels the more abstract meaning of the poem: voluntary actor becomes involuntary victim.

At the inter-clause level, another dimension of the prefix *ang-* on *anglakoni* possibly comes into play. Actions could, in older, written Javanese, be marked as

---

[15]For a fuller, more systematic description of modern Javanese verb morphology, see Uhlenbeck (1956:567–73). I am also indebted to Stuart Robson for allowing me to study his unpublished *A Simple Javanese Grammar* (1976), and for his patience.

background-continuous by an infix -*um*-, which appears frequently in Austronesian languages with a similar function. In modern Javanese this possibility is lost, though frozen remnants of the infix remain (prefixed as m- to vowel initial stems, having lost the u-). With the -um- infix, the subject could only be actor. The -*um* background-continuous infix was mutually exclusive with the subject set in Figure 3 (although it occurs with the adjunct set, Figure 4): its function was to mark that the predicate concerned was background to the discourse—or a continuous action extending over several other actions. Thus *ang*- contrasts with -*um*- not in marking clause level subject roles (they are identical) but inter-clause foregrounding or backgrounding.

Performative Contexts

Any text establishes relations between speakers and hearers (or writers and readers, readers and hearers, speakers and readers, writers and hearers, etc.). Layers of meaning build as one language act is embedded in another, as any student of text knows well. This metacommunication is an essential part of what any utterance means.

In the case of *anglakoni,* two things mark (or may mark) the relation of speaker to hearer and speaker to text. The first is the choice of verb root. In a stratified language like Javanese, the root itself is a part of a paradigm clearly marking levels of politeness and respect. Somewhat similarly in English, we might say to a woman, you have spilled some mustard on your tit/breast/chest/front. The choices range from potentially insulting to ultra-fastidious, from specific terms to more general, diffuse terms. In Javanese this system is more elaborate, and the different levels are named and commonly discussed. The root of the predicate under discussion here is a common one with many derivations: to walk, perform a role, conduct oneself, endure, etc. In some of these values it has a higher level counterpart, *lampah*. However, since the actor here is unspecified, to use the higher form would suggest that the actor was *not* the speaker, for to use a high-level form for oneself (including one's actions) is immodest. The lower form, however, when spoken indirectly or written, is not so restrictive as the higher form, and might be considered the unmarked choice. It allows the possibility that the speaker is talking about him/herself.

Within the period from Old Javanese to Modern Javanese, particularly in dealing with self-consciously archaic literary language, it is difficult to know just when grammatical possibilities change. In Bali, as a most striking instance, people still compose in Kawi (Old Javanese), somewhat as Edmund Spenser composed Chaucerian English in Elizabethan times, or as a city folksinger adopts an archaic rural dialect today. We all speak the past on occasion (e.g. Hell hath no fury. . .). It was part of macapat technique to affect Old Javanese—but not too much. Hence, to know what was frozen Old Javanese (e.g. The remnants of the -um- infix, perhaps), and what was self-consciously literary, is difficult. One of the major problems in this regard concerns the initial m- of the actor subject prefixes: *ma-* varies with *a-*, *mang-* varies with *ang-* (see Figure 3). While foreign scholars have tended to see it as insignificant, sometimes free, sometimes morphophonemic, some of the author's Javanese and Balinese friends have felt this variation marked the speaker's closeness (either physically or psychologically) to the action, as in Figure 5. (This notion is discussed, with Kawi examples, in Becker & Oka 1974).

| | ACTOR SUBJECT | |
	CLOSE	DETACHED
ACTIVE/TRANSITIVE	MANG-	ANG-
STATIVE/INTRANSITIVE	MA-	A-

FIGURE 5. Deictic Inflexion in Actor Subject Prefixes

Note that this variation is felt to mark the involvement of the speaker, not the actor, unless the two are identical (as in First Person discourse). This distinction is basic to the pronominal system of Old Javanese, and so not so odd as might first appear. It may be that *anglakoni* shows speaker detachment, or it may be that this distinction was lost by the time the poem was composed (1860).

Referential Contexts

If we look at the referential possibilities of *anglakoni,* two final features of its aspection appear. One of the most important coherence features of older Javanese discourse was a realis-irrealis distinction. Imperatives, conditionals, plans, future acts, etc. were marked by a suffix *-a* (or *-en* in non-Actor focus) which came at the end of the predicate, after the other suffixes. The predicate in line 6 (*kaliren*) carries this suffix: 'will/might be in need, will/might starve'. *Anglakoni,* on the other hand, is not irrealis. It is reported as a reality, not a possibility, in reference to the perceived world of the speaker.

The other referential feature of this predicate has to do with an interpretation of the velar nasal (e.g. in the prefix *ang-*) which, among other functions, distinguishes active and stative subject-actor prefixes (see Figure 5). A verb carrying the velar nasal prefix resembled a noun preceded by a definite marker (in Old Javanese also *ang* or *ng*). Definiteness of action parallels, in some ways, our past tense, since a definite act is one that has happened. If definiteness is involved here, it is a second relation of *anglakoni* to the perceived world.

The details of Figure 2 should now be clearer to the reader. The network of grammatical relations, within the text and outside it, matches in complexity the rhetorical structure (as in Figure 1), the syntactic structure, and the prosodic structure. Musically it is just as complex, particularly when accompanied by a full gamelan.[16]

CONCLUSION

The goal here has been to guide the reader on a philological journey, deeper and deeper into a non-English world—into a poem, into a single key word and its multi-leveled, multi-contexted system of aspection. The irony is that I have had to do this in English—often rather awkward, obscure English, where the temptation was to sacrifice too much Javanese richness to English clarity.

Rather than translate the poem, I have tried to describe it, and translate the reader, so that in the poem the reader can get a glimpse of the poetic and noetic power of literary Javanese to shape, bind, and communicate a particular bit of knowledge.

One final comment. The poem is said by some Javanese to be a prediction of a time of madness, by others to be a description of the life of a traditional scholar-poet in a royal court during the colonial period. The author, Ranggawarsita, was one of the scholars who, in the Surakarta court in the 19th century, compiled the *Pustaka Raja* (the prior texts of kings), a compendium of what we might see as myth, chronicle, cosmogony, and philosophy—a sort of canonic memory for the instruction and use of rulers. In a colonial setting, the compiling of an encyclopedic work, and indeed the very position of the traditionally learned man in an ultimately powerless court, was unstable. A new, distant set of prior texts (European) was relevant: one might imagine oneself having to learn not just new 'facts' but a new framework within which to make sense of them. In Ranggawarsita's poem we get a picture of a deeply learned man in a world no longer contained in the *Pustaka Raja*.

It may be significant, too, that he represented the elite of a chirographic culture under the sustained attack of a culture well into print.

REFERENCES

BECKER, A. L. 1979a. Text-building, aesthetics, and epistemology in Javanese Shadow Theatre. The imagination of reality, ed. by A. L. Becker and Aram A. Yengoyan, 211–243. Norwood, N.J.: Ablex.

———. 1979b. The figure a sentence makes. Discourse and syntax, ed. by Talmy Givon, 243–259. New York: Academic.

---

[16]For a description of the music of macapat, see Kartomi (1973:67–1 65). This work also contains transcriptions of words and music (with translat ions) of 147 Javanese macapat songs and 54 Sundanese macapat songs.

BECKER, A. L. AND I. G. NG. OKA. 1974. Person in Kawi: Exploration of an elementary semantic dimension. Proceedings of the First International Conference of Austronesian Comparative Linguistics. Honolulu. *Oceanic Linguistics* 13, 229–255.

DESHPANDE, MADHAV M. 1979. Sociolinguistic attitudes in India: An historical reconstruction. Ann Arbor: Karoma.

DREWES, G. W. J. 1974. Ranggawarsita, the Pustaka Raja Madya and the Wayang Madya. Oriens Extremus 21.

GONDA, J. 1973. Sanskrit in Indonesia. New Delhi. International Academy of Indian Culture.

JONES, LINDA. 1977. Theme in English expository discourse. Lake Bluff, Illinois: Jupiter Press.

KARTOMI, MARGARET. 1973. Matjapat songs in Central and West Java. Canberra: Australian National University Press.

LABOV, WILLIAM, AND JOSHUA WALETZKY. 1967. Narrative analysis: Oral versions of personal experience. Essays on the verbal and visual arts, ed. by June Helms. Seattle: University of Washington Press.

ONG, WALTER J., S. J. 1978. Interfaces of the word. Ithaca: Cornell University Press.

PIGEAUD, TH. 1967. Literature in Java. The Hague: Martinus Nyhoff, vol. 1.

PIKE, KENNETH L., AND EVENLYN G. PIKE. 1977. Grammatical analysis. Arlington, Texas: Summer Institute of Linguistics.

POLANYI, LIVIA. 1978. The American story. Ph.D. dissertation, University of Michigan.

UHLENBECK, E. M. 1956. Verb structure in Javanese. For Roman Jakobson. The Hague: Mouton.

YATES, FRANCES. 1966. The art of memory. Chicago: The University of Chicago Press.

ZOETMULDER, P. J. 1974. Kalangwan. The Hague: Martinus Nyhoff.

ZURBUCHEN, MARY S. 1978. Introduction to Old Javanese (Kawi) prose: An anthology. Ann Arbor: Center for South and Southeast Asian Studies.

13

Some of my Favorite Writers are Literate: The Mingling of Oral and Literate Strategies in Written Communication

Robin Tolmach Lakoff
University of California, Berkeley

INTRODUCTION

It is generally acknowledged that written and oral communication involve very different kinds of strategies: what works orally does not work in print, and vice versa. We know the reasons for this discrepancy, at least in part: oral communication works through the assumption of immediacy, or spontaneity; writing, on the other hand, is planned, organized, and non-spontaneous. Hence, the devices utilized in the two media for maximum effect can be expected to be different, and we may further suppose that the direct transposition of the devices of one medium to the other will not work, or even result in intelligible communication.

Overlaid on this distinction is a problem of judgment. For the past three thousand years, more or less, literacy has been in competition with non-literacy (or rather, perhaps, orality) for minds and souls: many commentators are not so much interested in the different values, the different advantages, of each medium, as in perceiving the two as locked in deadly combat. Lately, this conflict seems to be exacerbated. The verdict in educational circles, as well as the circles of prescriptive comment on language use, is pretty much in: literacy is dying, and as a result, civilization as we know it is doomed. Only with the preservation of literacy can we hope to preserve culture and civilization. This assumption rests on deeper unsupported beliefs; but much of the current unrelenting attack on non-literate media—earlier, comic books; currently, TV and movies—can be traced to the terror that we are about to regress as a civilization into a new Stone Age, bereft of logical linear thought, that literacy alone allows for sensitivity, intelligence and complexity of thought. Since there is much evidence that, in fact, literacy is diminishing, if we make the assumption that it is a necessary concomitant of civilized culture, indeed we have cause for fear.

In this chapter I want to take a couple of different tacks: to argue that, first of all, loss of literacy is not the same as loss of culture. I want to argue this from a specific point of view. In the past several hundred years, the reverse has been generally believed. In this time, we have been in the thrall of the assumption that written communication is primary and preferable. There is much evidence that, in the past couple of millennia in fact, at least in written media (which of course is all we have, to document bygone ages) the assumption has been made that the written form of communication is basic, is more valid than the oral, and that even originally oral discourse must be represented in terms of the rules of written communication to be valid and intelligible. But in the last generation or so, there is much to suggest that this position is being reversed; that the oral medium is considered more valid and intelligible as a form of communication than the written, and that even written documents are now tending to be couched in forms imitative of the oral mode. Moreover, the reasons for this are not mere decline of education, of mental sloppiness, but are rooted in technological progress—even as the advent of literacy was three millennia ago. I will present some discussion about the differences in ways of representing thought and discourse in the two media, and how the style of representing these ideas has been shifting, and why.

Lastly, I want to suggest that we must adapt to these changes rather than stand by and deplore them, nor can we turn the clock back by any means available to us. Literacy is useful in one sort of technology; but we may not require it any more. As one whose entire life has been grounded in the acquisition of literacy, and whose productivity resides in literate communication, I confess to a sense of horror and betrayal as I write these words, and of course I write them, in the hope that there are those who will read them, so it may be argued that I am—as my readers are—caught in a paradox. But we must recognize the paradox if we are to emerge from our confusion with honor.

We can see signs of change and confusion in a number of places, if we correctly interpret what we see. In this paper I want to bring together a group of seemingly unrelated or random facts that I have been noticing over the last couple of decades, with the intention of arguing that these illustrate the shift in our society from a literacy-based model of ideal human communication to one based on the oral mode of discourse.

This is not, of course, the only such changeover in our culture. We can be confident that several millennia ago contemporaneous civilization underwent an equally agonizing shift, only in the opposite direction, as writing became widespread and overtook oral modes of literature as a means of recording present and past events. Of course, we have no record of the wrenching effect of the changeover: the wrench would have principally affected the Old Guard—in this case, the nonliterate—and they, of course, being nonliterate, have left us no record of any pain they felt. More recently, within the past several centuries, a more minor change seems to have taken place. Within a culture prizing literacy for the recording of memorable events, there was a shift from a state where most people were in fact nonliterate or barely functionally literate, and depended on another, or scribal, class, to achieve their memorability for them, to one in which the majority of people were, in the worst case, at least expected to be literate, to make use of the written medium for information and amusement with relatively little effort. It is not clear whether, in fact, this ideal in fact ever actually existed, but it certainly has been present as an ideal.

SPONTANEITY VS. FORETHOUGHT

Linguists, psychologists, sociologists, and anthropologists who study communication strategies agree, as a truism, that the way we express and understand ideas in writing is in many crucial ways different from the way we express the same ideas in oral discourse. Actually, work on this topic tends to create a peculiar dichotomy: planned, nonspontaneous written discourse on the one hand, and spontaneous, direct oral communication on the other. It is unarguable that these represent the clearest cases, and the sharpest distinctions, and are worth studying therefore as ends of a continuum. But in order to understand how we utilize the various modes of communication to their fullest advantage, we must understand that there are other possibilities, and that some of the characteristics we have ascribed to 'oral' discourse, for example, are not necessarily characteristic of the oral medium per se, but rather their choice has more to do with immediate personal contact—eye contact, for instance—or the usefulness of an appearance of spontaneity, rather than to the use of the vocal channel itself.

The distinction between spontaneity—real or apparent—and forethought in discourse is often directly equated with the oral/written distinction. The relation is not as clear as it seems. True, in oral, conversational discourse we cannot plan in any real way—our utterances are too dependent on those of our interlocutors and on other shifting realworld circumstances. In print, on the other hand, we must plan. Our words are understood as being subject to editing and revision, as representing the considered preference of the writer and others among perhaps several alternatives, all of which have been weighted. Intuitive writers may not consciously make these selections, may go by 'feel'—but they are certainly doing some sort of editing, and are free to make substitutions later on.

But this distinction is not necessarily made in terms of the mode of communication itself; we can easily imagine—indeed, there exist—types of nonspontaneous oral discourse, and spontaneous written discourse. Of course, these are special—they do not fit our prototype. Indeed, they tend to be viewed with some suspicion, as if, by mixing alternatives like this, someone is trying to get away with something. For example, formal old-fashioned carefully crafted political rhetoric is viewed with some suspicion; when stream-of-consciousness prose was introduced as a literary device before the turn of the century, it evoked shrieks of protest, with the majority of contemporary readers evidently outraged at authors who dared to meddle with the conventions of the written medium, and in particular, the convention that writers appear to carefully and consciously select their words.

As spontaneity and forethought have their advantages, they have their equally inalienable disadvantages. Truly spontaneous discourse has an immediacy, and emotional directness, that is truly exhilarating; at the same time, it carries the burden of immediacy: lack of clarity, use of the wrong word or phrase, hesitation, repetition, and so on. These are necessary concomitants of true spontaneity: we cannot be spontaneous and polished at once. Planned discourse avoids these pitfalls; but at the same time, it necessarily lacks warmth, closeness, and vividness. These lacks are sometimes (e.g. by McLuhan) viewed as necessarily characteristic of print media; but it can be better argued that they are concomitants of nonspontaneous discourse, of which print is one example. But print—more than oral nonspontaneous media—exacerbates these difficulties because it lacks many of the devices oral present discourse utilized as carriers of emotional tone: intonation, pitch, gesture, eyes, and so on. On the other hand, nonspontaneous media, by their ability to capture, through planning, the appropriate mood, the description, may help the reader or hearer form an ultimately more lasting and more vivid memory in the mind, and allows a reader as well as a writer to rethink, re-experience, and revise impressions which, in traditional forms of oral discourse, are lost forever once uttered.

There are additional 'meanings' that we attribute to the choice of medium. Written communication is memorable, the stuff of history and reliability. Hence—and also because it is acquired and utilized with more difficulty—it is more formal, the bearer of respectability. Oral discourse can be colloquial or dialectal; the representation of nonstandard dialect in writing—as a reader of, say, Mark Twain or George Ade will attest—tends to give a reader a tired throat after a short period of reading: we cannot help subvocalizing as we read 'dialect'; it exists only in oral form.

Written discourse, then, is respectable; spoken, more heartfelt. A culture at any point in time has to decide whether the preferred mode of presentation of self is as a respectable or as a feeling creature. There may, at some times in some situations, be available the chance to be both at once, so that no such decision must be made. But in the matter of form of communication, a society must decide whether the ideal is that of writing or that of talking—reliability or warmth, respectability or ability to convey emotion. For the last several centuries, we have, where possible, opted for the first, assuming that the written channel was in some sense primary or preferable. For various reasons, some social, some technological, we are at present in the process of shifting, so that we prefer and respond most appropriately to communications in any mode couched in an oral framework. This switch, like any profound cultural revolution, is creating severe confusion and dislocation, especially in those who perceive themselves as holdovers of the old order. But rather than take moral or aesthetic positions in favor of one or the other, we will do better to examine the evidence of the claim that this change is in progress, and then consider why, if indeed it is, and what if anything we are to do in response.

If the written medium is primary, we can expect to find that even when people speak or are assumed to speak 'spontaneously', their contributions are represented via the conventions of the written mode. Thus quotations in biography or fiction can be expected generally to sound like 'written' discourse, to utilize its conventions. We might find other, special uses of an assumption of the primacy of writing: for instance, serious people, in serious situations, in a work of art, might be represented as adopting stylized 'written' modes of discourse even when they are supposed to be communicating orally; non-'serious' people, in non-'serious' situations, might utilize more characteristically 'oral' modes, again stylized.

We might consider Shakespeare the clearest piece of evidence for the existence of such a set of assumptions a few centuries back. Shakespeare has, basically, two modes of discourse: metrical lines and simple prose paragraphs. It is frequently noted that the former tend to be assigned to 'noble' characters—noble both in a social and a psychological sense. At the most climactic moments, the ends of crucial scenes, for instance, we frequently find not only iambic pentameter, but rhymed heroic couplets. But when 'commoners' speak, especially those who are comical, they tend to speak prose. Additionally of course, the 'noble' poetic utterances contain formal, elaborate language, complex sentence patterns, and other characteristics of planned and memorable speech, while the prose segments tend to be informal, colloquial, and even dialectal, and use much simpler vocabulary and sentences that are not necessarily shorter, but less complex: conjuction rather than complementation, for instance. (These are tendencies, of course, rather than absolutes, and have frequently been commented on by critics.)

In such dialog, we can look at meter as an idealization of 'fore-thought' discourse. For surely, more than any other type of discourse, metered utterances must be planned in advance: one cannot speak spontaneously and at length in meter. Rhyme compounds the plannedness, along with complex sentence structure and formal language. Thus, Shakespeare's poetic diction is meant as a sort of ideal model, a signal to his audience, 'We are speaking for history here' rather than as a literal transcription of real speech. (And the prose segments serve to accentuate this intention by their dissimilarity.) What I say here is true, of course, not only of Shakespeare but to some degree of playwrights until relatively recent times.

Or consider a less striking, but perhaps clearer case: Boswell's representation of Samuel Johnson's speech. Reading Boswell, we tend to be struck with awe at Johnson's ability to express ideas pithily and perfectly in apparently spontaneous conversation: it is the ultimate fantasy, l'esprit d'escalier, idealizing our feelings, on leaving a party — about why we couldn't, at the telling moment, find just the right words to say just the right thing, rather than the sloppiness, the hesitation we remember with chagrin. Perhaps in the spirit of sour grapes, I suggest that Boswell's representation of Johnson is as much an idealization as it is a faithful transcript. Johnson was no doubt better at epigrammatic oral conversation than most of us, indeed than most of his contemporaries, or Boswell would not have immortalized him thus; but he was probably not as good at it as the written evidence suggests: Boswell must have done a bit of judicious editing. He was enabled to do so—to delete the searchings, the hesitations and repetitions, the false starts—because the conventions of his age suggested that a good human being spoke without them, that the most intelligent, or most admirable person spoke like a printed page. If Boswell were immortalizing a contemporary Johnson, it is a safe bet that one would find just the reverse. Johnson's speech would probably be represented as colloquial, having hesitations and repetitions and so on, to show him as real, in keeping with our perception of our culture's ideal. ('Eloquence', since it entails planning, is a concept whose time has passed.)

TRANSFERRING SPOKEN DISCOURSE TO WRITING

Another window into contemporary idealizations of style is in representations in novels of spontaneous conversation. Here in fact we might consider ourselves faced with a sort of paradox, a paradox an author of fiction confronts constantly, and must deal with in his or her own idiosyncratic way. (This is true not only of novels, but of the screenplays of movies, or the scripts of plays.) Here we have the transfer of the oral, spontaneous mode, with all its implications, to either a written or a still-oral medium, but clearly one where there has been forethought. (Unless, of course, we are considering some of the cinematic works of people like Norman Mailer.) In one way, we can detect a striking change between novels and plays of the past, and the present, generally speaking (we still have throwbacks, for instance, Jacqueline Susann or the writers of Gothic fiction). In the past, novelists seem to have represented spoken discourse by the same rules by which the rest of the narrative exposition is unfolded. There are occasional deviations, scraps thrown to verisimilitude: the use of contractions, perhaps a few 'wells' here and there; but otherwise, one would be hard put to differentiate between the spoken dialog and the written exposition of most novels before the mid-twentieth century. (Again, there is sometimes a divergence between socially or psychologically 'serious' and 'nonserious' characters, the latter of whom are more prone to utilize nonstandard forms of speech.) More recently, we find attempts in fiction to represent 'real' dialog: more hesitation, sloppiness, errors of various kinds. But, as we shall see, even when these occur, they do not have the same meaning as they do in real spontaneous discourse. The devices of spontaneous (oral) speech are found, but in different circumstances and, indeed, with different meaning, than in ordinary spontaneous conversation or in transcripts derived from it.

This raises the problem that students of conversational strategy keep being bedeviled with: that conversation, as taken off tapes and represented in transcripts, is fiendishly hard to understand and very hard to keep paying attention to—and more, that the participants in such recorded conversations, including quite often the researchers, highly-educated people who take pride in their articulateness under pressure, come off sounding like oafs or morons, or as if they were under the influence of psychedelic substances. This problem is manifested, for instance, in published transcripts of the Watergate tapes, which irritatingly seem to present a much more fallible and human—in any case, bumbling and inarticulate—view of Nixon and his henchmen than most of us are happy to see. Indeed, it is an article of faith among liberals that Nixon's very glibness, his profound lack of spontaneity, did him in, and rightly. Anyone who plans his thoughts in advance as he is felt to have done cannot be worth saving. Yet the Watergate transcripts show a very different person: not lovable, but certainly fallible; not genuine, but not really calculating either. In general, transcripts do not feel to readers like 'real' conversation—they are not immediately intelligible like the dialogue in a novel or a movie, they don't get to a point, they don't really begin or end. Yet they are real, and constructed dialog is not. How can we understand this?

One source of our difficulty lies in the reader's interpretation of what lies on the page. As long as a written format is used to represent purely written discourse, there is no danger. But once we attempt to translate oral communication to the written page, we find ourselves having to translate meaning, as much as form. The characteristics that work in one medium are not necessarily ideal for the other; direct translation tends not to preserve sense, or effect. In fact, there are not many valid reasons for attempting to represent oral modalities directly in writing. One such reason, true since time immemorial, is the representation of originally spoken dialog in print.

QUOTATION MARKS

All writing systems I am conversant with have developed conventions to mark 'spoken' words from the body of the written text—for example, quotation marks. These signal: 'Here we are using writing in a special way, to represent oral discourse. Hence the representation may not be completely accurate, so be on guard.' Interestingly, we do not restrict quotation marks to this purpose. In many systems of writing, we find quotation marks setting off forms that are not intended to be understood as 'uttered'. The markings on the last word in the last sentence are a case in point. I don't mean that someone just came up behind me and uttered 'uttered' in my ear. Rather, such quotation forms are conventionally used to indicate the writer's abdication of responsibility for the locution so enclosed, a sort of ironic lift of the eyebrow in print: 'I represent it like this, but do not fully take responsibility for the sentiments thus expressed.' This usage shares one thing with the more direct convention: in both, quotation marks signal, This is not the writer's own. In the one case, it is because the words are, literally, someone else's; in the other, the writer is merely not fully sincere in using them. Hence, too, the use of quotation marks around nonstandard forms: dialect, slang, non-written register for example. 'I really know better than this,' the writer is saying. 'See, I'm literate—really I am.'[1] To the extent that a writer is insecure, such uses tend to proliferate. Therefore, as anyone who has spent time grading freshman themes knows, such writings teem with quotation marks which, to the literate eye, seem inexplicable if not downright execrable. We have seen, for instance, the use of quotations around nicknames, or even real names:

> On my summer vacation I went with my brother 'Bill' to 'Boy Scout' camp.

They are used to enclose, and exonerate, anything that might be considered non-literate form, however mildly colloquial:

> The 'sophs' really 'didn't' do it. They 'sure' didn't.

Or, indeed, they may be used to indicate anything that is, until entrusted to paper, information that only the writer, and not the reader, possesses.

> And that's how you make 'beef bourguignon'.

This use may seem to contradict the claim that these quotation marks indicate denial of responsibility; but in fact, information not certainly shared by the reader is apt to make a fledgling writer especially nervous.

One recent use of quotation marks outside of written communication is particularly noteworthy. Traditionally, of course, quotation marks are restricted to writing: they represent, as I said, the insertion of nonwritten discourse into communication in the written mode. Then what are we to make of this?

> "I'm cynical enough to understand. . . my name assures more press coverage. This is a logical place to use me. I'm a woman of a certain age and I'm independent. All the 'safe' "—she put down her glass of ice water and used her fingers for quotation marks—"accouterments."

(Interview with Ali McGraw, *San Francisco Chronicle*, 10/20/80.)

Here the secondary meaning of quotation marks becomes primary: their use in achieving non-responsibility or ironic distance. Not trusting to vocal inflections

---

[1] A striking example of this use of italics was seen in the television reports of the freeing of the U.S. hostages by Iran, 1/20/81. The hostages were welcomed to the U.S. military installation in Wiesbaden, Germany, by crowds some of whose members were carrying signs. The most prominent of these was one which said: 'Welcome Home!' (with the quotation marks).

or visual cues—traditionally the means of expressing these meanings—to establish ironic intent, the speaker borrows from written form a sort of 'fail-safe' device: the gesture of making quotation marks with the fingers is so strikingly noticeable that it cannot be overlooked by an interlocutor, as inflection or a lift of the eyebrow might. We can assume that as this device is becoming more common—and I have seen a good deal of it around, particularly on TV talk shows—because we are losing confidence in ourselves and others as interpreters of subtle signs. (I put quotation marks around 'fail-safe' above, by the way, partly because I was using a metaphorical term and was a little afraid about whether the metaphor was appropriate; and partly, I fear, to indicate that appreciation by the reader of that witty (or, rather, 'witty') gesture was in order, but of course I could only suggest that, if I at the same time delicately removed it from MY responsibility. Under other circumstances, I would hope to have edited the whole thing out in a later draft, but I leave it in to show how it works.)

This extension in the use of quotation marks, then, becomes one way writers can try to personalize their writing by bringing into it the emotional directness of oral speech. It is not the quotation marks per se that convey the emotional impact. Rather, they are a signal, unlike other analogous devices; they suggest to the reader: 'feel about what is enclosed in these marks as you would about oral discourse'.

ITALICS

Other devices, on the other hand, are more direct in their communicative effect, dictating a specific emotional response just as stress or pitch might, for instance, in oral discourse. This is a principal function of italics. Italics, like quotation marks, serve two distinct but related purposes. One, their speech-imitative use, and their direct rather than metaphorical interpretation in writing, is to provide simple emphasis, by means of suggesting the modes by which oral discourse is made emphatic: rise in pitch and loudness. This is clearly the use of italics in quoted oral discourse:

'Mary is *very* intelligent', he expostulated.

Closely related is the use of italics to stress some idea as important, for instance, in order to make contrasts, which might be expressed orally either by pitch-loudness changes or by gestures.

No, this is Mrs. Jones, and *that* is Mr. Smith, with the carnation in his lapel.

Both of these are direct representations of oral devices, translations into writing which we understand through reference to speaking. It is interesting to note that, as far as we can tell, there is no tradition of italics or anything analogous in ancient languages. One reason for this might be that these languages, being free-word order types, could achieve what English can only effect by stress and pitch through word-order, which can be represented directly in writing, and in fact is a device that is probably more usable in writing than in speech, given planning and processing constraints.

But just as quotation marks have a secondary usage in writing that stems from the fact that they represent emphatic discourse in the oral medium, italics too have derived meaning. Italics, because their use suggests the tonal and emotional range characteristic of oral discourse, can be used in writing to suggest something similar: the writing is made to seem fresher, more spontaneous, more emotionally open and direct. As with quotation marks, this is playing with communicative fire: it suggests the writer is not conversant with the devices available to writing to achieve these effects. Overuse is deadly. The magazine *Cosmopolitan* is perhaps the strongest exponent of the genre:

> As illnesses go, hypoglycemia has a good deal of flair, but another debility is *almost* as status-laden these days: low back pain. No one is sure *why* an aching back should have such panache. Perhaps the appeal of this disorder is that it has traditionally been associated with vigorous, earthy, *physical* types. . . . (' "In" diseases: A look at the Current Crop of Chic Complaints', Lee Coleman, *Cosmopolitan, July, 1980.)

The *Cosmo* italic is really a sort of amalgam of the two conventions I have identified. The reader is undoubtedly supposed to imagine the writer's voice rising to a squeal; but at the same time, the words italicized, as in the quotation above, would not normally receive unusual stress or pitch in speech. The italics then signal 'N.B.'

Italics, however, have a meaning not shared by quotation marks: they are popularly characterized as a written manifestation of 'woman's language'. It is popularly thought that women, when they write, overuse italics (for example, in letter-writing. This stereotype no doubt helps to account for the prevalence of italics in *Cosmopolitan*.) Presumably this accords with the wider inflectional range of woman's speech. As far as I know, no serious research has been done on the prevalence of italics in women's written prose. Any correlation with the wider range of oral intonational possibilities would be rather unexpected and inexplicable, unless we assume that in writing we literally encode a spoken 'voice' in our minds, which seems quite implausible. In any case, whether because of their association with 'feminine' style or because they too heavy-handedly attempt to manipulate the reader's emotional response, italics are much riskier in writing than their counterparts in speech.

CAPITALIZATION

We might compare with quotation marks and italics—conventions whose effect in writing is related to their invoking of oral equivalents—a third emphatic device, that of capitalization. This, when used outside of the normal convention of capitalizing proper nouns, has both a different origin and a very different feel from the others. Where quotation marks feel adolescent, and italics feminine, capitals feel childlike. But all are used to set the matter so marked off from the rest of the text, in one way or another. It is interesting that, while italics and quotations seem to have increased their range of usage in recent history, capitalization flourished in earlier periods much more than now. Seventeenth and eighteenth-century writing seems to have employed capitalization, especially of nouns, either in a manner reminiscent of modern German (all nouns capitalized) or as a marker of emphasis, not required but stylistically optional. Relics persist, particularly in children's writing (which may be why they have a childish flavor, or perhaps they are used in juvenile literature BECAUSE they have a childish flavor). Perhaps the clearest case is in A. A. Milne's *Winnie-the-Pooh* books:

> "Hallo, Pooh," he said. "How's things?"
> "Terrible and Sad," said Pooh, "because Eeyore, who is a friend of mine, has lost his tail. And he's Moping about it. So could you very kindly tell me how to find it for him?"
> "Well," said Owl, "the customary procedure in such cases is as follows."
> "What does Crustimoney Proseedcake mean?" said Pooh. "For I am a Bear of Very Little Brain, and long words Bother me."
> (Milne, *Winnie-the-Pooh*, p. 50.)

Here capitalization does indeed serve to mark the words of greatest significance in the narrative, rather like the *Cosmopolitan* italics. But it does so without recourse to spoken convention.[2]

NONFLUENCIES

There are still other devices of spoken language that are carried into written language, for example, ellipses, repetitions, and vocalized pauses. These, though, fall into a different category. Where the earlier types are intentionally used to create emotional involvement, these tend to be more or less involuntary. Indeed, encountering oneself on tape using them to excess frequently causes chagrin: "Do I talk like that?" They do not, typically, mark emotional directness, but rather simple unpreparedness—the negative side of spontaneity. For while in writing we can marshal our thoughts and present them in coherent and rhetorically effective order, in speech we seldom have the opportunity, and at least currently, if we do, we

---

[2]The reverse of A. A. Milne is, perhaps, e. e. cummings, who eschewed capitalization entirely. If Milne (and others) use capitals as directives to readers as to what is to be considered important, then we can take cumming's avoidance of the device as a kind of anarchy: readers are left to their own devices, with no authorial guidance.

try to look as if we are not making use of it. It is conventional—and, probably, realistic—to assume that the more emotionally involved one is, the more one's thoughts are confused, or at least presented linguistically in incoherent and rambling form. Therefore, the use of these devices, primarily resulting from the normal inability in spontaneous discourse to know in advance what to say, secondarily can signify emotional turmoil in oral communication, at least if carried to excess, or used in unusual places in the conversation.

Perhaps, in fact, it is this that gives metered dialog, in older dramatists, its sense of seriousness and majesty: if we are working within the constraints of iambic pentameter (for instance), the form cannot tolerate any additions or deletions, no vocalized pauses, hesitations, or repetitions. Distress must, then, be represented lexically and explicitly. In more modern forms of constructed dialog, however, we find these devices used for very specific effects. Soap opera is one genre that strives for the appearance of spontaneity, both to manipulate the audience's emotions and to increase the verisimilitude of the dialog. Besides, soap opera can afford it while other genres can't: a script aiming for artistic effect must compress and telescope its exposition, leaving explicit only what is necessary to further the development of the plot and the characters. Therefore, those aspects of spontaneous dialog that are truly random and accidental—the result of universal human difficulties in organization and memory, rather than problems specific to the character and his or her situation—are eliminated. But soap opera runs by different rules. Soap opera tries to provide a literal slice of true experience for its audience, so that life, and dialog, in that genre moves just as slowly as it does in real life. Hence there is a time for ellipsis, correction, hesitation, and so on.

One random episode in a randomly-chosen half-hour daily soap opera (*All My Children*) illustrates this aspect of soap-opera grammar interestingly. A male character has, in the way common to soaps, unbeknownst to himself fathered a daughter years ago by a woman who has since (as a result, we may surmise) become a nun. This girl and the man's legitimate son (unaware of course of their true relationship) are having an affair. They are somehow involved in a murder, and are in jail. The son, it is implied, has fallen into these bad ways as a result of his father's neglect, of which his father is keenly aware. In the randomly chosen segment, the father first encounters the nun, who indirectly informs him of the identity of the girl, and then encounters his son and the girl, separately, in jail. Thus, we have one character who, in the course of the episode, has increasingly more to feel uncomfortable about, and whose every confrontation with another character is wracking to him; and several other characters who, while they have their various guilts, have no guilt with respect to this particular character. This character, incidentally, is a lawyer and politician, so articulateness is expected of him. As the episode progresses, while the speech-patterns of the other characters remain more or less stable, only occasionally lapsing into real-speech conventions, the father progressively gets closer and closer to transcript-form.

Another interesting use of 'spontaneous' form in non-spontaneous oral media is seen principally in commercials. The commercial is, in one sense, the diametric opposite of the soap opera: time goes by in a flash; every micro-millisecond must count. At the same time, the actors must seem real, must be people the audience can identify or at least sympathize with. Because of the time-constraint, we see very little use of time-wasting oral devices. Rather, we get a different set of quasi-oral conventions. In true spontaneous discourse, sentence-structure such as is expected in written prose is not strictly adhered to. We find run-ons and fragments quite typically. So one way to approximate spontaneous speech is via telegraphic fragments:

> Mm! Light, crispy! Glad I discovered it!
>   It's as nutritious as grape-nuts!
>   As grape-nuts?

Aside from the question of whether normal adults ever really find themselves conversing at length about breakfast cereal, this passage is unnatural in a couple of respects. If telegraphic fragments do in fact occur in ordinary conversation, they tend to occur in the body of the discourse—not as introductions, where the topics of discourse tend to be made explicit. It also seems to me that the third contribution is unlikely: repetitions of this type normally signal serious disagreement, not merely the need for a bit of amplification (for which 'Oh, really?' normally suffices). But in the commercial, every syllable must add to the informational content. Finally, notice the word *crispy*. This is certainly not a word characteristic of formal written register—in fact, *crispy* is not oral colloquial American English: I don't think I have ever heard it uttered spontaneously. It is one of a set of words used only, or almost exclusively, in writing to suggest oral register, but in fact seldom or never in true spontaneous oral discourse (*tyke* is another.)

I have contrasted these special narrative conventions with transcripts, and indeed if we continue this comparison we can begin to understand why, accustomed to these narrative conventions, we find accurate transcripts of spontaneous conversation especially hard to interpret. We have been trained to believe that, when we encounter these devices in written communication, we must translate them as signals of emotional intensity. But in ordinary transcripts, we find them in every sentence, in every context. Either we are dealing with a feverish emotional pitch—belied by other clues in the recorded conversation—or we are truly contending with a foreign language, or perhaps a pidgin—as indeed a transcript is, half-written and half-spoken grammar.

In general, then, the borrowing of a device from one medium into another is always overdetermined: it carries with it the communicative effect, or 'feel', of one medium into another (the metacommunicative effect) and at the same time attempts to utilize the language of one mode to communicate ideas in another (the communicative effect). It is no wonder that this sort of translation can create confusion in readers (or hearers), and can also create in them very strong feelings—typically negative.

THE COMIC STRIP

The negative impact of such borrowings, particularly from the oral to the written mode, is exacerbated by the fact that the least 'desirable' forms of communication are the first to show the traces—or perhaps this is the effect of the derogation of oral style, rather than the cause of its initial appearance in unrespectable places. One of the earliest forms of communication to attempt to convey essentially oral concepts in print was the comic strip. Interestingly, in the newer and more sophisticated strips (e.g. Doonesbury) the conventions of the old strips are missing, and we have, as it were, reverted to the 'respectability' of print convention. But the strips I remember reading as a child, though they utilized print, actually approximated in many ways a blend of oral and literate culture. It is easy to recall examples: the fact that comic book sentences never ended with a period but, if not questions, with an exclamation point, seems to have been an attempt analogous to the use of italics or initial capitals to impart importance and emotional immediacy to the text. (Alas, with overkill it lost its potential force.) There were frequent attempts to reproduce oral self-correction devices, for emotional effect, e.g. pauses and repetition. Additionally, there was the attempt to reproduce nonstandard dialect and colloquialism. Very commonly, this was done by 'dropping g's' from the suffix -ing, but rather more interesting were other attempts to create the same effect.

I remember as a child trying to imagine pronouncing some of the comic book writers' attempts at 'natural' speech. There were basically two types of problems. One occurred when the form could not in fact be pronounced as written by anyone with the normal articulatory apparatus; the other involved spelling representations that, in fact, represented the only way a form could be pronounced at all, outside of profound affectation, so that it was hard to see what was gained by the special 'colloquial' spelling. In fact, it sometimes led to more confusion than necessary. Examples of the first type include the dropping of vowels to form impossible consonant clusters: 'T' th' store'; of the second, spellings like *yuh* or *ya* for unstressed *you* (always pronounced /yə/.); *ta* for *to;* and the mysterious (to me for years) locution *Omigosh,* which I perceived then as an exotic exclamation /ámigaš/ (years later, I realized that it was intended to represent the much less interesting *Oh, my gosh*). But running it together as a single word (which led to my confusion) served the purpose of making it seem more quickly articulated, hence more exciting as well as more 'colloquial'. We sometimes find phonetic spelling used to represent slang, although the word itself would not be pronounced differently in standard and nonstandard dialects: *wuz* for *was,* for example. In all these cases, then, special spellings are used not simply as a guide to pronunciation, but as a way of indicating, 'Since this representation is different from the "formal" forms of written language, it is to be taken as "oral", i.e. immediate, emotional, colloquial.'[3]

Abuse of the trust thus engendered is always a temptation. I remember a striking case from the 1964 Presidential primary campaign. George Wallace was running in this campaign, a fact the *New York Times,* for reasons good and bad, viewed with dismay. Wallace was perceived as a redneck, an illiterate—a far cry from the hallowed JFK, and not even up to the style of the folksy, but nonetheless minimally literate LBJ. At one point the *Times* attributed to Wallace, in an interview, a locution the *Times* represented as *could of.* What is remarkable is that the newspaper was thereby representing an utterance that could not in fact have been pronounced, in non-stilted speech, by a native speaker of English in any way other than /kúdəv/ or, even more colloquially, /kúdə/. It corresponded, of course, to the written form *could have,* but would never normally have actually been pronounced that way. So the *Times* was engaging essentially in comic-strip tactics, representing a form via nonstandard spelling not in order to accurately distinguish a special pronunciation from the standard, but for some other reason. I would argue that the reason was to make Wallace look like an illiterate redneck; that if someone of unimpeachable intellectual credentials, say Adlai Stevenson, uttered the same phonetic segments, they would have been represented as 'could have'; had they been uttered by the informal but respectable Lyndon Johnson, perhaps as 'could've'; but 'could of' marked Wallace as unmistakably of the booboisie, an implicit editorialization in the paper of record's news columns.

So anything deviating from the written medium and its ways of expression has tended to be viewed as suspect, a bad second-best, certainly not to find its way into respectable print. Indeed, a good part of the fashionable outcry against comics of the 1950's (a campaign superseded now by similar cries of outrage against television) can probably be traced to the fear that they were corrupting our youth

---

[3]On the Phil Donahue show of 1/23/81, Donahue read a letter from a viewer whose essence was this: She had always found the show one of the most 'literate' on television. Recently she had received her first transcript of the show, and was dismayed to discover that Donahue is cited as saying *ya* and +-in'—e.g.:

'I have to tell ya'
'It's comin' to the time. . . .'

There are two relevant points here. First, it is perhaps curious that transcripts of the Donahue show provide this sort of close phonetic transcription (and even more curious that their fidelity appears somewhat selective: if *ya,* why not *hafta* or *haveta*?); second, it is striking that—as my foregoing discussion would predict—the viewer was perfectly comfortable with [yə] and [kʌmɪn] in oral discourse, but reinterpreted these forms when they were encountered in print.

by confounding written and spoken styles and thereby destroying the culture's literacy. Then we have a right to be surprised, perhaps, and certainly to want an explanation when serious stylists, writers of fiction and nonfiction who are reviewed by and taken seriously in reputable intellectual journals, emerge in the '60s and '70s with a style reminiscent of nothing so much as the despised comics. In novels, particularly, this is indicated by the way dialog is represented: in older fiction, dialog appears not very different in style from the rest of the narrative exposition: sentences are finished and not run-on; there are few indications of hesitation or self-correction. But in more experimental recent work, often the dialog is strikingly different in form from the rest of the text. For example, from Thomas Pynchon's *The Crying of Lot 49:*

> "But," began Oedipa, then saw how they were suddenly out of wine.
> "Aha," said Metzger, from an inside pocket producing a bottle of tequila.
> "No lemon?" she asked, with movie-gaiety. "No salt?"
> "A tourist thing. Did Inverarity use lemons when you were there?" (p. 19)

Here we see an attempt at representation of informal (and somewhat intoxicated) conversation, giving an impression of sentences trailing off into nowhere. The writer is trying to draw the reader into the complete context, much as an oral storyteller might by intonation and gestures.

But these are still attempts to represent originally-oral discourse. More striking is the use of oral devices in nonfiction, nondialog narrative exposition. Here the line between oral and written communication blurs irrevocably. We might expect this from inexpert writers, setting down on paper exactly what they envision themselves as saying—for example, schoolchildren or students in college remedial-composition courses. But in fact, this is seldom what we find in such artless or 'natural' writers. They, it seems, are overawed by being faced with the need to communicate for posterity, on paper, and their style typically is anything but colloquial. If we would search for the relics of a bygone age, although misunderstood and misused, we would be most apt to find them in the writings of neophytes. Informal, or colloquial style, in a written text, is not natural, is not the mark of one unfamiliar with the distinctions between the media. Rather, it shows up only in the works of writers of great subtlety and skill, who deliberately obscure the age-old distinctions—and why, indeed, would they do that, unless there were some reward? In a writing-based culture, there is of course no discernible reward, and this is why we have encountered writings of this type only very recently.

The work of Tom Wolfe is representative of the genre, indeed its most striking exemplar. In *The Right Stuff,* his style is strongly and intentionally reminiscent of comic books. (We might suppose that the subject-matter, the astronauts, contributes to this choice of action-packed breeziness as a style, except that it is characteristic of his writing in general.) Scattered plentifully through the text we find italics, quotation marks, capitalization, other aberrant punctuation devices, ellipses, fragments, expletives, dialectal and colloquial forms, and much, much, more:

> The thing was, he said, the Mercury system was completely automated. Once they put you in the capsule, that was the last you got to say about the subject. *Whuh!* —
> "Well," said Yeager, "a monkey's gonna make the first flight."
> *A monkey?*
> The reporters were shocked. . . .Was this national heresy? What the hell was it? . . . .
> But f'r chrissake. . . . (pp. 105-106)

or:

> And in this new branch of the military, *no one outranked you.* (p. 115)
> Sympathy. . . because *our rockets all blow up.* (ibid.)
> He had literally *written the book* on the handling characteristics of aircraft. (ibid.)

In all the last three examples, italics are used to indicate, almost paradoxically, a sort of ironic detachment: 'They keep saying this, this is a cliche.' Sometimes, too, they mirror directly the vocal inflections of incredulity:

> . . .their religious affiliations (re*lig*ious affiliations?). . .(p. 95)

The italics here can represent nothing but vocal intonation, since in writing italics are never used to underline part of a word, except to indicate, for instance, misspelling—deviations from written convention.

Examples could be multiplied at will to illustrate the really shocking change that Wolfe has visited on English narrative prose convention. What is surprising is that it works. Purists may complain, but Wolfe has had a profound impact as a contemporary stylist. My feeling is that a style such as his—while it is perhaps the style of tomorrow, rather than today—could not have been utilized, however experimentally, until very recently. Even stream-of-consciousness, as in Joyce, does not bring the conventions of oral discourse so directly into the narrative segments of written prose. Wolfe is not only inviting us to share a particular sort of emotional relationship—with him, as well as with his subject—but is also informing us that the relation between written and spoken discourse is not as it has always been, that we have to rethink our ideas about the primacy of writing. For Wolfe, it is evident, talking is primary, and writing is successful to the extent it captures the nuances of speech. (For Boswell, two centuries ago, we assume precisely the reverse was true: a man was a dazzling oral stylist precisely to the extent that his 'spontaneous' oral epigrams resembled the productions of a careful writer, although they were perhaps valued more than they might have been had they been original in writing, for much the same reason that Dr. Johnson himself alleged a female preacher, or a dog walking on its hind legs, would be admired—because the trick was done against heavy odds, contrary to normal expectation.)

Even in oral media, style changes to reflect our new preference for the products of 'spontaneity': The tradition of the political orator goes back, in this country, several centuries. But where once—as in old Fourth-of-July orations that have been preserved for our delectation— the orator strove to deliver a polished speech, every word considered for effect, nothing accidental, now such an oration would be viewed with suspicion if not derision. Now a political speaker must seem to be holding a conversation, even if there is not much turn-taking in evidence. He can hesitate, he can change his mind about words, he can use vocalized pauses. We can see the change in our own time. Franklin D. Roosevelt, by all the evidence available to us, was a dazzlingly successful orator of the 'polished' school. (Churchill was even more so, of course.) Eisenhower was viewed by large segments of the populace as incompetent as a speaker, incomprehensible. (Yet, if we listen to tapes of his speeches today, they don't sound nearly as confused as they were supposed to have sounded.) He was forgiven, of course, because he was quintessentially a man of action. Stevenson, of the other hand, was Johnsonian (Samuel, that is)—a speaker of wit and grace. He lost to Eisenhower, the bumbler, perhaps setting into motion, or at least giving the nod to, a profound reevaluation of discourse strategies. Kennedy, universally accounted a good and powerful oral stylist, nonetheless ushered in a new mode. He, and his brothers as well, used a great deal of hesitation and, even more, vocalized pauses of the 'er' variety. While these were made fun of, the fun was benevolent, and none of the Kennedys were faulted as orators on these grounds. Nixon, interestingly, attempts to be a throwback to the old 'polished' and nonspontaneous style, but is not successful at it. Jimmy Carter is an exponent of the new, simple-conversation style of oratory, and his resounding defeat may indicate that we are not quite ready for this cataclysmic changeover at the highest levels of leadership just yet. However, the style has been tried and shown to be possible if nothing else.

THE PRIMACY OF ORAL MODES

So there is evidence all around us that as a culture we are contemplating—if we have not taken already—a leap from being written-oriented to being oral-oriented. Our stylistic preferences naturally are shifting along with our values, although we have not consciously been aware of a shift in either. Publicly and outwardly, we are a people who prize literacy: we believe that all children must be taught to read and write, and we recoil in despair at the evidence piling up that, in ever larger numbers, they achieve neither. We cast about for scapegoats: the decline of education, the failure of parental discipline, the rise of television. But these are better viewed as effects, not causes. In fact, deep in our hearts, we are no longer a society which values literacy. Compare the sales of books with the Nielsen ratings, or box-office attendance at movies; and the only books that do sell are those that hardly can be said to be read, their style and plot are so simple. Or, more and more often, best-selling books are those that are reconstructed, under contract, from the screenplays of movies, novelizations rather than novels. You read them after you see the movie, rather than the other way around, as it used to be.

Our first temptation is to view this imminent changeover as profoundly threatening. We are tempted to try to turn it around—say, by pouring millions into the teaching of writing, as educational organizations have done of late. But perhaps this is not a farsighted approach, perhaps all the untold billions at our disposal cannot make a significant difference. Perhaps, too, it is just as well, and there is nothing to bemoan. Literacy may be going the way of the horse-and-buggy; and while there are those who bewail the switch from horse and buggy to automobile, it is also argued that, had the horse not been replaced by the motorcar, cities today would be buried under horse manure. Just as no language change occurs unless there exists in the language the potential to express the same range of ideas in another way, so communicative change—change of communicative style—will not occur, I would propose, if something were to be irrevocably lost. Language changes nothing before its time. Thus, if we look at what literacy has achieved for humanity in the past—as well, by the way, as what the advent of literacy has cost us, for there have indeed been costs—we may well find that there are now other means at our disposal to achieve these same benefits, perhaps with fewer unfortunate side-effects; and that, in fact, the new mode that is gaining strength at the expense of literacy will enable us to communicate more beautifully and forcefully with one another than can be envisioned now. Since the change is barely in its infancy, is in fact still in gestation, we cannot see the final product yet. But we can at least take a different tack in viewing the oral/literate dichotomy. Rather than wringing our hands about the loss of literacy, let us ask what is replacing literacy, and why this change is occurring, and finally, what the gains as well as losses are apt, in the long run, to be.

While most of what we encounter contrasting literate with oral culture, or discussing the apparent decline of literacy among ourselves, explicitly or implicitly assumes that literacy is the desirable state, and to forswear it is to invite the return of the Dark Ages, there are other possible points of view. Marshall McLuhan, for example, has argued in his writings (e.g. 1964) that a literate culture loses something: immediacy, warmth—the qualities I have been suggesting we are trying to put back into our literate productions, albeit not really successfully. McLuhan suggests that the coming of literacy caused great, and undesirable, changes in human character and social behavior: we retreated, physically and emotionally, from one another. But now that nonliterate media are gaining influence at the expense of literacy, we are beginning to see the return of the old virtues. McLuhan, then, sees literacy and nonliteracy as heavily influencing character and behavior, as well as less-clearly-social psychological attributes.

On the other hand, it is sometimes argued that scientific progress, in terms of linear logical thought, can only be found where there is literacy; that the written word, in fact, and its linear syntactic arrangement into sentences going from one side of the page to the other (or, for that matter, up-and-down, but in any case, in a visually perceptible pattern implying sequencing) has formed our thought and enabled us to formulate concepts like logical causality and temporal sequentiality. Without literacy, the argument continues, we would lose all ability to think logically, and revert to a state of animistic savagery.

To my knowledge, no evidence for either position, in any empirical sense, has surfaced. A fairer representation may be found in the writing of scholars like Olson (1977), who sets forth advantages and disadvantages in cognitive style for both states. In particular they note that members of nonliterate societies have far better short-term memory capacity—as indeed they must if they cannot rely on written lists or memoranda. Literature in such societies has a different relation to its creators and audience than in ours: in some ways, it is continually being created afresh by each new teller of tales; members of such societies, then, learn to abstract, to get the gist of ideas, to discover what, in a list of items or a work of art, is crucial and unchangeable, and what can be altered and embroidered at will. We do not develop such critical skills; for us, stories exist in books, to be reproduced aloud only under special circumstances, and then preferably word-for-word. A moderately skillful 'singer of tales' probably cannot be said ever to flub his lines—he is supposed to improvise. But an actor in our culture, reading from a teleprompter or memorizing a written script, is not expected to deviate from the unchangeable text, and even if he might get away with it because the audience is not familiar with it, he is nonetheless apt to show his anxiety at the knowledge that he has altered a line, and manifests his nervousness so that it is apparent to all.

In any event, the relation between literacy and high culture is not as clear as many have supposed it to be. The acquisition of literacy clearly entails loss as well as gain. We can imagine, if we like, rock-ribbed conservatives of Homeric times grousing as literacy swept like a noxious firestorm over the young. Only a fad, they said at first, hopefully. Decadent foreign ways. But as the fad persisted, as the younger generation ceased to pay attention to the older educational system and found their own sources of enlightenment, the scorn no doubt turned to fear, and rationalizations set in. The acquisition of this book-learning is a real danger. . .soon, none of our young people will be able to produce a decent rendition of the *Iliad*, by Zeus, without consulting (sneer) a book! What if they were out on a moonless night and needed to refer to a passage in the epic? They'd be lost—unable to cope, unable to participate as intelligent human beings and make use of the riches with which their society has so generously endowed them. . .And so on. In fact, the plaints of the elders would sound astonishingly like the Jeremiads of some of our own culture critics, mutatis mutandis.

CONCLUSION: A NEW NONLITERACY

I certainly don't mean, in a written document no less, to denigrate literacy. But I am arguing that all points of view that represent the two positions in terms of value-judgments are dangerously misleading and make it impossible to understand what is really going on. What is clear is that, for whatever reason, societies give literacy and nonliteracy moral and intellectual values that there is no real evidence to support; and indeed, one could argue that at different times, in different cultures, the influential powers could take diametrically opposed views on the issue, and feel just as smugly and self-righteously guardians of the old, right way of living. It also seems true that the issue arises in a culture only occasionally: when its members have reason to be uncertain as to which mode of expression is preferable. Clearly, in Homeric times, there was no choice: since there was no literacy, there was no controversy. Then, of course, partially aided by the advent of literacy, partly by other factors, life and society became more complex, and by recent times, we came to feel we could exist as full-fledged human beings only if literacy, in some sense, were more or less universal, at least as an ideal. There was no other way to assure that the tremendous amount of information necessary to survive in times like ours could be assimilated and utilized. But currently, that whole assumption is called into question by the development of the first new informational technology since the advent of literacy (perhaps excluding the invention of the printing press). Now access to all the information one previously achieved through literacy can be gained by other means, via newer media, and we see that it is the younger people who are the first to recognize this and become able to take advantage of it. Literacy shortly will not be essential for simple survival any more, nor will there be any need to preserve it except as a curiosity or an atavistic skill, like quiltmaking, learned and proudly practiced by a few. Indeed, with sophisticated information-processing and audio-visual technology, we will have achieved a sort of meeting of the fullest benefits of literate and non-literate forms of information-sharing. We will have at our disposal the emotional closeness of the oral channel, its immediacy, its ready accessibility. And at the same time we will have the preservability, the historical accuracy, the immortality of print, because tapes, like books, can be stored. So rather than the epic singer's approximation to replication of his tales, we will have absolutely accurate reproduction of works of art or sources of information, just as we do now with writing. With some improvement in technology, it is hard to see why literacy per se should be crucial for survival in the future.

It is this shift toward which our more innovative writers are tending. They are developing a style for a nonliterate age, although they are doing so, rather paradoxically, in a literate medium. We might think of the first writers of prose, as opposed to poetry, as operating under analogous assumptions—trying to adapt their techniques to a new medium. Poetry was devised for oral transmission, for memorability. Prose works best as a literate device, since it cannot be easily remembered nor reduced to formulas. Similarly, the contemporary introduction of oral devices into written communication suggests the merging of the oral and literate traditions—although oral-style-on-paper is really only a metaphorical evocation of written-memorability-through-the-voice—and therefore, the experiments and special uses I have been discussing in this chapter represent an attempt to come to terms with the future.

REFERENCES

McLuhan, Marshall. 1964. Understanding Media: The Extensions of Man. New York: McGraw-Hill.

Milne, A. A. 1926. Winnie-the-Pooh. London: Dutton.

Olson, David R. 1977. From utterance to text: The bias of language in speech and writing. Harvard Educational Review 47: 257–81.

Pynchon, Thomas. 1966. The Crying of Lot 49. New York: Bantam.

Wolfe, Tom. 1979. The Right Stuff. New York: Bantam.

Author Index

Page numbers in *italics* indicate where complete references are listed.

A

Adams, M. J., 112, *116*
Agar, M., 167, 168, *169*
Aissen, J., 120, *152*
Anderson, A. B., 93, *116*
Anderson, R. C., 21, *32*
Aronowitz, R., 13, *15*

B

Banfield, A., 121, 129, *152*
Baron, N., 92, *116*
Bartlett, F. C., 19, *32*
Bateson, G., 2–3 *15*, 217
Becker, A. L., 218, 234, *237, 238*
Begg, I., 19, *32*
Berger, N. S., 20, 22, 30, *32*
Berkowitz, A., 19, *32*
Bernstein, B., 14, *15*
Bolinger, D., 120, *152*
Borkin, A., 151, *152*
Bourdieu, P., 92, *116*
Bower, G. H., 19, 23, *32*
Brewer, W., 135n, 142, *152*
Bright, W., 35, 173, 174, 183, *184*
Brooks, L. R., 25, *32*

B (cont.)

Brown, A. L., 20, 22, 30, *33*
Brown, P., *32*

C

Calhoun, D., 114, *116*
Campion, J. C., 20, 22, 30, *33*
Carlton, R., 98, *116*
Carothers, J. C., 112, *116*
Cazden, C., *15*
Chafe, W. L., 4, 14, *15*, 36n, 37, 49, 50, *52*, 56, 57, 60, 61, 68, 70, 71, *76*, 192, *197*
Christensen, F., 186, 187, 195, *197*
Cicourel, A. V., 111n, *116*
Clancy, P. M., 4n, 63n, 65, 71n, *76*
Clark, H. H., 192, *197*
Cole, M., 1, *15, 16*
Collins, J., 4n, 13, *16*
Cook-Gumperz, J., 1, 3, 13, *15*, 111n, *116*
Cressy, D., 113, *116*
Culler, J., 191, *197*

D

Davis, N., 113, *116*
Davison, A., 151, *152*

261

Subject Index